What We Have Seen and Heard

What We Have Seen and Heard

—————— Fostering Baptismal Witness in the World

EDITED BY

Michael E. Connors, C.S.C.

PICKWICK *Publications* · Eugene, Oregon

WHAT WE HAVE SEEN AND HEARD
Fostering Baptismal Witness in the World

Pickwick Publications
An Imprint of Wipf and Stock Publishers
199 W. 8th Ave., Suite 3
Eugene, OR 97401

www.wipfandstock.com

PAPERBACK ISBN: 978-1-5326-0199-6
HARDCOVER ISBN: 978-1-5326-0201-6
EBOOK ISBN: 978-1-5326-0200-9

Cataloguing-in-Publication data:

Names: Connors, Michael E., editor.

Title: What we have seen and heard : fostering baptismal witness in the world / edited by Michael E. Connors.

Description: Eugene, OR: Pickwick Publications, 2017 | Includes bibliographical references.

Identifiers: ISBN 978-1-5326-0199-6 (paperback) | ISBN 978-1-5326-0201-6 (hardcover) | ISBN 978-1-5326-0200-9 (ebook).

Subjects: LCSH: Baptism | Initiation rites—Religious aspects—Christianity | Vatican Council (1st : 1869-1870 : Basilica di San Pietro in Vaticano).

Classification: BV811.2 W42 2017 (print) | BV811.2 (ebook).

Manufactured in the U.S.A.   04/25/17

Contents

Preface

GODFREY DIEKMANN († 2002), Benedictine monk and one of the fathers of the twentieth-century liturgical movement, once remarked that the single greatest achievement of the Second Vatican Council was "the restoration of the baptismal dignity of the laity."[1] More than fifty years after the close of the council, we may fairly ask not only whether Diekmann was right, but how well that restoration is faring in the church of the early twenty-first century. Today the church is guided by an apostolically oriented Jesuit, the first pope since the council who did not participate directly in the event. This moment invites a reconsideration and re-energized focus on the mission shared by all the baptized.

The Council Fathers' intention to focus their work on the mission and dignity flowing from baptism was clear from early on. Diekmann himself helped to author the first great text of the council, *Sacrosanctum Concilium: The Constitution on the Sacred Liturgy* (1963), which he later termed "a Magna Carta of the laity."[2] In a memorable passage, the council stated:

> It is very much the wish of the church that all the faithful should be led to take that full, conscious and active part in liturgical celebrations which is demanded by the very nature of the liturgy, and to which the Christian people, "a chosen race, a royal priesthood, a holy nation, a redeemed people" (1 Pet. 2:9, 4-5), have a right and to which they are bound by reason of their Baptism.
>
> In the restoration and development of the sacred liturgy the full and active participation by all the people is the paramount

---

1. Reported in Johnson, *Rites*, 386; a personal conversation between Johnson and Diekmann.

2. Roberts, "Battle Lines."

concern, for it is the primary, indeed the indispensable source from which the faithful are to derive the true Christian spirit. Therefore, in all their apostolic activity, pastors of souls should energetically set about achieving it through the requisite formation.[3]

Full, conscious, and active participation in the liturgy is not the exclusive domain of the clergy or other religious professionals, but belongs to all the baptized faithful.

The key thrust of *Sacrosanctum Concilium* was carried through in other major documents of the council, where it remained grounded in baptism but increasingly took on an outward character. Devoting an entire document to the theme, the bishops stressed the church "can never be without the lay apostolate," since "it is something that derives from the lay person's very vocation as a Christian."[4] For the lay baptized, the apostolic mission is exercised primarily in the "secular" or "temporal order":

> The characteristic of the lay state being a life led in the midst of the world and of secular affairs, lay people are called by God to make of their apostolate, through the vigor of their Christian spirit, a leaven in the world . . . They do not separate their union with Christ from their ordinary life, but actually grow closer to him by doing their work according to God's will.[5]

The goal of the baptismal apostolate is nothing less than "the renewal of the temporal order."[6] Moreover, the council insisted on the universality of the mission, both in its incumbency upon every baptized person and in its direction to the entire world: "On all Christians, accordingly, rests the noble obligation of working to bring all people the whole world over to hear and accept the divine message of salvation."[7]

These sentiments would be echoed in other central documents of Vatican II. For example, in speaking about the church, the council said: "The laity are called to participate actively in the entire life of the church; not only are they to animate the world with the spirit of Christianity, they are to be witnesses to Christ in all circumstances and at the very heart of the

---

3. Second Vatican Council, *Sacrosanctum Concilium*, 14. All quotations from Vatican II in this preface are from Flannery, *Vatican Council II*.

4. Second Vatican Council, *Apostolicam Actuositatem*, 1.

5. Ibid., 2, 4. The document avoids a strict sacred/secular dualism, making it clear elsewhere that the laity exercise their gifts both in the church and in the world, though primarily the latter.

6. Ibid., 7 and elsewhere.

7. Ibid., 3.

human community."[8] In taking up the missionary activity of the church, the Fathers claimed: "The church on earth is by its very nature missionary . . . All Christians by the example of their lives and the witness of the word, wherever they live, have an obligation to manifest the new person which they put on in baptism."[9] Service and mission go hand-in-hand with verbal witness to the living presence of God.

But, if all of this attests to the validity of Diekmann's claim about Vatican II's greatest achievement, it may also be true that the renewal of baptismal witness in and to the secular world remains the largest unmet challenge of Vatican II. To be sure, there have been a number of exciting and creative developments over these five decades—one can point to the flourishing of social ministries, for example. These developments deserve to be celebrated and better known. Yet the challenge remains; too few baptized Catholics actively believe and feel themselves to be "on mission" to the world around us each day, especially in their secular occupations. Reflection on this challenge in the context of the secularization, cultural diversity and globalized commerce and communication of the twenty-first century is surely needed. To put it another way, how might we cultivate a broad ecclesial "culture of witness" flowing from baptism?

Pope Francis has made clear his own interest in this subject and in stimulating the church's witness to the "joy of the gospel."

> In virtue of their baptism, all the members of the People of God have become missionary disciples (cf. Mt 28:19). All the baptized, whatever their position in the Church or their level of instruction in the faith, are agents of evangelization . . . The new evangelization calls for personal involvement on the part of each of the baptized. Every Christian is challenged, here and now, to be actively engaged in evangelization; indeed, anyone who has truly experienced God's saving love does not need much time or lengthy training to go out and proclaim that love. Every Christian is a missionary to the extent that he or she has encountered the love of God in Christ Jesus.[10]

In nearly every speech and homily he gives, Francis reminds us of our baptismal dignity and obligations, and summons us to a faith active through both words and deeds in the world.

As a preacher, I am prone to lay awake at night, pondering the next homiletic challenge I face. I ponder the scriptural texts, their original

---

8. Second Vatican Council, *Gaudium et Spes*, 43.

9. Second Vatican Council, *Ad Gentes*, 2, 11.

10. Francis, *Evangelii Gaudium*, 120.

meanings and their possible meanings for today. I ponder the nature of the community I will address, their needs, hopes, pains, joys, expectations, longings. I ponder my own limitations as one deputized to speak. I ponder strategies and methods for getting my central point across through the rough instrument of words. I ponder the mystery of God hovering around both me and my hearers. But few questions vex me more than this one: *How can I preach in a way that animates, stimulates, calls forth, or focuses the proclamation of the Good News by all the baptized outside the doors of the church, in their families, in their places of work, and in society?* Baptism unites us and is the ground of all preaching, liturgical and non-liturgical. It is the sacrament by which we are called into the Christian life and sent into the world as witness-servants. Thus, my preaching from the ambo must be in service to the call of all the baptized to live out their vocation as God's witnesses.

In the pages that follow, you will not find a simple answer to the question above. What you will find, I hope, is an invitation to let that question "get under your skin" and join an ongoing conversation. This book emerged from such a conversation that took place at a conference with the same title as this volume, "'What We Have Seen and Heard': Fostering Baptismal Witness in the World," held at the University of Notre Dame in June of 2015. There are many people to thank for making the rich dialogue of those days possible, most especially the contributors to this volume, but also the attendees, who came eager and open to be full and active participants. Thanks are owed to the editors of Wipf & Stock for their support of this project, and to Mary Reardon, our tireless copy editor. Finally, none of this would have been possible without the generosity of Virginia Marten, to whom this work is dedicated. The whole Marten family reminds me visibly that preaching does indeed matter to the People of God.

We can honor the Second Vatican Council no more aptly than to ponder again, and rededicate ourselves to, its chief challenge: to live the full meaning of baptism into Jesus Christ.

Michael E. Connors, C.S.C.

The John S. Marten Program in Homiletics and Liturgics,
University of Notre Dame

Bibliography

Flannery, Austin, *Vatican Council II: The Basic Sixteen Documents*. Rev. ed. Northport, NY: Costello, 1996.

Francis. *Evangelii Gaudium*. November 24, 2014. w2.vatican.va/content/francesco/en/apost_exhortations/documents/papa-francesco_esortazione-ap_20131124_evangelii-gaudium.html.

Johnson, Maxwell E. *The Rites of Christian Initiation: Their Evolution and Interpretation*. Collegeville, MN: Liturgical, 1999.

Roberts, Tom. "Battle Lines in the Liturgy Wars." *National Catholic Reporter*. March 1, 2010. www.ncronline.org/news/faith-parish/battle-lines-liturgy-wars.

Contributors

J. Matthew Ashley is the chair of the Department of Theology at the University of Notre Dame. He earned a PhD at the University of Chicago Divinity School and an MTS from Weston School of Theology. Ashley's scholarly interests include science and theology, political and liberation theology, and Christian spirituality. He is the author of *Interruptions: Mysticism, Politics, and Theology in the Work of Johann Baptist Metz, Take Lord and Receive All My Memory: Toward an Anamnestic Mysticism*, and numerous articles.

Ann W. Astell is a professor of theology at the University of Notre Dame, where she was appointed after serving as professor of English and chair of Medieval Studies at Purdue University. A member of the Schoenstatt Sisters of Mary, Astell is the author of six books, including *The Song of Songs in the Middle Ages, Joan of Arc and Sacrificial Authorship,* and her most recent, *Eating Beauty: The Eucharist and the Spiritual Arts of the Middle Ages.*

Rev. Stephen Bevans, S.V.D., is a priest in the missionary congregation of the Society of the Divine Word and professor emeritus at Catholic Theological Union, Chicago. He has written or co-written six books and has edited or co-edited ten, mostly on issues around the church's mission. He is past president of the American Society of Missiology and a member of the World Council of Churches' Commission on World Mission and Evangelization.

Kristin M. Colberg is an assistant professor of theology at Saint John's University and the College of Saint Benedict, Minnesota. She received her doctorate at the University of Notre Dame and is the author of several articles on the Second Vatican Council that have appeared in journals such as *The*

Heythrop Journal, Horizons and *Missiology*. She is co-editor of a *Festschrift* in honor of Cardinal Walter Kasper.

Rev. **Michael E. Connors**, C.S.C., earned a ThD at the Toronto School of Theology and now teaches homiletics at the University of Notre Dame, where he also directs the John S. Marten Program in Homiletics and Liturgics. Father Connors is the author of *Inculturated Pastoral Planning: The U.S. Hispanic Experience*, and editor of *We Preach Christ Crucified* and *To All the World: Preaching and the New Evangelization*.

Tom Corcoran received his bachelor's degree from Loyola University of Maryland. Tom has served Church of the Nativity in Timonium, Maryland, in a variety of roles that give him a unique perspective on parish ministry and leadership. Along with Father Michael White, Tom is the author of *Rebuilt: Awakening the Faithful, Reaching the Lost and Making Church Matter*, and *Tools for Rebuilding: 75 Really, Really Practical Ways to Make Your Parish Better*.

Rev. **Donald Cozzens** is writer in residence and adjunct professor of theology at John Carroll University in Cleveland, Ohio. He has lectured widely on issues relating to church renewal and the priesthood. His awarding-winning books include *The Changing Face of the Priesthood, Sacred Silence: Denial and the Crisis in the Church, Freeing Celibacy,* and *Notes from the Underground: The Spiritual Journal of a Secular Priest*.

Michael Downey has served as professor of theology and spirituality at universities and seminaries in North America and abroad. Downey's theological concern for the wounded and marginalized has brought him to serve the church most in need in impoverished areas throughout the world. The author or editor of more than twenty books, Downey is the founding North American editor of *Spirituality*, an international journal of the spiritual life. Dr. Downey is Professor of Theology at the Catholic Institute of Vietnam, a graduate school of theology in Ho Chi Minh City (Saigon).

Rev. **Anna Carter Florence** is the Peter Marshall Associate Professor of Preaching at Columbia Theological Seminary in Decatur, Georgia. She is an ordained minister in the Presbyterian Church (USA) and holds degrees from Yale College and Princeton Theological Seminary. Her books include *Preaching as Testimony, Inscribing the Word,* and *The Repertory Church,* based on her 2012 Lyman Beecher Lectures on Preaching at Yale Divinity School.

Zeni Fox, professor of pastoral theology at Seton Hall University, earned an MA in religious education and PhD in theology from Fordham University. She is the author of *New Ecclesial Ministry: Lay Professionals Serving the Church*. For over ten years, she served as an advisor to the Bishops' Subcommittee on Lay Ministry as they developed *Co-Workers in the Vineyard of the Lord: A Resource for Guiding the Development of Lay Ecclesial Ministry*. She lectures frequently throughout the country on lay ministry, lay spirituality, and lay leadership.

Elizabeth Groppe is associate professor of theology at Xavier University. She is the author of *Yves Congar's Theology of the Holy Spirit* and *Eating and Drinking*. Her articles on topics including Trinitarian theology, Catholic-Jewish relations, and care for God's creation appear in *Theological Studies, Modern Theology, Horizons*, and other journals.

Edward P. Hahnenberg is the Breen Chair in Catholic Theology at John Carroll University in Cleveland, Ohio. He taught previously at Xavier University in Cincinnati and at the University of Notre Dame, where he received his PhD in 2002. Hahnenberg is the author or co-editor of five books and numerous articles in academic and pastoral journals. He is a delegate to the U.S. Lutheran–Catholic Dialogue and was a theological consultant to the U.S. Bishops' Subcommittee on Lay Ministry in its preparation of the document *Co-Workers in the Vineyard of the Lord*.

Jack Jezreel is the founder and president of JustFaith Ministries, which supports faith-based justice education processes. After earning an MDiv from the University of Notre Dame, he spent six years in a Colorado Catholic Worker community providing services to homeless men and women, before directing his attention to transformative education, mostly focused on how to encourage Catholics to engage in outreach and social change. He is a popular national speaker and teacher.

Rev. **Maxwell E. Johnson** is a professor of theology at the University of Notre Dame. He was president of the North American Academy of Liturgy in 2014–15. Johnson's research interests are in the origins and development of early Christian liturgy and in the history and theology of the rites of Christian initiation. His book, *The Rites of Christian Initiation: Their Evolution and Interpretation*, revised and expanded edition (Pueblo, 2007), is widely used in schools of theology and seminaries.

Timothy Matovina is professor of Theology and executive director of the Institute for Latino Studies at the University of Notre Dame. He works in the area of theology and culture, with specialization in U.S. Catholic and U.S. Latino theology and religion. His *Latino Catholicism: Transformation in America's Largest Church* has won five book awards, including selection as a CHOICE Outstanding Academic Title for 2012. Matovina offers presentations and workshops on U.S. Catholicism and Latino ministry and theology throughout the United States.

Timothy P. O'Malley is director of the Notre Dame Center for Liturgy and a concurrent assistant professional specialist in the Department of Theology. He teaches and researches in the area of liturgical-sacramental theology, theological aesthetics, as well as catechesis and history of preaching. He is the author and co-editor of numerous books. His present research includes a book entitled *On Praise: Cultivating Liturgical Desire in a Secular Age.*

Rev. **Peter-John Pearson** is the chairperson of the Working Group and the director of the Southern Africa Catholic Bishops' Conference's Parliamentary Liaison Office. Under his direction, the office provides an avenue for the Catholic Church, as part of civil society, to contribute to debates on issues of public policy, exerting an influence for the common good. Fr. Peter-John also teaches Catholic social teaching and is a founding member of AFCAST, the African Forum for Catholic Social Teaching.

Danielle M. Peters, a member of the Secular Institute of the Schoenstatt Sisters of Mary, received degrees from the Pontifical International Marian Research Institute (IMRI) in Dayton, Ohio, and is a fellow at the Institute for Church Life at the University of Notre Dame. Her former assignments include professor at IMRI, lecturer at the Athenaeum in Cincinnati, Ohio, and employment at the Congregation for the Doctrine of the Faith.

Most Rev. **Joseph W. Tobin**, C.Ss.R., was named Cardinal and archbishop of Newark, New Jersey, by Pope Francis in 2016, after four years as archbishop of Indianapolis and two years as archbishop secretary of the Congregation for Institutes of Consecrated Life and Societies of Apostolic Life in Rome. He is a former parish pastor and was superior general of the Redemptorist Congregation from 1997 to 2009.

Rev. **Michael White** is pastor of the Church of the Nativity in Timonium, Maryland. During his tenure the church has almost tripled in weekend attendance and the commitment to the mission of the church has grown, evidenced by the significant increase of giving and service in ministry. Father White, along with Tom Corcoran, is the author of *Rebuilt: Awakening* *the Faithful, Reaching the Lost, and Making Church Matter,* and *Tools for Rebuilding: 75 Really, Really Practical Ways to Make Your Parish Better.*

Rev. **Oliver F. Williams**, C.S.C., is associate professor of management in the Mendoza College of Business at the University of Notre Dame, where he also directs the Center for Ethics and Religious Values in Business. His areas of expertise include business ethics, corporate governance, sustainability, and Catholic social teaching. In 2006, Father Williams was appointed a member of the three-person board of directors of the United Nations Global Compact Foundation.

Wendy M. Wright is professor of theology at Creighton University. She earned her PhD in late medieval/early modern contemplative studies at the University of California at Santa Barbara. Professor Wright's areas of expertise include the history of Christian spirituality, family spirituality, and the Catholic devotional tradition. Her scholarly work has focused on the Salesian spiritual tradition founded by Francis de Sales and Jane de Chantal. Wright co-hosts the weekly Creighton University podcast "Catholic Comments" with her colleague Dr. John O'Keefe.

Intensifying the Apostolic Activity of God's People[1]

—Joseph W. Tobin, C.Ss.R.

I AM GRATEFUL FOR this opportunity to celebrate the fiftieth anniversary of the close of the Second Vatican Council. My reflection recalls a particular interest of the council: the desire to recognize the dignity of all the baptized and to empower them to fulfill their vocation in the church.

All forms of Christian preaching ultimately are grounded in baptism, the sacrament by which we are called into the Christian life and sent into the world as witnesses and servants. For the baptized, this witness does not take place primarily within the church's liturgy, but rather, facing the world and immersed in the world. Here service and mission will go hand in hand with spoken witness to the living presence of God.

Three conciliar documents will illuminate this claim: the *Pastoral Constitution on the Church in the Modern World, Gaudium et Spes*; the *Decree on the Mission Activity of the Church, Ad Gentes*; and the *Decree on the Apostolate of the Laity, Apostolicam Actuositatem*. I will limit this modest contribution to the last of the three.

---

1. Second Vatican Council, *Apostolicam Actuositatem*, 1. See www.vatican.va/. Scripture quotations in this chapter are taken from the *New American Bible, revised edition* © 2010, 1991, 1986, 1970 Confraternity of Christian Doctrine, Washington DC. and are used by permission of the copyright owner. All Rights Reserved. No part of the New American Bible may be reproduced in any form without permission in writing from the copyright owner.

If we were to consider simply the path of the *Decree on the Apostolate of the Laity, Apostolicam Actuositatem,* from the introduction of its schema into the council on October 6, 1964, through its solemn promulgation by Paul VI on November 18, 1965, this chapter would be considerably shorter. Important though the schema was, it was for the most part non-controversial, and the discussion in the plenary session lasted only a week.[2] During that debate, the intervention that may have raised the greatest number of episcopal eyebrows was made by a bishop from Croatia, Stjepan Bauerlein, who proposed that the "first and principal task" of the lay apostolate was the begetting of children, since one reason for the shortage of vocations to the priesthood was the low birthrate in Christian families![3] Even without including that practical prescription, the decree eventually was approved with 2,305 votes in favor and only six opposed.[4]

When *Apostolicam Actuositatem* encouraged lay people to take an active role in the work of the church, it was carried by momentum already underway. The decree affirmed that the laity have an apostolate in the church that has its sacramental basis in baptism and confirmation. The apostolate of the church and of all its members is "primarily designed to manifest Christ's message by words and deeds and to communicate His grace to the world."[5]

The role of the laity and their participation in the ministry of the church has evolved considerably over the last five decades. Consider, for example, the growth in this country of a particular form of the lay apostolate, lay ecclesial ministry.[6] A survey by the Center for Applied Research in the Apostolate (CARA), published in 2011, underscored the sheer number of people enrolled in lay ecclesial ministry formation programs.[7] Over a ten-year period, even at its lowest point, the number of candidates in such programs was well above the combined enrollments in seminary and diaconate

2. O'Malley, *What Happened,* 229–30.

3. Ibid., 230.

4. Ibid., 282.

5. Second Vatican Council, *Apostolicam Actuositatem,* 6.

6. The phrase "lay ecclesial ministry" is intended to be a generic term, not a specific role description or title. A statement of the United States Conference of Catholic Bishops, *Co-Workers in the Vineyard of the Lord* (2005) states that the ministry is lay "because it is service done by lay persons [including vowed religious]. The sacramental basis is the Sacraments of Initiation, not the Sacrament of Ordination." It is ecclesial "because it has a place within the community of the church, whose communion and mission it serves, and because it is submitted to the discernment, authorization, and supervision of the hierarchy." It is ministry "because it is a participation in the threefold ministry of Christ who is priest, prophet and king." See *Co-Workers,* 11.

7. CARA, "Catholic Ministry Formation Enrollment: Statistical Overview for 2010–2011."

formation programs. After peaking in the early 2000s, the total number dropped sharply until stabilizing more recently; lay ecclesial ministry formation enrollments are more volatile than enrollments in seminary and diaconate formation programs. The study highlighted another interesting factor related to the number of lay ecclesial ministers enrolled in formation programs—the number of available programs themselves. When the number of programs drops, the number of students drops; the initial drop in programs precedes the drop in enrollments.[8]

In 2014–15, CARA identified 215 active lay ecclesial ministry formation programs and received program information from 187. The number of candidates enrolled in degree and certificate programs in 2014–15 was 22,145, slightly above the five-year average of 20,689 from 2010–2015. This year, 17,104 (77 percent) are working toward a certificate in ministry and 5,041 (23 percent) are working toward a graduate degree in ministry.[9]

As impressive as the development of lay ecclesial ministry has been,[10] in my opinion, it would be myopic for the church to bet the farm on this particular form. Allow me to tell you why by means of a little parable about preaching. I will then inflict on you another story with the hope of showing a way forward for our reflection.

Two Stories about Preaching

Talking to Ourselves

The first story is set in Chicago where, twenty-five years ago, I pastored a parish on the North Side. I still have contact with many of those parishioners and, last spring, a young dad wrote to tell me about a conversation he had with his seven-year-old son, walking home after Sunday mass. It seems that Tom, the dad, couldn't quite figure out what Father was trying to say in the homily. So, he consulted young Sam, who paid close attention

---

8. Ibid.

9. CARA, "Catholic Ministry Formation Enrollment: Statistical Overview for 2014–2015."

10. Professor Edward Hahnenberg, a recognized expert on the theology of vocation and ministry, has characterized lay ecclesial ministry as "as one of the top three or four most important ministerial shifts of the past two-thousand years, on a historical par with—and in fact may even eclipse—the changes to the church brought about by the rise of communal forms of monasticism in the 5th century, the birth of mendicant orders in the 13th century, or the explosion of women's religious communities in the 19th century." See Hahnenberg "The Holy Spirit's Call," 1–2.

to everything going on in church, since he was preparing to make his first communion later that spring.

Tom asked, "Sam, who do you think Father was talking to today, the grown-ups or the kids?" Sam pondered this weighty question, then looked up with a big smile and replied, "I think he was talking to himself!"—thereby putting his young finger on an occupational hazard for preachers.

The United States Conference of Catholic Bishops (USCCB) has given high priority to lay ecclesial ministry as a "great gift to the church, arising from the distinct vocation and mission of the laity."[11] Ten years ago, the bishops issued a resource to guide the development of lay ecclesial ministry entitled *Co-Workers in the Vineyard*,[12] which was the subject of several symposia, including a study day that preceded the spring assembly of the episcopal conference just two weeks ago. There is no doubt that the different forms of lay ecclesial ministry are a gift to mission of the church in this country.

However, I wonder if the trenchant observations of a statement made thirty-eight years ago by a group of prominent Catholics in Chicago might not still be valid. Their statement, entitled "Declaration of Concern by 47 Chicago Area Catholics: Devaluing the Role of the Laity," was issued on December 12, 1977, and later published in *Origins*.

Commenting on the contemporary emphasis placed on new ministries in the church, the signers stated, "It is our experience that a wholesome and significant movement within the church—the involvement of lay people in many church ministries—has led to a devaluation of the unique ministry of lay men and women." Lay ministry is now often viewed as "the laity's participation in work traditionally assigned to priests or sisters," according to the statement. Today, "the impression is often given that one can work for justice and peace only by stepping outside one's ordinary role in the business world, as a mayor, a factory worker or a government worker," the statement continues. The best insights of Vatican II regarded the church as present to the world in the ordinary roles of lay Christians as it is in the ecclesiastical roles of bishop and priest, and "rejected the notion that church is to be identified exclusively with hierarchical roles."[13]

Two hundred years before Vatican II's Dogmatic Constitution on the Church, *Lumen Gentium*, described the universal call to holiness, the

11. Bishop Richard J. Malone, chairman of the U.S. Bishops' Committee on Laity, Marriage, Family Life and Youth, addressing a plenary session of the USCCB, November 11, 2014.

12. Found at www.usccb.org/upload/co-workers-vineyard-lay-ecclesial-ministry-2005.pdf.

13. Ibid.

founder of my religious family, Saint Alphonsus Liguori, wrote: "God wishes all to be Saints, and each one according to his state of life: the religious as a religious; the secular as a secular; the priest as a priest; the married as married; the man of business as a man of business; the soldier as a soldier; and so of every other state of life."[14] In other words, we do not become holy by living someone else's life. God's grace literally reaches us "where we live." Similarly, the "faithful are called to engage in the apostolate as individuals in the varying circumstances of their life."[15] Although a small portion of the baptized will minister with the authorization of the hierarchy to serve publicly in the local church, faithfulness to the saving plan of God as well as the particular challenges of evangelization demand that we work to intensify the apostolic activity of *all* God's people. Otherwise, bishops and other leaders in the church will end up talking to ourselves.

How can we promote the unique ministry of all God's People? I propose we learn a new language. I hope a second story might help to illustrate my point. I am going to ask another, more experienced bishop to help me.

Talking a Language that Can Be Understood

This second story took place in 2013 at the conclusion of a trip to Rome, where I received the pallium from Pope Francis on June 29, the Solemnity of Saints Peter and Paul. One of the final nights there, I went for supper with some family and friends. We dined at a little trattoria not far from the Vatican. Its three waiters knew me from my former life and quickly gathered around our table, chattering excitedly about the unbelievable difference the new pope was already making just three months after his election. Great crowds of people were pushing into the Eternal City each week, hoping to glimpse Pope Francis at the Wednesday audience or during the angelus at noon on Sundays. The waiters judged that this was a wonderful development for the church and—coincidentally, of course—a good boost for business.

Aware that the pushback against Pope Francis was already beginning to coalesce—usually manifest in the form of snide articles, authored by self-proclaimed "vaticanologists" (who are fed by the not-so-loyal opposition in the Roman Curia)—I decided to try out some of the principal criticisms leveled at the Holy Father. "That's all well and good," I informed my friends, "but—let's be honest—*il Papa* really isn't a theologian. And he talks off the cuff a lot. And he repeats himself . . ." Each pronouncement evoked an increasingly more puzzled look from the waiters; as if an alien being had

---

14. Liguori, *Practice* 4.2.1.

15. Second Vatican Council, *Apostolicam Actuositatem*, 18.

replaced the "Padre Giuseppe" they had once known. Finally, one blurted emphatically, "But he's speaking a language we can understand!"

I agreed.

There is little doubt that the immediate predecessors of Pope Francis were great teachers, but I will argue that none of them equaled the present pontiff's ability to speak a language that combines a pedagogy of verbal communication and prophetic gesture. This eloquent blend speaks to faithful within the church as well as alienated Catholics, other Christians, "nones" and nonbelievers.

I propose to examine very briefly some of the constituent elements of the "language" of Pope Francis. From the point of view of homiletics, an appropriation of these elements will help preachers speak a language that people can understand. These same elements can shape the witness of the baptized in the actual circumstances of their lives, thus serving to intensify the apostolic activity of God's people. It is instructive to recognize how profoundly the doctrine of the Second Vatican Council resonates in the "language" of the Holy Father.

I will touch upon three essential elements of the "language" of Pope Francis:

- The necessity of an experience of Christ
- His self-identification as a sinner who has found mercy
- His passionate advocacy for a "culture of encounter"

Taken together, these elements can help preachers touch the hearts of men and women with an invitation to become missionary disciples of Jesus Christ and thus realize the vision of the decree *Apostolicam Actuositatem*.

An Experience of Jesus

The first element of the "language" of Francis has been a common theme in Latin American pastoral theology and found eloquent expression in a recent ecclesial event in which the future pope played a crucial role. The final document of the Fifth General Conference of the Bishops of Latin America and the Caribbean (CELAM), held in May 2007 in Aparecida, Brazil, articulated the necessity of an experience of Christ as a condition for discipleship. The bishops elected Cardinal Jorge Bergoglio to chair the important committee charged with drafting the final document.[16]

---

16. "V General Conference of the Bishops of Latin America and the Caribbean Concluding Document," hereafter *Aparecida*.

The bishops of Latin America and the Caribbean underscored the erosion of religious traditions across the continent; as a result, the Aparecida document calls for a personal encounter with Jesus Christ: "The very nature of Christianity consists, therefore, in recognizing the presence of Jesus Christ and following him."[17] The Christ event will give birth "to this new man that appears in history and which we call a disciple."[18] Restating the beginning of Pope Benedict XVI's encyclical *Deus Caritas Est*, the Aparecida document recognizes that: "Being Christian is not the result of an ethical choice or a lofty idea, but the encounter with an event, a person, which gives life a new horizon and a decisive direction."[19] The document proclaims, "[K]nowing Jesus Christ by faith is our joy, following Him is our grace and transmitting this treasure to others is a mission that the Lord, by choosing and calling us, has entrusted with us."[20]

At a time when religious traditions have lost much of their force, Pope Francis proposes an experience: an encounter with Jesus that transforms a Christianity that is based on tradition to a Christianity that is founded on conviction. Who can ignore the audacious claim made by the opening salvo of his first programmatic statement, the apostolic exhortation *Evangelii Gaudium*?

> The joy of the gospel fills the hearts and lives of all who encounter Jesus. Those who accept his offer of salvation are set free from sin, sorrow, inner emptiness and loneliness. With Christ, joy is constantly born anew . . . I wish to encourage the Christian faithful to embark upon a new chapter of evangelization marked by this joy, while pointing out new paths for the church's journey in years to come.[21]

Fifty years ago, *Apostolicam Actuositatem*, taught that Christ, sent by the Father, is the "source and origin of the whole apostolate of the church." Hence, "the success of the lay apostolate depends upon the laity living union with Christ, in keeping with the Lord's words, 'He who abides in me, and I in him, bears much fruit, for without me you can do nothing.'"[22]

An encounter with Christ transforms the person into a missionary disciple. The Gospel of Mark offers a succinct formula for such transformation: "He went up the mountain and summoned those whom he wanted

17. *Aparecida*, 244.

18. *Aparecida*, 243.

19. Benedict XVI, *Deus Caritas Est*, 1; *Aparecida*, 12.

20. *Aparecida*, 18.

21. Francis, *Evangelii Gaudium*, 1.

22. See Second Vatican Council, *Apostolicam Actuositatem*, 4.

and they came to him. He appointed twelve [whom he also named apostles] that they might be with him and he might send them forth to preach and to have authority to drive out demons" (Mark 3:13–15). People will come to Christ insofar as they recognize themselves as "summoned" and "wanted" by Christ. The binary, "missionary-disciple," implies "following him, living in intimacy with him, imitating his example and bearing witness."[23] Homiletics will contribute to intensifying the missionary activity of the People of God, first and foremost, if preaching promotes an encounter with Jesus. The encounter reveals not only the Redeemer, who summons those he wants, but also the nature of those whom he calls. Let us look at the second element of the "language" of Pope Francis.

A Sinner Who Has Found Mercy

At the beginning of his pontificate, Francis gave a remarkable interview to his Jesuit confrere, Father Antonio Spadaro.[24] The first question Father Spadaro posed was "Who is Jorge Mario Bergoglio?" Francis replied, "I am a sinner. This is the most accurate definition. It is not a figure of speech, a literary genre. I am a sinner." The reader is tempted to dismiss the answer as pious self-effacement. After all, the pope's admissions and gestures of humility have become one of his trademarks. If he had opened with an impressive CV or psychobabble, then that might have been news.

Francis' humility, however, is not like Uriah Heep's—a formalistic display of being "ever so 'umble." Instead, his self-understanding expresses a central conviction of the Christian faith. As we now know, Cardinal Bergoglio accepted his election to the papacy with the words: "I am a sinner, but I trust in the infinite mercy and patience of our Lord Jesus Christ." These whispered words illuminate his later choices to spurn the pomp in favor of simplicity. Francis "smells like the sheep" because he has been lost and experienced being found by the Shepherd of his soul.

For the Christian, the searing guilt one feels for one's sins is, or ought to be, underwritten with hope in the One "who is rich in mercy" (Eph 2:4). With great sorrow at having sinned, comes the greater appreciation of God, who does what only God can do. Francis echoes the famous words of 1 Tim 1:15: "The saying is sure and worthy of full acceptance, that Christ Jesus came into the world to save sinners—of whom I am the foremost." Or as

---

23. *Aparecida*, 3.

24. A translation of the interview can be found at w2.vatican.va/content/francesco/en/speeches/2013/september/documents/papa-francesco_20130921_intervista-spadaro.html.

Paul writes in Romans, "where sin increased, grace abounded all the more" (Rom 5:20). From Paul and Augustine, right down to Dorothy Day and Mother Teresa, it is always the saints who are most painfully aware of how sinful they are, of how desperately they need God's mercy.[25]

Significantly, the pope criticizes not only rigoristic confessors, but also the one who is "too lax," who "washes his hands by simply saying, 'This is not a sin.'" Francis' field hospital, in common with its consultant Physician, is there to heal wounds, not deny that they exist.[26]

In Antonio Spadaro's extraordinary interview, Francis identifies with Caravaggio's St. Matthew, the tax collector: "That's me. I feel like him . . . Here, this is me, a sinner on whom the Lord has turned his gaze." This is true humility, the same humility we see in a different tax collector in the gospels—the one in the temple, crying out "God, be merciful to me, a sinner!" (Luke 18:9–14). Only the one who truly feels in need of mercy can announce, with joy and relief, that "the grace of our Lord overflowed for me with the faith and love that are in Christ Jesus" (1 Tim 1:14). This is the "good news"—what Francis means when he talks about "the first proclamation . . . the proclamation of salvation," that which "there is nothing more solid, deep and sure." And this, for once, really is a headline-worthy bombshell, no less now than it was almost 2,000 years ago.

Culture of Encounter

On May 22, 2013, during his morning Mass, Pope Francis offered a reflection that caught the attention of many people. In his homily, Pope Francis said that "doing good" is a principle that unites all of humanity, beyond the diversity of ideologies and religions, and creates the "culture of encounter" that is the foundation of peace. Let me quote just a portion of this provocative homily.

> The Lord created us in His image and likeness, and we are the image of the Lord, and He does good and all of us have this commandment at heart: do good and do not do evil. All of us. "But, Father, this [one] is not Catholic! He cannot do good." Yes, he can. He must. Not can: must![27]

The Holy Father continued:

25. Bullivant, "I Am a Sinner."

26. Ibid.

27. Vatican Radio, "Pope at Mass."

The Lord has redeemed all of us, all of us, with the Blood of Christ: all of us, not just Catholics. Everyone! "Father, the atheists?" Even the atheists. Everyone! And this Blood makes us children of God of the first class! We are created children in the likeness of God and the Blood of Christ has redeemed us all! And we all have a duty to do good . . . We must meet one another doing good. "But I don't believe, Father, I am an atheist!" But do good, we will meet one another there.

Not surprisingly this brief homily created a bit of a stir—and not just among Catholics! Did the pope say that all atheists are going to heaven? As David Perry commented in a subsequent article in the *Atlantic*:

Perhaps the focus on atheism, as breathtaking as this issue has proven to be for the media and blogosphere, misses the more powerful concept at the core of Francis' homily: the culture of encounter. In the documents from the Second Vatican Council, as well as much older texts, one finds numerous explicit statements about our shared humanity, universal rights, and the necessity to find common ground. This idea of encounter lays out a pathway for us to locate and recognize those commonalities.[28]

I recently heard Sotirios Athanassoulas, the metropolitan archbishop for the Greek Orthodox church in Canada, state: "there are many sins that afflict the church; however, there is no more grievous wound to the Body of Christ than the division among Christians."

Pope Francis is inviting us to expand the space in which a "culture of encounter" might flourish. Expanding that space provides the locus where the apostolate of all the baptized can intensify. We ought to meet each other doing good. During our childhood, when quarrels arose among my siblings and me, our mother would serenely state that if we had time to squabble, we simply did not have enough to do.

Conclusion

What can I leave you, after this long and rambling reflection? I ask you to consider the language we employ in speaking about the mission of the baptized. This mission is not an invitation to create a new caste of "professionals" who will supply for a diminishing number priests and religious. We do not become holy by living someone else's life. What, then, should this new language aim to do? Following the inspiration of Pope Francis, I suggest

28. Perry, "No, the Pope."

that without an experience of being called by Jesus to be with him and then being sent forth, it will be difficult for any of us to sustain a missionary life. Without a love for the Cross, we will never endure the disappointments that inevitably come. Suffering and disappointment will finally rob us of that most precious gift: joy.

There is no doubt that Francis supports the goal of our reflection here, to contribute to the strengthening of the apostolic activity of the People of God. In a recent address to the bishops of Italy, the pope asked that the "essential role" of the laity be "reinforced" so that the laity "take on the responsibilities that they have."[29] Laypeople who have "an authentic Christian formation should not need a helmsman-Bishop, or pilot-monsignor, or the input of clergy in order to take on their proper responsibilities at all levels, from the political to the social, from the economic to the legislative! They have, rather, the need of a Pastor Bishop!"

The pope is proposing an ecclesial model that envisions a bishop-pastor and a free and responsible laity. Bishops need not try to act like a "pilot" and steer the laity's choices into the areas he is in charge of. Laity need not demand an endless stream of support and blessings for their apostolic activity nor complain about the hierarchy not underscoring certain hot-button issues on a weekly basis, as unfortunately still happens.

Most of all, bishops should avoid talking to themselves. "A conference or event is organized, which by giving prominence to the usual voices, thus narcotizes communities, homogenizing choices, opinions and people, instead of allowing ourselves to be transported toward those horizons where the Holy Spirit is calling us to go."[30]

May we glimpse where the Holy Spirit is calling us to go!

Bibliography

Benedict XVI. *Deus Caritas Est.* December 25, 2005. w2.vatican.va/content/benedict-xvi/en/encyclicals/documents/hf_ben-xvi_enc_20051225_deus-caritas-est.html.

Bullivant, Stephen. "I Am a Sinner." *America.* September 25, 2013. americamagazine.org/issue/%E2%80%98i-am-sinner%E2%80%99.

CELAM. "V General Conference of the Bishops of Latin America and the Caribbean Concluding Document." www.aecrc.org/documents/Aparecida-Concluding%20Document.pdf.

Center for Applied Research in the Apostolate. "Catholic Ministry Formation Enrollment: Statistical Overview for 2010–2011." Washington, DC: CARA, 2011. cara.georgetown.edu/Publications/MFDOverview2010-11.pdf.

29. Francis, *Address.*
30. Ibid.

————. "Catholic Ministry Formation Enrollment: Statistical Overview for 2014–2015." Washington, DC: CARA, 2011. cara.georgetown.edu/Publications/MFDOverview2010-11.pdf.

"Declaration of Concern by 47 Chicago Area Catholics: Devaluing the Role of the Laity." *Origins* 7.28 (December 29, 1977) 440–42.

Francis. *Address of His Holiness Pope Francis to the 68th General Assembly of the Italian Episcopal Conference.* May 18, 2015. w2.vatican.va/content/francesco/en/speeches/2015/may/documents/papa-francesco_20150518_conferenza-episcopale-italiana.html.

Francis. *Evangelii Gaudium.* November 24, 2014. w2.vatican.va/content/francesco/en/apost_exhortations/documents/papa-francesco_esortazione-ap_20131124_evangelii-gaudium.html.

Hahnenberg, Edward. "The Holy Spirit's Call: The Vocation to Lay Ecclesial Ministry." Paper delivered at National Symposium on Lay Ecclesial Ministry, St. John's University, Collegeville, MN. August 1, 2007. www.csbsju.edu/Documents/SOT/Events/2007Symposium/8.Hahnenberg-SpiritsCall.pdf.

Liguori, Alphonsus. *Practice of the Love of Jesus Christ* 4.2.1. London: Aeterna, 2016.

O'Malley, John W. *What Happened at Vatican II.* Cambridge, MA: Belknap, 2008.

Perry, David M. "No, the Pope Didn't Just Say All Atheists Go to Heaven." *The Atlantic,* May 24, 2013. www.theatlantic.com/international/archive/2013/05/no-the-pope-didnt-just-say-all-atheists-go-to-heaven/276214/.

Second Vatican Council. *Apostolicam Actuositatem.* November 18, 1965. www.vatican.va/archive/hist_councils/ii_vatican_council/documents/vat-ii_decree_19651118_apostolicam-actuositatem_en.html.

Spadaro, Antonio. Radio interview with Pope Francis. August 19, 2013. w2.vatican.va/content/francesco/en/speeches/2013/september/documents/papa-francesco_20130921_intervista-spadaro.html.

United States Conference of Catholic Bishops. *Co-Workers in the Vineyard of the Lord.* www.usccb.org/upload/co-workers-vineyard-lay-ecclesial-ministry-2005.pdf.

Vatican Radio. "Pope at Mass: Culture of encounter is the foundation of peace." May 22, 2013. en.radiovaticana.va/storico/2013/05/22/pope_at_mass_culture_of_encounter_is_the_foundation_of_peace/en1-694445.

2

The Ecumenical Renewal of Baptismal Spirituality

Foundation for Ministry

—*Maxwell E. Johnson*

"Ecumenical Renewal of Baptismal Spirituality" is a topic very near and dear to my heart, both because it is about baptism and because it is about ecumenism, two themes that have occupied part of my scholarly attention over the past almost twenty-five years.[1] And, of course, such an approach is foundational to the overall theme of this volume, as reflected, first, in *Ad Gentes:* "The church is missionary by her very nature . . . all Christians, wherever they live, are bound to show forth, by the example of their lives and by the witness of the word, that new man put on at baptism."[2] And, second, in Pope Francis' encyclical, *Evangelii Gaudium*: "In virtue of their baptism, all the members of the People of God have become missionary disciples (cf. Mt 28:19). All the baptized, whatever their position in the Church or their level of instruction in the faith, are agents of evangelization

---

1. Cf. Johnson, *Rites,* 451–78; "Loss of a Common Language." Another version of this essay appeared in *Studia Liturgica* 37 (2007) 55–72; Johnson, "Building Christian Unity"; Johnson, "Not 'Sheep Stealing'"; Johnson, "'Satis Est'"; Johnson, "Liturgy and Ecumenism"; Johnson, "Romans 6"; Johnson, "Let's Stop"; Johnson, "Planning and Leading"; and, more recently, Johnson, *Church in Act.*

2. Second Vatican Council, *Ad Gentes,* 1.2; 2.11.

... Every Christian is a missionary to the extent that he or she has encountered the love of God in Christ Jesus."[3]

Further, I am reminded of a comment made to me by the great Benedictine patristics and liturgical scholar Fr. Godfrey Diekmann, OSB, in a conversation about this very issue some twenty years ago: "The greatest achievement of Vatican II was the restoration of the baptismal dignity of the laity, an achievement even greater than episcopal collegiality."[4]

In this chapter I will focus on this "greatest achievement of Vatican II" in two distinct ways. First, I will look directly at the ecumenical recovery of a baptismal spirituality, or, better, the recovery of an *ecumenical* baptismal spirituality and its implications for a baptismal ecclesiology flowing from this. Second, I will focus on the implications of this for ministry, for the witness of the church and all its members in the world. Finally, I will offer briefly a conclusion on the meaning and hope of a baptismal ecclesiology.

Recovery of a Baptismal Spirituality

I have often argued that what is needed in our own day is the recovery of a baptismal spirituality and ecclesiology, which, by definition, can be nothing other than an ecumenical spirituality and ecclesiology as well. The language of the New Testament could not be clearer here: "there is one body and one Spirit, just as you were called to the one hope of your calling, one Lord, one faith, one baptism, one God and Father of all, who is above all and through all and in all" (Eph 4:4-6). Through water and the Spirit in baptism all are incorporated into the *one* Christ, the *one* church, the *one* Body of Christ. And because of this, Christian unity is, above all, not a demand, not a call, but already a gift of baptism itself to be received and further realized gratefully. That is, all of the baptized, in a very real way, already belong to the same church! It is this sacramental bond of "real" communion that must be on the forefront of any discussion of visible Christian unity today. In 1995 encyclical on Christian unity, *Ut Unum Sint*, Pope John Paul II, in fact, underscored the baptismal basis for Christian unity precisely in this way when he asked: "How is it possible to remain divided if we have been 'buried' through Baptism in the Lord's death, in the very act by which God, through the death of his Son, has broken down the walls of division? Division 'openly contradicts the will of Christ, provides a stumbling block to the

---

3. Francis, *Evangelii Gaudium*, 20.
4. Godfrey Diekmann, personal conversation.

world and inflicts damage on the most holy cause of proclaiming the good news to every creature."[5]

Similarly, the 1982 Faith and Order statement of the World Council of Churches, *Baptism, Eucharist, Ministry*, also highlights this ecumenical foundation of baptism well: "When baptismal unity is realized in one, holy, catholic, apostolic Church, a genuine Christian witness can be made to the healing and reconciling love of God. Therefore, our one baptism into Christ constitutes a call to the churches to overcome their divisions and visibly manifest their fellowship."[6] The *Catechism of the Catholic Church* draws attention to the ecumenical nature of the church due to baptism, while acknowledging the tragic divisions that continue to exist:

> Baptism constitutes the foundation of communion among all Christians, including those who are not yet in full communion with the Catholic Church: "For men who believe in Christ and have been properly baptized are put in some, though imperfect, communion with the Catholic Church. Justified by faith in Baptism, [they] are incorporated into Christ; they therefore have a right to be called Christians, and with good reason are accepted as brothers by the children of the Catholic Church." "Baptism therefore constitutes *the sacramental bond of unity* existing among all who through it are reborn."[7]

And listen more recently to the baptismal basis and orientation of the recent 2013 document produced jointly by the Lutheran World Federation and the Pontifical Council for Promoting Christian Unity, *From Conflict to Communion: Lutheran-Catholic Common Commemoration of the Reformation in 2017*. First, in claiming baptism as the basis for unity and common commemoration, we read:

> 219. The church is the body of Christ. As there is only one Christ, so also he has only one body. Through baptism, human beings are made members of this body.

> 220. The Second Vatican Council teaches that people who are baptized and believe in Christ but do not belong to the Roman Catholic church "have been justified by faith in Baptism [and] are members of Christ's body and have a right to be called Christian, and so are correctly accepted as brothers by the children

---

5. John Paul II, *Ut Unum Sint*, 6.

6. World Council of Churches, "Baptism," D.6.

7. *Catechism of the Catholic Church*, §1271, p. 323 [emphasis is original].

of the Catholic Church" (UR 1.3). Lutheran Christians say the same of their Catholic fellow Christians.

> 221. Since Catholics and Lutherans are bound to one another in the body of Christ as members of it, then it is true of them what Paul says in 1 Corinthians 12:26: "If one member suffers, all suffer together; if one member is honored, all rejoice together." What affects one member of the body also affects all the others. For this reason, when Lutheran Christians remember the events that led to the particular formation of their churches, they do not wish to do so without their Catholic fellow Christians. In remembering with each other the beginning of the Reformation, they are taking their baptism seriously.[8]

And, second, one of the ecumenical imperatives arising from this is as follows:

> 238. Catholics and Lutherans realize that they and the communities in which they live out their faith belong to the one body of Christ. The awareness is dawning on Lutherans and Catholics that the struggle of the sixteenth century is over. The reasons for mutually condemning each other's faith have fallen by the wayside.

> 239. Lutherans and Catholics are invited to think from the perspective of the unity of Christ's body and to seek whatever will bring this unity to expression and serve the community of the body of Christ. Through baptism they recognize each other mutually as Christians. This orientation requires a continual conversion of heart.

Hence: "Catholics and Lutherans should always begin from the perspective of unity and not from the point of view of division in order to strengthen what is held in common even though the differences are more easily seen and experienced."[9] What might be accomplished if we begin from the perspective of our baptismal unity rather than division? In a 1997 *Worship* article "Forum: Confusion Over Confirmation,"[10] Paul Turner called for Roman Catholic recognition that not only baptism but what Roman Catholics consider to be the *fullness* of Christian initiation already exists liturgically within the baptismal rites of other Christian traditions, especially today

---

8. Lutheran World Federation and Pontifical Council for Promoting Christian Unity, *From Conflict to Communion*, 80.

9. Ibid, 87.

10. Turner, "Forum: Confusion."

where, increasingly, the equivalent to Roman Catholic confirmation (hand-laying prayer for the Spirit's sevenfold gift and, often, an anointing related to the Spirit's seal) appears as the regular post-baptismal rites within most contemporary Protestant worship books. He concluded by saying, "We need better ecumenical conversation on baptism, profession of faith, eucharistic communion, and orders. We yearn for the day when confirmation will not be necessary for those who share our Christian faith and wish to share our table."[11] Turner's statement calling for "better ecumenical conversation on baptism, profession of faith, eucharistic communion, and orders" spells out a complete agenda for where we now need to go, especially in light of recent ecumenical agreements. In short, although he does not use these terms, Turner calls here for precisely a foundational-ecumenical baptismal spirituality[12] and a baptismal ecclesiology. Indeed, our ecclesial identity as church, as the corporate Body of Christ, as dead, buried, and risen in Christ, as born anew and adopted through water and the Spirit, and as signed and sealed by the Holy Spirit for life, witness, and mission in the world is given to us freely in baptism. From baptism the various orders of ministry flow. And back to baptism, to our freely given baptismal identity, the Eucharist and other sacraments lead and direct us. "Better ecumenical conversation on baptism, profession of faith, eucharistic communion, and orders" is precisely the call for better ecumenical conversation about what the "sacramental bond of unity" constituted by baptism actually implies.

I would suggest, above all, then, that it is the development of a clear baptismal ecclesiology, rather than starting elsewhere, that will bring Christians closer to a common eucharistic table. For it is baptism itself that must frame the conversation and it is baptism that serves to raise all other ecclesiological questions anew. As Pope Francis said in May 2015:

> The unity that is budding among us is that unity which begins under the seal of the one Baptism we have all received. It is the unity we are seeking along a common path. It is the spiritual unity of prayer for one another. It is the unity of our common labor on behalf of our brothers and sisters, and all those who believe in the sovereignty of Christ. Dear brothers and sisters, division is a wound in the body of the Church of Christ. And we do not want this wound to remain open . . . I am convinced it won't be theologians who bring about unity among us. Theologians help us, the science of the theologians will assist us, but

11. Ibid., 545.

12. I tried to sketch out eight implications for such a baptismal spirituality in my 1997 article, "Back Home to the Font: Eight Implications of a Baptismal Spirituality." This essay also appears as the final chapter in my *Rites of Christian Initiation*.

if we hope that theologians will agree with one another, we will reach unity the day after Judgment Day. The Holy Spirit brings about unity. Theologians are helpful, but most helpful is the goodwill of us all who are on this journey with our hearts open to the Holy Spirit![13]

What kind of church would we be and what kind of Christians would we form if we took our baptismal death as death in Christ seriously, if we, as church, fully aware that we are a "dead church" living *after* life, chose to focus on what is truly essential in our postbaptismal life? That is, if we mean what we say and so are truly "dead" and "buried" by our baptism into Christ's Paschal Mystery, then we can afford to be a church, a "dead church," which understands itself as already having death in its past and walking now in "newness of life" as the result only of a most gracious, freely given, and divine gift. If we as church are truly crucified, dead, and buried in Christ so much so that, to paraphrase St. Paul, "it is no longer we who live but Christ who lives in us" (see Gal 2:20), then there is nothing left to hold on to other than this, nothing left to lose of ourselves and identity that cannot be risked in service to the reign of God as we follow the way of the cross, which we know of and embrace as the only and ultimate way to life. For, if we as church are already dead, then how can even death itself possibly any longer pose a threat to us? The reflections of Joseph Cardinal Bernardin published shortly before his death remind us strongly that the experience of impending death itself has a way of confronting us with the need to focus only on what is truly essential in life and "how much of what consumes our daily life is trivial and insignificant."[14] Is this not equally true in terms of ecclesiology, that so much of what consumes our ecclesial life is often trivial and insignificant in comparison to what and who baptism has already made us to be?

An ecclesiology flowing from baptism, I believe, would lead to an understanding of the church much like that already envisioned in *Lumen Gentium* 18, where the church is spoken of in rather Lutheran-sounding terms of its identity as simultaneously "holy" and in constant need of purification, where, like all the baptized, so also the church itself is called to continual repentance, reform, and renewal as it seeks to put the "old Adam" to death daily in order that Christ, and Christ alone, may come to life within it. *Lumen Gentium* 18 states clearly, "The Church . . . clasping sinners to her bosom, at once holy and always in need of purification (*sancta simul et semper purificanda*), follows constantly the path of penance and renewal."[15] In

13. Vatican Radio, "Pope sends greetings."

14. Bernardin, *Gift of Peace*, 109.

15. English translation in Flannery, *Vatican Council II*, 358.

such an ecclesiology, I believe that questions of ecumenism, the inclusive-catholic nature of the Church, and its mission and priestly service in the world, and even ecumenical questions about liturgy would seem to be of paramount importance as the baptismal image of the crucified and risen Christ is continually formed and reformed by the Holy Spirit in the church's members.

In his study of liturgical ecclesiology, Lutheran liturgist Gordon Lathrop asked, "If Baptism constitutes the assembly that is the church, ought not the Christians in a given locality enact that truth? Can we not do much of the process of Baptism together? Could a renewed catechumenate be undertaken by many or even all of the Christian assemblies in a given local place? Could we be present at each other's baptisms? Could we do baptisms on the great feasts and do them side by side? Could we even consider constructing a single font for the local churches in our towns and cities?"[16] And, as many know, it was Walter Cardinal Kasper who suggested that the time was ripe for the development of an ecumenical catechism among Roman Catholics, Anglicans, Lutherans, Methodists, and members of the Reformed churches, based on "an ecumenism of basics that identifies, reinforces and deepens the common foundation" of faith in Christ and belief in the tenets of the creed.[17]

Such are the very questions that should arise for us when we take baptism seriously for the continued life of the ecumenical church. And, as Paul Turner has said [emphasis mine]:

> The ecumenical movement longs for the day when the rites which prepare baptized Christians for full communion will be ripped from our books, and the catechumenate now so freely adapted for the *baptized* may become again the proper province of the unbaptized . . . When the disciples warned Jesus that some who were not of their company were exorcising demons in his name they expected him to put a stop to it. Jesus tolerated strange exorcists with the simplest of aphorisms: "If they're not against us, they're for us." The [Catholic] church tolerates baptisms. Is it too much to ask that we tolerate confirmations as well? Our churches are irresponsibly dawdling toward a common table.[18]

But can we not go even further here? In light of the continued ecumenical dialogues, even Roman Catholic recognition of Lutheran "orders," for example, is not out of the question with regard to the "validity" of the Eucharist

16. Lathrop, *Holy People*, 146–47.

17. *Catholic News Service*, "Cardinal Asks."

18. Turner, *Confirmation*, 129.

among Lutherans. The recent Lutheran-Catholic dialogue, *The Church as Koinonia of Salvation*, certainly shows that from a Catholic perspective there is even hope here for some kind of resolution. According to this statement:

> Catholic judgment on the authenticity of Lutheran ministry need not be of an all-or-nothing nature. The Decree on Ecumenism of Vatican II distinguished between relationships of full ecclesiastical communion and those of imperfect communion to reflect the varying degrees of differences with the Catholic Church. (164) The communion of these separated communities with the Catholic Church is real, even though it is imperfect. Furthermore, the decree positively affirmed: "Our separated brothers and sisters also celebrate many sacred actions of the Christian religion. These most certainly can truly engender a life of grace in ways that vary according to the condition of each church or community, and must be held capable of giving access to that communion in which is salvation." (165) Commenting on this point, Joseph Cardinal Ratzinger, prefect of the Congregation on the Doctrine of the Faith, wrote in 1993 to Bavarian Lutheran bishop Johannes Hanselmann: "I count among the most important results of the ecumenical dialogues the insight that the issue of the eucharist cannot be narrowed to the problem of 'validity.' Even a theology oriented to the concept of succession, such as that which holds in the Catholic and in the Orthodox church, need not in any way deny the salvation-granting presence of the Lord [*Heilschaffende Gegenwart des Herrn*] in a Lutheran [*evangelische*] Lord's Supper." (166) If the actions of Lutheran pastors can be described by Catholics as 'sacred actions' that 'can truly engender a life of grace,' if communities served by such ministers give 'access to that communion in which is salvation,' and if at a eucharist at which a Lutheran pastor presides is to be found 'the salvation-granting presence of the Lord,' then Lutheran churches cannot be said simply to lack the ministry given to the church by Christ and the Spirit. In acknowledging the imperfect *koinonia* between our communities and the access to grace through the ministries of these communities, we also acknowledge a real although imperfect *koinonia* between our ministries."[19]

Further, again it was Cardinal Kasper, who, in his 2004 study, *Sacrament of Unity: The Eucharist and the Church*, drew attention to John Paul II's *Ut Unum Sint*, saying:

---

19. *The Church as Koinonia of Salvation*, 107.

The pope offered a more spiritual description of the meaning of the prescriptions of canon law: "It is a source of joy to note that Catholic ministers are able, in certain particular cases, to administer the sacraments of the Eucharist, Penance, and Anointing of the Sick to Christians who are not in full communion with the Catholic Church but who greatly desire to receive these sacraments, freely request them, and manifest the faith which the Catholic Church professes with regard to these sacraments" [*Ut unum sint*, par. 46]. It is clear that this affirmation was very important in the pope's eyes, for he repeated it literally eight years later in his encyclical on the Eucharist [*Ecclesia de Eucharistia*, par. 46].[20] Not only did John Paul say that such a practice was a *source of joy* [emphasis mine] but in both texts he even changed slightly the requirements of Canon Law by no longer specifying that one of the conditions for reception is that of being unable "to approach a minister of their own community."[21]

Such a subtle and widely unknown change may truly be viewed as a sign of ecumenical hope.

Baptismal Foundation for Ministry

What, then, does this mean for ministry, for the missionary vocation of all the baptized in the world? Let me suggest that baptism grafts us into a priestly vocation, it initiates us into a community of priests and this community of priests, the royal priesthood of the faithful, offers itself in union with Christ *the* Priest for the life of the world. Probably nothing in the contemporary rites of baptism better expresses this understanding than the postbaptismal anointing in the current Roman Rite, an anointing which, unfortunately, is customarily omitted in favor of confirmation in the case of adult initiation:

> The God of power and Father of our Lord Jesus
> Christ has freed you from sin
> and brought you to new life
> through water and the Holy Spirit.
> He now anoints you with the chrism of salvation
> so that, united with his people,
> you may remain forever a member of Christ,
> who is Priest, Prophet, and King.[22]

20. Kasper, *Sacrament of Unity*, 72–73. See also Seasoltz, "One House."

21 *Code of Canon Law*, 321.

22. *Rites of the Catholic Church*, vol. 1, §319, 208.

A similar understanding of this priestly identity of the church appears as well in the words that introduce a welcome spoken to the newly baptized by the assembly at the conclusion of the baptismal rite in the *Lutheran Book of Worship*: "Through Baptism God has made *these* new *sisters and brothers* members of the priesthood we all share in Christ Jesus, that we may proclaim the praise of God and bear his creative and redeeming Word to all the world."[23]

Because it is the Body of *Christ* into which the baptized are incorporated all are initiated by baptism into a royal and prophetic priesthood. As such, the community of the church is a particular kind of community that knows itself as engaged in active priestly ministry and self-sacrificial service in the world. The Body of Christ is not a community bent on its own survival or self-preservation. The Body of Christ, who is Priest, Prophet, and King, exists that it may die in Christ, so that it may extend itself for the life of others as it continues its baptismal pilgrimage through death to resurrection. The current *Catechism of the Catholic Church* expresses this baptismal-ecclesiological dimension well:

> The baptized have become "living stones" to be "built into a spiritual house, to be a holy priesthood." By Baptism they share in the priesthood of Christ, in his prophetic and royal mission. They are "a chosen race, a royal priesthood, a holy nation, God's own people, that [they] may declare the wonderful deeds of him who called [them] out of darkness into his marvelous light." *Baptism gives a share in the common priesthood of all believers.*[24]

In other words, baptism itself is an "ordination" to priesthood and the church itself is a nothing other than a royal, prophetic, and communal priesthood itself. In an article devoted in large part to precisely this priestly identity of the baptized, Aidan Kavanagh writes:

> A baptismal element needs to be introduced into our contemporary discussion of ministry . . . But while one cannot discuss baptism without ministerial implications arising, it has unfortunately become usual to discuss ministries without ever feeling it necessary to enter into the implications of this discussion for baptism. That holy orders are rooted in baptism never seems to cross our minds. I suggest that it must . . . [T]he Church baptizes to priesthood: it ordains only to executive exercise of that priesthood in the major orders of ministry. Indeed *Ordo Romanus XI*

23. *Lutheran Book of Worship*, 124. This language of priesthood, unfortunately, no longer appears in the parallel welcome in *Evangelical Lutheran Worship*, 231.

24. *Catechism of the Catholic Church*, §1268, p. 323 [emphasis is original].

of the ninth century has the baptized and anointed neophytes vested in stole and chasuble as they are presented to the Bishop of Rome for consignation prior to the beginning of the Easter Eucharist. The point being that *sacerdotium* (priesthood) in orthodox Christianity is not plural but single. It is that of Christ, shared among those in solidarity with whom . . . he was himself baptized in the Jordan, and also in solidarity with whom he now stands as both sacrifice and sacrificer in heaven . . . While every presbyter and bishop is therefore a sacerdotal person, not every sacerdotal person in the Church is a presbyter or bishop. Nor does sacerdotality come upon one for the first time, so to speak, at one's ordination. In constant genesis in the font, the Church is born there as a sacerdotal assembly by the Spirit of the Anointed One himself. *Laos* [laity] is a priestly name for a priestly person.[25]

He continues:

In baptism by water and the Holy Spirit . . . one is anointed with as full a sacerdotality as the Church possesses in and by the Anointed One himself. Ordination cannot make one more priestly than the Church, and without baptism ordination cannot make one a priest at all. Becoming a Christian and becoming a sacerdotal being are not merely correlative processes, they are one and the same.[26]

To be baptized, therefore, to be incorporated by baptism into the Body of Christ, is to become a priest within a community of priests in Jesus Christ, our great High Priest. Indeed, all theological consideration of ordination and ministry flows from our theology of baptism. For does not ordained ministry itself exist to serve all the baptized?

Now this priestly people constituted by our baptismal plunge into the Paschal Mystery is of course a servant people of God involved in Christ's own mission of service in the world. In a pastoral letter to his archdiocese, written in 1966, Richard Cardinal Cushing wrote:

Jesus came not only to proclaim the coming of the Kingdom, he came also to give himself for its realization. He came to serve, to heal, to reconcile, to bind up wounds. Jesus, we may say, is in an exceptional way the Good Samaritan. He is the one who comes alongside of us in our need and in our sorrow, he extends himself for our sake. He truly dies that we might live and

25. Kavanagh, "Unfinished," 267–69.
26. Ibid., 270–71.

he ministers to us that we might be healed . . . So it is that the Church announces the coming of the Kingdom of God not only in word, through preaching and proclamation, but more particularly in work, in her ministry of reconciliation, of binding up wounds, of suffering service, of healing . . . As the Lord was the "man for others," so must the Church be "the community for others."[27]

Similarly, Lutheran theologian and martyr Dietrich Bonhoeffer wrote in his classic work, *The Cost of Discipleship,* that the call of Christ is always a call to death in Him:

When Christ calls a man, he bids him come and die. It may be a death like that of the first disciples who had to leave home and work to follow him . . . But it is the same death every time— death in Jesus Christ, the death of the old man at his call. Jesus' summons to the rich young man was calling him to die, because only the man who is dead to his own will can follow Christ. In fact every command of Jesus is a call to die, with all our affections and lusts. But we do not want to die, and therefore Jesus Christ and his call are necessarily our death as well as our life. The call to discipleship, the baptism in the name of Jesus Christ means both death and life . . . If we refuse to take up our cross and submit to suffering and rejection at the hands of men, we forfeit our fellowship with Christ and have ceased to follow him. But if we lose our lives in his service and carry our cross, we shall find our lives again in the fellowship of the cross with Christ. The opposite of discipleship is to be ashamed of Christ and his cross and all the offence which the cross brings in its train . . . Discipleship means allegiance to the suffering Christ, and it is therefore not at all surprising that Christians should be called upon to suffer. In fact it is a joy and token of his grace.[28]

And, with regard to the mission of the church itself, Bonhoeffer could write in his famous *Letters and Papers from Prison* that "The Church is the Church only when it exists for others. To make a start, it should give away all its property to those in need . . . The Church must share in the secular problems of ordinary human life, not dominating but helping and serving."[29]

A church "dead" and "buried" by baptism into Christ is liberated from the fear of death itself and, therefore, can dare to risk itself in a mission

27. Cushing, *Servant Church,* 6–8.

28. Bonhoeffer, *Cost of Discipleship,* 99, 101.

29. Bonhoeffer, *Letters and Papers,* 203–4.

of suffering service in the world because it knows and seeks to know only the cross and suffering with the world as the way to resurrection. You see, death has a way of setting one free from all kinds of constraints, laws, plans, priorities, and old ways of doing things. So, if the church is truly dead and buried in Christ then there is nothing left to lose in offering itself in service in union and solidarity with the crucified Christ himself. What can possibly happen any longer to an individual or a church who know themselves to be already dead? Absolutely nothing, of course! And, as such, the church has been set free by its baptismal death and burial to become truly this "community for others" in the world.

One in our own day who came to understand the mission of the church and his own episcopal ministry within the church in precisely this way was, of course, the Salvadoran martyr, Archbishop, now Blessed, Oscar Arnulfo Romero (1917–1980), champion of El Salvador's poor, oppressed, and disappeared. As is well known, Romero boldly faced the numerous death threats he encountered in response to his ministry in a way that can only be characterized as baptismal: "If they kill me I shall rise in the Salvadoran people." Only one who knew himself already dead and buried in Christ could make such a bold assertion about his own future. But Romero is not alone. Those who suggest that, rather than the patristic era, it is actually our own time that should be termed the "age of the martyrs" are undoubtedly correct. In this year we cannot but think of the recent canonization of the Martyrs of the Armenian Genocide by the Armenian Apostolic Church and, among others certainly, the martyrdom of the twenty-one Coptic Christians at the hands of ISIS. And if the third-century theologian Tertullian was right in his own day of claiming that "blood of the martyrs is the seed of the Church," then it is also true that this "seed" of the church is precisely that which is planted still today by our baptismal plunge into Christ's death and burial. As Pope Francis has reminded us, "The ecumenism of suffering and the ecumenism of martyrdom, the ecumenism of blood is a powerful call to journey along the road of reconciliation among the Churches, with decision and with trusting abandonment to the action of the Spirit."[30] Indeed, from that watery grave of Baptism emerges a priestly-servant community of the cross, which expects nothing other than what its Servant-Master himself endured and experienced. Who knows what kind of church might yet arise when such baptismal-Paschal Mystery imagery is embraced by the baptized themselves?

30. Vatican Radio, "Pope Francis to Armenian Catholicos," August 5, 2014.

Conclusion

There is no question but that since Vatican II a "communion ecclesiology" has been a dominant theological concern and an increasingly popular, even ecumenical way of approaching the theology of the church. Such an ecclesiology, however, is often closely connected to divisive ecumenical issues, such as orders (especially the historic episcopacy) and the Eucharist, and so often has limited value. Hence, a *baptismal* ecclesiology, as the absolute foundation and source for all theological reflection on the church, may be much more fruitful as a foundational approach out of which other divisive issues can be addressed anew. Not only would such an approach to understanding the church be ecumenically helpful, but it could well serve to underscore boldly the very nature and identity of the church and its mission in the world as that which is given precisely in baptism already. That is, Eucharist is the means by which our *baptismal* identity is continually renewed, reconstituted, and strengthened. Our ecclesial identity as church, as the corporate Body of Christ, as dead, buried, and risen in Christ, as born anew and adopted through water and the Spirit, and as signed and sealed by the Holy Spirit for life, witness, and mission in the world is given to us freely in baptism. From baptism the various orders of ministry flow. And back to baptism, to our freely-given baptismal identity, the Eucharist and other sacraments lead and direct us. There is a real sense in which our life in Christ is always about baptism and its implications. We are always walking wet with Christ, never quite getting out of the font!

Finally, baptism, of course, is not merely about what happens or is supposed to happen to baptized individuals. Death, burial, and resurrection in Christ through baptism is about the birthing of that community of grace called the church. That is, baptism is the paradigm for the church itself. It is not just baptized individuals but it is the *church* that is called to die constantly in order to live. The kind of Church a baptismal ecclesiology may well yet engender in our own world is an ecumenical Church, an inclusive-catholic Church, and a Church on mission knowing that its true identity and life only comes when it gives itself up in death, only when it realizes that it is already dead and buried so that it may rise always to newness of life and be the Church that baptism calls into being.

Bibliography

Bernardin, Joseph Cardinal. *The Gift of Peace*. Chicago: Loyola, 1997.

Bonhoeffer, Dietrich. *The Cost of Discipleship*. Unabridged ed. New York: Macmillan, 1963.

———. *Letters and Papers from Prison*. Rev. ed. New York: Macmillan, 1967.

Canon Law Society of America. *Code of Canon Law: Latin-English Edition*. Washington, DC: Canon Law Society of America, 1983.

Catholic News Service. "Cardinal Asks Dialogue Partners If an Ecumenical Catechism Might Work." Feb. 8, 2010. www.catholicnews.com/data/stories/cns/1000540.htm.

Cushing, Richard Cardinal. *The Servant Church*. Boston: Daughters of Saint Paul, 1966.

Evangelical Lutheran Worship. Minneapolis: Augsburg Fortress, 2006.

Francis, *Evangelii Gaudium*. November 24, 2013. w2.vatican.va/content/francesco/en/apost_exhortations/documents/papa-francesco_esortazione-ap_20131124_evangelii-gaudium.html.

Inter-Lutheran Commission on Worship. *Lutheran Book of Worship*. Minneapolis: Augsburg, 1978.

John Paul II. *Ut Unum Sint*. May 25, 1995. w2.vatican.va/content/john-paul-ii/en/encyclicals/documents/hf_jp-ii_enc_25051995_ut-unum-sint.html.

Johnson, Maxwell E. "Back Home to the Font: Eight Implications of a Baptismal Spirituality." *Worship* 71 (1997) 482–504.

———. "Building Christian Unity." In *The Oblate Life*, edited by Gervase Holdaway, 231–35. Collegeville, MN: Liturgical, 2008.

———. *The Church in Act: Lutheran Liturgical Theology in Ecumenical Conversation*. Minneapolis: Fortress, 2015.

———. "Ecumenism: Gifts, Challenges, and Hopes for a Renewed Vision." Godfrey Diekmann Lecture. *Worship* 80 (2006) 2–29.

———. "Let's Stop Making 'Converts' at Easter." *Catechumenate: A Journal of Christian Initiation* 21, no. 5 (1999) 10–20.

———. "Liturgy and Ecumenism: Gifts, Challenges, and Hopes for a Renewed Vision." The Godfrey Diekmann Lecture. *Worship* 80, no. 1 (2006) 2–29.

———. "The Loss of a Common Language: The End of Ecumenical-Liturgical Convergence?" Aidan Kavanagh Lecture, October 10, 2006. In *Colloquium: Music, Worship, and the Arts*, 27–39. New Haven: Yale Institute of Sacred Music, 2010.

———. "Not 'Sheep Stealing': Christ Calls Us to Be One/No Es Robar Ovejas: Cristo Nos Llama a la Unidad." *¡Oye! 2008* 4 (2007) 24–25.

———. "Planning and Leading Liturgical Prayer in an Ecumenical Context." *Pro Ecclesia* 8 (1999) 187–200.

———. *The Rites of Christian Initiation: Their Evolution and Interpretation*. 2nd rev. ed. Collegeville, MN: Liturgical, 2007.

———. "Romans 6 and the Identity of the Church: Towards a Baptismal Ecclesiology." *Catechumenate: A Journal of Christian Initiation* 22 (2000) 22–36.

———. "'Satis Est': Ecumenical Catalyst or Narrow Reductionism?" In *Liturgy in a New Millennium, 2000–2003*, edited by Rhoda Schuler, 158–72. Institute of Liturgical Studies Occasional Papers 11. Valparaiso: Institute of Liturgical Studies, 2006.

Kasper, Walter. *Sacrament of Unity: The Eucharist and the Church*. New York: Crossroad, 2004.

Kavanagh, Aidan. "Unfinished and Unbegun Revisited." In *Living Water, Sealing Spirit: Readings on Christian Initiation*, edited by Maxwell E. Johnson, 259–73. Collegeville, MN: Pueblo, 1995.

Lathrop, Gordon, *Holy People: A Liturgical Ecclesiology*. Minneapolis: Fortress, 1999.

Lutheran-Catholic Dialogue in the *United States. The Church as Koinonia of Salvation: Its Structures and Ministries; Common Statement of the Tenth Round of the U.S. Lutheran-Roman Catholic Dialogue*. Washington, DC: USCCB, 2005.

The Lutheran World Federation and The Pontifical Council for Promoting Christian Unity. *From Conflict to Communion: Lutheran-Catholic Common Commemoration of the Reformation in 2017*. Leipzig: Evangelische, 2013.

Pratt Green, Fred. "The Church of Christ, in Every Age." Hymn #433. In *Lutheran Book of Worship*. Minneapolis: Augsburg, 1978.

The Rites of the Catholic Church. Vol. 1. Collegeville, MN: Pueblo, 1990.

Seasoltz, R. Kevin. "One House, Many Dwellings: Open and Closed Communion." *Worship* 79 (2005) 405–14.

Turner, Paul. *Confirmation: The Baby in Solomon's Court*. Mahwah, NJ: Paulist, 1993.

———. "Forum: Confusion over Confirmation." *Worship* 71 (1997) 537–45.

United States Conference of Catholic Bishops. *Catechism of the Catholic Church*. Collegeville, MN: Liturgical, 1994.

Vatican Council II: The Conciliar and Post Conciliar Documents. Vol. 1. Translated by A. Flannery. Collegeville, MN: Liturgical, 1984.

Vatican Radio. "Pope Sends Greetings for US Christian Unity Event." May 23, 2015. en.radiovaticana.va/news/2015/05/24/pope_sends_greetings_for_us_christian_unity_event/1146375.

Vatican Radio. "Pope Francis to Armenian Catholics: Blood of Martyrs is Seed of Unity." August 5, 2014. en.radiovaticana.va/storico/2014/05/08/pope_francis_to_armenian_catholicos_blood_of_martyrs_is_seed_of_unity/en1-797476.

World Council of Churches. *Baptism, Eucharist and Ministry*. Geneva, 1982.

3

A Wider Witness

From "Lay Vocation" to the Call of Missionary Discipleship

—Edward P. Hahnenberg

> I dream of a "missionary option," that is, a missionary impulse capable of transforming everything, so that the Church's customs, ways of doing things, times and schedules, language and structures can be suitably channeled for the evangelization of today's world rather than for her self-preservation.[1]
>
> —POPE FRANCIS

IN HIS APOSTOLIC EXHORTATION *Evangelii Gaudium* (The Joy of the Gospel), Pope Francis picks up the "new evangelization" begun by his predecessors and places it squarely within the context of a broader "missionary transformation" of the church itself. This transformation is nothing less than a conversion of hearts, minds, institutions, and practices so as to make "missionary outreach . . . *paradigmatic for all the Church's activity.*"[2] In this call, Francis caps a development in official church teaching a century in the

1. Francis, *Evangelii Gaudium*, 27.
2. Ibid., 15; emphasis in original.

making—confirming with confidence and joy a basic shift in the church's self-understanding, the shift from "drawing in" to "going out."

One way to see this shift is through the lens of the laity. In what follows I would like to chart a trajectory over the past fifty years, beginning with the awakening of the laity that marked mid-century Catholicism, continuing through the Second Vatican Council's ecclesiological vision, and concluding with the call to become missionary disciples that has been such a central message of Pope Francis. I will conclude with some brief reflections on what all of this might mean for the ministry of preaching.

Vatican II's Theology of the Laity

Godfrey Diekmann, the Benedictine theologian and pioneer of the liturgical movement, once observed that the greatest achievement of the Second Vatican Council "was the restoration of the baptismal dignity of the laity."[3] Vatican II stands apart from all previous general councils in the amount of attention it gave to the life and activity of laypeople in the church. After centuries of neglect, the laity were brought to the center of the church's consciousness and placed at the heart of its most official pronouncements.

Given this historic shift within an institution so shy of change, what is remarkable is how uncontroversial the whole question of the laity was at the council itself. The initial draft of Vatican II's document on the church, which in all other respects was roundly criticized, already contained within it a quite positive chapter on the laity. Though the document was rejected and sent back to committee, the original core of the chapter on the laity survived. Throughout the various revisions of this chapter, reactions came mostly in the form of speeches that praised the laity's contributions to the church and the world. Bishops wanted more said about the laity, not less. The final version of the chapter on the laity passed almost unanimously, with only eight negatives out of 2,236 votes cast.

This dramatic affirmation was the culmination of decades of expanding lay engagement in the church. Often grouped together under the title "Catholic Action," a variety of sodalities, guilds, and lay associations—some of which were already active in the 1920s and 1930s—exploded in size and energy following the Second World War. Bishops and pastors endorsed these groups, major conferences were held at the Vatican in 1951 and 1957, and theologians showed unprecedented interest in all things lay.

As theologians like Karl Rahner, Edward Schillebeeckx, Gerard Philips, and, above all, Yves Congar began to craft a theology of the laity, they

---

3. Reported in Johnson, *Rites*, 386.

discovered little attention to the topic in classic sources. This lacuna was brought home during the council debates when Bishop Stephen László of Austria provided a concrete example. In a speech from the council floor, Bishop László described going to look up the word "laity" in the *Kirchenlexikon*—a multi-volume theological encyclopedia from the nineteenth century. The entry on "Laity" read simply: "See clergy."[4] There was no positive treatment. The laity were defined in terms of their subordination to the hierarchy.

The Second Vatican Council sought out a more positive theological description of the lay person. It did so in two ways.

First, the council affirmed unambiguously that the mission of the laity is rooted in our shared baptism. Baptism (followed by confirmation and Eucharist) initiates us into a community. As members of this community, we all have an active role to play. We all share in this community's mission to serve and celebrate the reign of God in our midst. Over the centuries, baptism had been reduced to an almost magical rite, hastily administered after birth, whose sole purpose was to wipe away original sin. Vatican II recovered a more ancient vision: baptism draws us into a community and sends us out—in a variety of ways, over the course of our lives—on a mission to share the Gospel with others.

Baptism brands everyone an apostle. Baptism calls all of us to spread the Good News. Thus the mission of the church does not trickle down from Christ to the hierarchy to the laity.[5] Our Catholic leaders do not "own" Christ's mission and then beneficently bestow it on the people in the pews. The laity do not "help out" with work that belongs to someone else. According to Vatican II, baptism brings us all into the Body of Christ and the people of God. Through baptism, Christ himself calls each of us to serve.

As the *Decree on the Apostolate of the Laity* put it: "Lay people's right and duty to be apostles derives from their union with Christ their head. Inserted as they are in the mystical body of Christ by baptism and strengthened by the power of the Holy Spirit in confirmation, it is by the Lord himself that they are assigned to the apostolate."[6]

---

4. Wetzer and Welte, *Kirchenlexikon*, 1323. This telling entry appears to have been first noticed by R. Müller in "Der Laie." Congar often cited the entry, and may very well have been the one to inspire Bishop Stephen László's intervention. See Sauer, "Council Discovers," vol. 4, 256.

5. Pope Pius XI defined Catholic Action as "the participation of the laity in the apostolate of the Church's hierarchy." See Pius XI, "Discourse."

6. Second Vatican Council, *Apostolicam Actuositatem*, 3. References to the documents of Vatican II are from Flannery, ed., *Vatican Council II.*

Second, the council offered a more positive theology by describing the secular world as the graced context that gives distinctive shape to the lay apostolate. The laity are *secular*—and that is not a slur. For the secular is understood here not as some God-forsaken wasteland separate from the church. Instead, the bishops at Vatican II used that word to talk about ordinary life. In the world of family and friends, work and recreation, politics and culture, God must be present.

> [The laity] live in the world, in each and every one of the world's occupations and callings and in the ordinary circumstances of social and family life which, as it were, form the context of their existence. There they are called by God to contribute to the sanctification of the world from within, like leaven, in the spirit of the Gospel, by fulfilling their own particular duties.[7]

Overcoming centuries of Christian spirituality that had reduced "the world" to a site of sin and temptation, Vatican II saw it as the positive context that both informs the life of the laity and is itself transformed by their Christian witness. But even as the council described the "secular characteristic" of the laity, it did not insist on a rigid dichotomy between clergy in the church and laity in the world. The documents easily admit that priests sometimes hold secular jobs. And the council affirms the many contributions that the laity were just beginning to make to important ministries within the church.

Toward a Total Ecclesiology

Almost as soon as the council ended, questions about this "theology of the laity" began to surface. The most important questions came from those who had done so much to promote the laity prior to the council; and their critique came out of a growing appreciation for the council's broader ecclesiological vision. At a 1966 symposium held at the University of Notre Dame, Abbot Christopher Butler observed: "I should like to suggest that this question of the definition of the laity is a completely false problem. There is no definition of laity. There is a definition of a Christian. We have a definition of a priest or of a minister in holy orders. There is no third definition of the laity. A member of the laity is very simply a Christian."[8] Richard McBrien, then teaching at Pope John XXIII National Seminary in Weston, began a 1969 article, titled "A Theology of the Laity," by saying:

---

7. Second Vatican Council, *Lumen Gentium*, 31.
8. Cited in Miller, *Vatican II*, 269.

I should regard this essay a success if it becomes the last article ever written on the theology of the laity. Otherwise, I shall have contributed one more item to a body of literature which, as a systematic theologian, I can find little reason to justify. The topic itself betrays an understanding of the Church which is simply untenable; namely, that the non-ordained constitute a special segment of the Body of Christ whose vocation, dignity, and mission are somehow regarded as a limited aspect of the total vocation, dignity, and mission of the church.[9]

Butler and McBrien were just two voices in a chorus of European and North American theologians drawing attention to the fact that—despite all the positive things Vatican II had to say about laypeople—the category of layperson itself remains basically negative. It is a remainder concept, a left-over term. It names something over against something else: The laity are not clergy. In light of the broader ecclesiological revolution confirmed by the Second Vatican Council, these theologians had begun to question the value of building a theology on a basic and non-biblical distinction between two groups in the church.

Yves Congar, who wrote the first major theology of the laity in the 1950s, later acknowledged the limitations of his earlier work.[10] In a 1971 essay, he admitted that his preconciliar writing on the laity had distinguished things "too nicely," thus leading to a linear scheme in which "Christ makes the hierarchy and the hierarchy makes the Church as community of faithful."[11] Despite his efforts to promote the laity, Congar recognized that, simply by the way he framed the question, he had inadvertently perpetuated a theological subordination of laity to clergy, and thus of baptism to ordination. He then suggested that the decisive pair for a truly postconciliar theology of ministry was no longer "clergy-laity" but "ministries-community."[12] In that one line, Congar captured the fundamental sea change taking place in the theology of church and ministry after the council: a shift from a linear model putting clergy over against laity to a model of two concentric circles, where various ministries are seen within the whole church community and

---

9. McBrien, "Theology," 73.

10. Congar, *Lay People*.

11. Congar, "My Path-Findings," 174–75.

12. Ibid., 176. The English translation of this passage obscures Congar's point. His phrase "*ministères ou services-communauté*" becomes "ministries/modes of community service," instead of "ministries or services/community." The emphasis in the original is not to distinguish ministries from services, but to place a variety of ministries and other services within the context of the church community. Congar, *Ministères*, 17.

its mission in the world.[13] What is needed is not a theology of the laity, Congar concluded, but a "total ecclesiology."[14]

Toward a Church of Missionary Disciples

Vatican II's *Dogmatic Constitution on the Church, Lumen Gentium*, presents a vision of church as the whole people of God, the Body of Christ and home of the Spirit, a communion of disciples called by Christ, through baptism, to share in his priestly, prophetic, and royal work. In this vision, the Second Vatican Council laid a foundation for the "total ecclesiology" called for by Congar.

But even Vatican II did not construct that comprehensive and systematic "total ecclesiology." The German theologian Hermann Pottmeyer offers a wonderful image of the council as "an unfinished building site"—a daring project that has not been completed.[15] The council participants may have set the foundation and delivered the materials, but they left the rest of the work to us.

As I look back on the work that has been done over the past fifty years—this long building project, with its bursts of progress and long construction delays—my image is not that of a modern skyscraper going up according to the plan of a detailed blueprint. Rather, my metaphor is a medieval cathedral, whose original inspiration evolves organically over time as each generation adapts to changing dreams and changing demands. As economic conditions improve, one spire becomes two. Stonework changes color when a quarry closes and another opens. Windows are added after a new patron arrives, and walls are removed if they fail to bear weight. The final edifice is the result of the original vision that inspired it, even if it takes shape in ways that were never anticipated.

The construction of our postconciliar church has unfolded in a similar organic way. In terms of our topic here, I note two significant adaptations. The first is the shift we saw in Congar and others, namely, the shift from focusing on a theology of the layperson to developing a "total ecclesiology." As I suggested, this adaptation is not a departure from the council, but a reflection of its deeper vision. Indeed, by placing the laity within the whole people of God, *Lumen Gentium* made this shift possible. But just as *Lumen*

13. Congar's model of concentric circles was developed and fruitfully applied to the North American context by O'Meara, *Theology*. See Hahnenberg, *Ministries*, 7–38.

14. In 1971, Congar admitted, "I have not written that ecclesiology." See Congar, "My Path-Findings," 174.

15. Pottmeyer, *Towards a Papacy*, 110.

Gentium located the laity within the context of the church, two other council documents, *Gaudium et Spes* and *Ad Gentes*, placed the church itself within the wider context of its mission in the world. This is a second adaptation, turning the focus from the nature of the church to its mission. Given these two adaptations, it seems to me that the important question to ask today, fifty years after the close of Vatican II, is not, "What does it mean to be a *layperson* in the *church?*" The question to ask is, "What does it mean to be a *disciple* on *mission?*"

To illustrate how we might begin to address this question, I would like to turn our attention to the words and example of the bishop of Rome, Pope Francis, who has made the call to become missionary disciples a hallmark of his papacy.

When Francis went back to South America for the first time as pope, he added a stop that was not on Pope Benedict's original itinerary for World Youth Day. Before joining the crowds in Rio de Janeiro, Francis traveled 150 miles southwest to visit the Marian shrine at Aparecida, Brazil. At the heart of this shrine, which boasts the second largest basilica in the world (after St. Peter's) and welcomes over ten million pilgrims a year, is a little image of the Virgin known as "Our Lady of Aparecida." Legend has it that in 1717 three fisherman discovered the broken pieces of a statue of a dark-skinned Madonna in the Paraíba River. This discovery was followed by a miraculous catch of fish, further miracles, and wide-spread popular devotion. According to tradition, the statue is black because Our Lady identifies with the oppressed; it was found in pieces to symbolize the broken lives of slaves.

Francis went to Aparecida not only because the place is important to the people of Brazil, but also because the place is important to the person of the pope. It was at this shrine in 2007 that Cardinal Jorge Mario Bergoglio joined bishops from across Latin America for the Fifth General Conference of Bishops of Latin America and the Caribbean (CELAM). Continuing the legacy of the ground-breaking gatherings at Medellín (1968) and Puebla (1979), Aparecida sought to examine the signs of the times in light of the Gospel. Embracing the "see–judge–act" methodology of those earlier meetings,[16] the bishops at Aparecida looked out on a continent still suffering under the historical weight of colonial exploitation, political oppression, environmental degradation, and massive, death-dealing poverty. They also noted a new reality: the rapid erosion of local religious cultures, now in danger of being completely washed away in the maelstrom of the global market.[17] Such realities, when read through the lens of faith in Christ, called

16. CELAM. "V General Conference," 9.

17. Ibid., 38–39.

for a renewed dedication to the "preferential option for the poor" and a new commitment to stand as a church in "permanent mission."[18] The final document of Aparecida called all of the faithful to become "missionary disciples"—a phrase that runs throughout the text, claiming it as the fundamental identity and the principle vocation of Christians today. The man who wrote this final document, who gathered together the discussion at Aparecida, was none other than the cardinal from Buenos Aires, Cardinal Bergoglio.[19]

In an interview shortly after the gathering at Aparecida, Cardinal Bergoglio talked about his experience there. He identified three themes that offer insight into what it might meant to be "missionary disciples" today. First, the future Pope Francis stressed the spirit of genuine collaboration and mutual respect that characterized the work of the bishops at Aparecida. This was a process "that moved from below upwards, not vice versa."[20] Nothing was imposed from above, there was no prepackaged text. Instead, discussion began with each of the twenty-three presidents from the different episcopal conferences simply sharing what they had learned from the people of God in their various countries and contexts. As the conversation progressed, the editorial committee sought to draw these different motifs into creative harmony. Bergoglio, who chaired this committee, was convinced that this harmony could only be explained as the work of the Spirit, who "can stir diversity, plurality, multiplicity and at the same time make unity."[21]

The second key point about Aparecida is that, for the first time, the Latin American bishops gathered at a Marian shrine. For Bergoglio, the importance of this fact should not be overlooked. He told the reporter that, "Celebrating the Eucharist together with the people is different from celebrating it amongst us bishops separately. That gave us a live sense of belonging to our people, of the Church that goes forward as People of God, of us bishops as its servants."[22] After Mass, the bishops went down to meet in a hall directly below the sanctuary, and throughout their deliberations, they

18. "Message of the Fifth General Conference," in CELAM, "V General Conference," 17.

19. Bergoglio was elected to chair the drafting committee, a committee that also included the Honduran Cardinal Oscar Rodríguez Maradiaga, whom Pope Francis would later choose to lead the Council of Cardinal Advisers (the "G-8"). Also on this advisory council is Cardinal Francisco Javier Errázuriz of Chile, who, as co-president of CELAM, was a major force in bringing Aparecida to fruition.

20. Cited in Sefania Falasca, "What I Would Have Said."

21. Ibid.

22. Ibid.

heard the constant prayer of the pilgrims, the hymns of the faithful. Much of the document—and, in particular, its positive treatment of devotions and popular religiosity—came out of this experience of praying with the people.

Finally, Aparecida opens out into *mission*. Discipleship demands mission; mission requires discipleship. For Bergoglio, this is what lies at the heart of the call to become missionary disciples: "To remain faithful we need to go outside. Remaining faithful one goes out."[23] Later in the interview, the cardinal pointed out that sociologists say the influence of a parish extends to a radius of only about 600 meters (about 650 yards). But in Buenos Aires, there are more than 2,000 meters between one parish and the next. So he told his priests, "If you can, rent a garage and, if you find some willing layman, let him go there! Let him be with those people a bit, do a little catechesis and even give communion if they ask him." When a priest challenged the cardinal by saying, "But Father, if we do this the people then won't come to church," Bergoglio replied, "But why? Do they come to Mass now?"[24] This emphasis on mission is inseparable from the theme of mercy that runs throughout the Aparecida text. Cardinal Bergoglio drew attention to the importance of mercy by citing the biblical story of Jonah. When the interviewer offered the opinion that Jonah ran away from a difficult mission, Bergolgio interrupted: "No. What he was fleeing was not so much Nineveh as the boundless love of God for those people." He continued:

> [Jonah] wanted to do things his way, he wanted to steer it all. His stubbornness shut him in his own structures of evaluation, in his pre-ordained methods, in his righteous opinions. He had fenced his soul off with the barbed wire of those certainties that instead of giving freedom with God and opening horizons of greater service to others had finished by deafening his heart.[25]

Mission and mercy often make a mess. But what is the alternative? Better to be bruised and dirty because you've been in the streets than to waste away inside, sadly clinging to the comforts of one's own security.[26] "Our certainties can become a wall, a jail that imprisons the Holy Spirit."[27]

23. Ibid.
24. Ibid.
25. Ibid.
26. Francis, *Evangelii Gaudium*, 49.
27. Cited in Falasca, "What I Would Have Said."

Conclusion: Implications for Preaching

What Aparecida reveals to us, according to the Peruvian theologian Ernest Cavassa, SJ, is that behind the witness and words of Pope Francis are not only an undeniable personal style but also an ecclesial tradition.[28] The themes that have come to characterize the pontificate of Francis—collaboration and collegiality, a fundamental trust in the faith of the people, mercy, and, above all, a missionary spirit calling the whole church to the peripheries—these themes are not the high notes of a solo performer. They are the song of a whole chorus—a whole continent—inviting the universal church into a new self-understanding and sense of purpose. We are not, first and foremost, clergy and laity, priests and people, ordained and non-ordained; we are, first and foremost, a community of missionary disciples. Our purpose is not self-preservation, but self-gift—sharing with all people the profound truth of the Gospel that "life is attained and matures in the measure that it is offered up in order to give life to others."[29]

What might this mean for the ministry of preaching? The journey from the "lay vocation" to the call of missionary discipleship—which is, in many ways, the journey from Vatican II to CELAM V, from Rome to Aparecida—is an invitation to foster baptismal witness in the world. Pope Francis has some very particular and very practical advice for preachers, and great hopes for moving beyond the profound suffering that is the homily. ("The laity suffer from having to listen to these homilies, the clergy suffer from having to preach them!"[30]) However, there may be a more fundamental orientation here, an approach to proclaiming the Gospel in the spirit that Cardinal Bergoglio experienced at Aparecida.

First, preaching begins below, in the Spirit of God at work among ordinary people living ordinary lives. A text written in abstraction and obsessed with ideas can only become an imposition from above, proposing answers to questions that nobody asks.[31] Second, the preacher ministers among the people. Just as the bishops were inspired by praying alongside the faithful at Aparecida, so the preacher grows as a preacher through shared life, shared prayer, shared celebration, and shared pain with the people of God. Finally, both the preaching and the preacher become evangelical by turning toward the peripheries. These peripheries are geographic and economic, and they are social, cultural, and existential. They can be found wherever people suf-

---

28. Cavassa, "On the Trail."
29. Francis, *Evangelii Gaudium*, 10.
30. Ibid., 135.
31. Ibid., 155.

fer and starve. But they can also be found wherever people live on the edge of sin, pain, injustice, ignorance, indifference to religion, or any form of human misery.[32]

This mission to the margins cuts both ways. In *preaching*, we invite others to "go out," to discover the joy and the heartbreak that comes when we "cross over," like the Good Samaritan, in order to be present to the abused and neglected one on the side of the road. But as *preachers*, we ourselves are challenged to do the same, to give witness to the death of self and the new life in Christ that is the promise of our own baptism—to preach constantly, and only occasionally use words.

At the end of his reflections on the experience of Aparecida, Cardinal Bergoglio offered this bit of advice to those who have the audacity to preach the good news:

> Look at our people not for what it should be but for what it is and see what is necessary. Without preconceptions and recipes but with generous openness. For the wounds and the frailty God spoke. Allowing the Lord to speak . . . In a world that we can't manage to interest with the words we say, only His presence that loves us, saves us, can be of interest.[33]

Bibliography

Cavassa, Ernesto. "On the Trail of Aparecida." *America*. October 30, 2013. americamagazine.org/trail-aparecida.

CELAM. "V General Conference of the Bishops of Latin America and the Caribbean Concluding Document." www.aecrc.org/documents/Aparecida-Concluding%20 Document.pdf.

Congar, Yves. *Lay People in the Church*. Translated by Donald Attwater. 1956. Westminster, MD: Newman, 1965.

———. "My Path-Findings in the Theology of Laity and Ministries." *Jurist* 32/2 (1972) 169–88.

———. *Ministères et communion ecclésiale*. Paris: Cerf, 1971.

Falasca, Sefania. "What I Would Have Said at the Consistory: An Interview with Cardinal Jorge Mario Bergoglio." *30Giorni* 11 (2007). www.30giorni.it/articoli_ id_16457_l3.htm.

Francis. *Evangelii Gaudium*. November 24, 2014. w2.vatican.va/content/francesco/ en/apost_exhortations/documents/papa-francesco_esortazione-ap_20131124_ evangelii-gaudium.html.

---

32. See Cardinal Bergoglio's intervention at the consistory of cardinals before the conclave that would elect him pope: "Bergoglio's Intervention."

33. Cited in Falasca, "What I Would Have Said."

Flannery, Austin, ed. *Vatican Council II: The Basic Sixteen Documents*. Northport, NY: Costello, 1996.

Hahnenberg, Edward P. *Ministries: A Relational Approach*. New York: Crossroad, 2003.

Johnson, Maxwell. *The Rites of Christian Initiation: Their Evolution and Interpretation*. Collegeville, MN: Liturgical, 1999.

McBrien, Richard P. "A Theology of the Laity." *American Ecclesiastical Review* 160 (1969) 73–85.

Miller, John H, ed. *Vatican II: An Interfaith Appraisal*. Notre Dame: University of Notre Dame Press, 1966.

Müller, R. "Der Laie in der Kirche." *Theologische Quartalschrift* 130 (1950) 184–96.

O'Meara, Thomas F. *Theology of Ministry*. Rev. ed. New York: Paulist, 1999.

Pius XI, "Discourse to Italian Catholic Young Women." *L'Osservatore Romano*. March 21, 1927. p. 14.

Pottmeyer, Hermann. *Towards a Papacy in Communion: Perspectives from Vatican Councils I and II*. New York: Crossroad, 1998.

Sauer, Hanjo. "The Council Discovers the Laity." In *History of Vatican II*, edited by Giuseppe Alberigo and Joseph A. Komonchak. Maryknoll, NY: Orbis, 2003.

Vatican Radio. March 27, 2013, "Bergoglio's Intervention: A Diagnosis of the Problems in the Church." en.radiovaticana.va/storico/2013/03/27/bergoglios_intervention_a_diagnosis_ of_the_problems_in_the_church/en1-677269.

Wetzer, Heinrich J., and Welte, Benedict, eds. *Kirchenlexikon, oder Encyklopädie der katholischen theologie und ihrer hülfswissenschaften*. Vol. 8. Freiburg: Herder, 1891.

4

Gaudium et Spes

Reconsidered and Re-Projected

—Kristin Colberg

No aspect of the Catholic Church's life remains untouched by the Second Vatican Council in the fifty years since its final session. The council invited and guided the church to know itself and its relation to the world more deeply, and the implications of this invitation continue to unfold today. One thing that on-going study of the council increasingly reveals is that the trajectory out of the council was influenced in a profound way by the *Pastoral Constitution on the Church, Gaudium et Spes.* Many of the shifts in style, tone and content that were groundbreaking elements of this text in 1965 have become fundamental and familiar aspects of the church's approach to the world today. In fact, *Gaudium et Spes's* innovative and revolutionary character is often lost on contemporary readers precisely because its description of the church and the nature of the church-world relationship so closely mirrors current ecclesial self-understandings that its vision now seems self-evident. A renewed appreciation for *Gaudium et Spes's* distinctive development and impact provides an important lens for understanding key aspects of the text itself as well as Vatican II's on-going significance.

This chapter explores *Gaudium et Spes* and its anticipation of developments in the post-conciliar church in three sections. The first looks back at the genesis of *Gaudium et Spes* and its place within the overall theology of Vatican II. It highlights the way that the evolution of this text coincides with the council's discerning and embracing its own identity. Attention in the second section shifts to a consideration of three key aspects of *Gaudium et Spes*'s form and content, which help express its central theological commitments: its dialogical style, anthropological starting point and attention to concrete issues. The final section looks beyond the council to examine how *Gaudium et Spes* exerts a tremendous influence on the papacies of John Paul II, Benedict XVI, and Francis. Recognizing the common, although distinctive, reliance on *Gaudium et Spes* among these three popes demonstrates important, and sometimes surprising, continuity in their thought and underscores the nature of Vatican II's reception. Ultimately, examining *Gaudium et Spes* both retrospectively and prospectively underscores the fact that while the constitution's fiftieth anniversary celebrates a milestone in the council's history, its teachings and style continue to orient the church today as it looks toward the future.

The Emergence of *Gaudium et Spes* and the Theology of Vatican II

Considerable evidence attests to the fact that, from the earliest stages of his thinking, John XXIII understood one of Vatican II's primary aims as developing a more adequate description of the church-world relationship. The idea of holding a council arose early in Pope John's pontificate during a conversation with the Vatican secretary of State, Domenico Tardini, regarding the crises facing the modern world and how the church might lend its assistance.[1] While considering how the church could serve as a model of peace in a wider climate of anxiety, Pope John had the idea, which he later described as a "flash of heavenly light," to convene an ecumenical council.[2] John XXIII recognized that the world was undergoing dramatic social, political, and religious changes, and moreover, that it stood at the threshold of a new era. As a historian he understood that councils often coincided with the great turning points in history, and in the signs of the times he saw a crucial opportunity for the church to "define clearly and distinguish between what is sacred principle and eternal gospel and what belongs rather to

---

1. For an account of the pope's decision to call a council, see Hebblethwaite, *John XXIII*.

2. In subsequent reflections on this decision, Pope John noted that he had not considered holding a council prior to this "unexpected illumination." He commented: "I do not like to appeal to special inspiration. I am satisfied with the Orthodox teaching that everything is from God. In light of that teaching I regarded the idea of a Council as likewise an inspiration from heaven." See Alberigo, "Announcement," 3–8.

the changing times."[3] Unlike previous councils that had reacted to historic trends or doctrinal controversies by issuing condemnations and distancing the church from the world and its corruptions, Pope John envisioned a council that would bring the church up-to-date so as to transcend divisions and offer its service in dealing with a myriad of contemporary challenges. Therefore, the idea for the twenty-first ecumenical council was, from its very inception, linked to the notion of engaging the modern world and the concrete problems faced by men and women.

The significance of John XXIII's undertaking and how his vision might be realized were not immediately clear as preparations for the gathering began. While reaching out to the world was a central aspect of Pope John's hopes for the council, this theme did not appear frequently in the *vota* submitted by the bishops. In fact, very few of the *vota* addressed contemporary issues and those that did generally did so to recommend that the council issue a strong condemnation of modern errors. After receiving approximately two thousand *vota*, the lengthy process of organizing and considering them in order to develop the council's preparatory documents or schemata took place between June 1960 and February 1962.[4] This process resulted in the production of seventy schemata, only one of which had any significant engagement of questions related to the social order. Despite the enormous amount of work devoted to the production of these texts, they were generally greeted with dissatisfaction. Representing the views of many, Yves Congar criticized the schemata for their "neglect of the substantive content of the Gospel, negative view of the contemporary world, abstract and scholastic style, and omission of crucial current issues and lack of ecumenical interest."[5] Many worried that the schemata would not allow for the type of deliberation or renewal that John XXIII had signaled and, on the contrary, that they would further entrench the church in its defensive posture and negative assessment of the world.

Alarmed by the state of the preparatory texts and the failure to "formulate a radical strategy, a single main plan," Cardinal Leon Joseph Suenens, cardinal-archbishop of Malines, Belgium, spoke with Pope John about these issues in an audience in March of 1962.[6] Suenens expressed concern that the schemata were too numerous, inconsistent in quality, and focused on

---

3. Ibid., 3–4.

4. This complex task is well-documented by Komonchak in his chapter "Struggle," 167–356.

5. Ibid., 234.

6. Suenens, "Plan," 88.

particulars rather than basic principles.[7] He urged that their number be reduced and that the remaining texts be arranged in an order that would reflect a coherent direction for the gathering.[8] Upon hearing Suenens's concerns, John XXIII asked the cardinal if he would be willing to devise such a plan. Acting quickly, Suenens submitted a proposal to the pope in July of 1962. Suenens recommended streamlining the bishops' efforts by centering all of their deliberations on a single question: "How is the Church of the twentieth century measuring up to the Master's last command: 'Go, therefore make disciples of all nations. Baptize them in the name of the Father and of the Son and of the Holy Spirit and teach them to observe the commands I gave you'?" (cf. Matt 28:19).[9] This command, Suenens argues, leads to the "basic idea" of his plan, namely that the council's deliberations should be organized into two main categories: considering the church in its own internal life (*ad intra*) and considering the church's relation to the world (*ad extra*). With Suenens's plan to structure Vatican II around the two pillars of the church *ad intra* and the church *ad extra*, Pope John's idea for a council that would engage the problems of the modern world took significant steps towards its realization. Nevertheless, because the proposal was developed only two months before Vatican II's opening, it came too late to exercise a decisive impact on the agenda for the council's first session.

As Vatican II opened in October of 1962, two facts soon became obvious. The first was that the issue of the church's relation to the world would be a major theme of the council. The second was the general dissatisfaction with the way in which this topic had been treated in the preparatory texts. As the official meetings got underway, many participants expressed frustration by what they perceived as a discontinuity between John XXIII's desire to bring the church up-to-date and the material presented in the prepared schemata. A particular source of tension was the fact that the preparatory texts only gave brief consideration to the church-world relationship and failed to offer a comprehensive or consistent account of this locus. While many of the Council Fathers communicated their dissatisfaction to the pope about this piecemeal approach, one bishop in particular, Dom Helder Camara of Brazil, is often identified as providing an important catalyst for the decision to begin production of a separate schema on the world. During a particularly fiery address, Camara asked, "Are we to spend our whole time discussing internal church problems with two-thirds of humanity dying of hunger? Will

7. Ibid.
8. Ibid., 89.
9. Ibid., 101.

the council express its concern about the great problems of mankind?"[10] Finally he asked, "Is the shortage of priests the greatest problem in Latin America? No! Underdevelopment!" In addition to agreeing with Camara about the urgency of contemporary issues, many bishops realized that if the council wanted to show the church's ability to speak meaningfully to the modern world, it would have to demonstrate an awareness of the concrete problems it faced. In response to speeches like Camara's and the growing support for an explicit consideration of the church-world relationship, a mixed commission was established shortly after the end of the First Session to consider this question.

The series of events that culminated in the decision to draft a separate document on the church-world relationship highlights the nature of Vatican II as an "event."[11] The evolution of this document reflects the truly deliberative nature of the council and the way in which it did not limit itself to fixed answers or pathways; rather, it remained open to the Holy Spirit working among the bishops. *Gaudium et Spes* is a result of this experience and would not exist without it. As such, this text reflects the council's goals in a distinctive way and provides an important lens for understanding not just Vatican II's teaching on the nature of the church-world relationship, but its theology as whole.

Three Key Aspects of the Theology of *Gaudium et Spes*

Gaudium et Spes was promulgated on December 4, 1965, the day before Vatican II's conclusion. It is fair to say that no document had a more complex path to its realization or went through as many revisions.[12] The final text makes many critical theological contributions to the church's self-understanding, which are expressed both in its style and in its content. Three characteristic elements of *Gaudium et Spes*'s theology—its dialogical style, anthropological starting point, and focus on concrete issues—illumine the distinctive ways in which the constitution approaches the church-world relationship.

One of the first questions pursued as part of the new schema asked: to whom shall it be addressed? That this issue was raised so early in the text's development underscores the fact that, from the very beginning, *Gaudium et*

10. Moeller details Camara's address and describes its impact in his chapter "History," 10–12.

11. For an excellent article on the character of Vatican II as an event, see Komonchak's "Vatican II as an Event."

12. Hahnenberg, *Concise Guide*, 58.

Spes was conceived in a manner distinct from previous conciliar statements. Rather than assuming that the document would follow the traditional pattern wherein the church would instruct the faithful on a particular topic, the bishops recognized that the nature of their task necessitated a break from protocol in favor of a more flexible means of engaging modern concerns.[13] The decision to address all men and women of goodwill meant that the document would not be an instance of the church talking *at* the world but of speaking *to* the world as an invitation to dialogue. Such an approach had a two-fold significance. One the one hand, it demonstrated humility on the church's part, a departure from previous images of the church as a supreme teacher or a perfect society. It implied that the church needed to articulate its ability and role in engaging modern problems.[14] On the other hand, this spirit of reciprocity also affirmed the value of the world's potential contributions, and it recognized the places where the secular realm had made advances ahead of what the church had realized. *Gaudium et Spes*'s efforts to initiate a dialogue with "people everywhere" represents not only a shift away from traditional content, but perhaps more importantly, an effort to find a new language for embracing the world (GS 2).

A second critical element of *Gaudium et Spes*'s approach to the world is its consideration of concrete problems in the economic, social, and political realms. That such matters would be considered in the constitution of an ecumenical council was groundbreaking and, for some, controversial. Amidst discussions regarding the appropriate form and content of this document, several bishops remained unconvinced about the appropriateness of developing such a text. Emblematic of these concerns, the archbishop of Zaragoza, Pedro Cantero Cuadrado, asked whether "the Church was not here occupying itself with temporal problems for which it has neither the authority nor the necessary special knowledge?"[15] Questions such as these prompted the Council Fathers to be more explicit about their intentions for this document and offer a clear justification for its engagement with concrete issues. Congar explained the rationale for the decision to speak to temporal realities in his commentary on *Gaudium et Spes*:

13. Many bishops were influenced by the wide and generally positive response to John XXIII's encyclical *Pacem in Terris,* which was issued in April of 1963. Many held up this document as an example that employing language that is not overly theological or technical and, instead, using concrete situations as a starting point could generate tremendous interest and support. For a more detailed account of the way that *Pacem in Terris* had an impact on *Gaudium et Spes*, see Moeller, "History," 12–15.

14. Hollenbach develops this idea in his chapter "Church's Social Mission."

15. Congar. "Role of the Church," 202.

What then is the basis of the relation between the Church and the world? The basis is man, the fact that Christianity concerns man and that the articles of faith affect him . . . The Church is inserted into the history of men because it is formed of men (art. 1); therefore the world is both the scene of human history and the realization of God's saving plan (art. 2). It is a matter of saving man; man asks himself a question to which the Gospel has the answer (art. 3); faith throws light on man's destiny (arts. 11 and 21).[16]

Thus, as Congar highlights, in *Gaudium et Spes* the church reaches out to the world because it is the place where men and women encounter and respond to God's call. Women and men move towards their fulfillment in the context of social, political and economic realities that facilitate or impede their full development. As such, the church must be closely attuned to helping develop practices, systems, and structures that promote human flourishing.

With this justification, *Gaudium et Spes* turns in its second part to addressing matters related to marriage and family, culture, economic, and social life, the political community, and fostering peace among nations. It treats these issues carefully seeking to avoid exceeding its competency, but still offering a meaningful perspective on contemporary challenges. The goal of the text is not to provide a theological treatise on these subjects; rather it seeks to present an objective description of certain modern realities with some consideration of the wisdom that the church can offer these situations. In doing so, the council saw itself as providing points of contact between the church and the modern world. This strategy was inspired by French Dominican Marie-Dominique Chenu, who employed the image of "toothing stones" used by builders to "jut out from the end of a building or wall in anticipation of an addition."[17] *Gaudium et Spes* offers "toothing stones" between the church and the world as places where a dialogue between them could begin.

A third crucial aspect of *Gaudium et Spes*'s engagement with the modern world is its use of an anthropological starting point. The church's and world's common commitment to a successful future establishes fertile common ground for dialogue. Joseph Ratzinger, shortly after the council, observed that the "hinge" of the discussion between the church and the world is "man's full development as man" and noted that "the whole Pastoral Constitution might therefore be described in this light as a discussion between the Church and the unbeliever on the question of who and what

---

16. Ibid., 220.
17. Hahnenberg, *Concise Guide*, 59.

man really is."[18] By selecting an anthropological starting point, *Gaudium et Spes* implicitly assigns a positive value to modernity's questions about human flourishing, and it demonstrates a willingness to engage a modern and *ad extra* audience in mutually intelligible terms.[19] Starting with human experience underscores a recognition that the church's traditional starting points often appear as "non-starters" to modern men and women and that a coherent presentation of the church's teachings requires attention to the questions and assumptions of a contemporary audience.

At the heart of *Gaudium et Spes* is the idea that human beings are inherently spiritual and temporal. By illuminating this reality, the church believes it can make a genuine contribution to alleviating modern problems. *Gaudium et Spes* argues that many of the challenges facing men and women are rooted in the fact that the modern world ignores or denies the spiritual dimension of human existence, occupying itself with a "painstaking search for a better material world, without a parallel spiritual advancement" (GS 4). The separation of the two fundamental dimensions of human personhood is a primary cause of the unhappiness and sense of fragmentation that plagues the modern society; if the world's responses to modern problems isolates women and men from the source of true meaning in their lives, it inhibits authentic human flourishing. Yet, as *Gaudium et Spes* points out, despite the modern world's efforts, men and women still retain an innate experience of their own transcendence. Article 14 asserts:

> For by their power to know themselves in the depths of their being they rise above the universe of mere objects. When they are drawn to think about their real selves they turn to those deep recesses of their being where God who probes the human heart awaits them, and where they themselves decide their own destiny in the sight of God. So when they recognize in themselves a spiritual and immortal soul, this is not an illusion, a product of their imagination, to be explained solely in terms of physical or social causes. On the contrary, they have grasped the profound truth of the matter.

Gaudium et Spes uses this universal experience of longing and sense that the meaning of one's life is found outside of one's self as the foundation for its dialogue with the world. The council believes that shedding light on the

---

18. Ratzinger, "Dignity," 124.

19. Kasper gives an excellent analysis of the theological anthropology of *Gaudium et Spes* and the implications of this starting point in his article "Theological Anthropology," 129–38.

authentic nature of human personhood can make a profound contribution to advancing the common goals shared by the church and the world.

Gaudium et Spes and the Trajectory out of the Council

Looking at the church in the decades following the council, it becomes clear that *Gaudium et Spes* pioneered many of the developments that fundamentally inform its life today. The full extent of the text's significance cannot be explored here; instead, three key aspects of its impact on the papacies of John Paul II, Benedict XVI and Francis will be explored as a way of highlighting its influence throughout the last fifty years.

Anthropological Starting Point

Anthropological arguments have dominated the church's approach to contemporary issues since Vatican II. This approach is at the heart of much of John Paul II's work, a fact that is not surprising given his role in the development of *Gaudium et Spes*.[20] Utilizing a central theme in *Gaudium et Spes*, John Paul II emphasizes that the sense of homelessness and fragmentation experienced by modern men and women results from a loss of a sense of the transcendent depths of human existence. This concern is at the root of his famous distinction between a culture of life and a culture of death. *Evangelium Vitae* asserts:

> In seeking the deepest roots of the struggle between the "culture of life" and the "culture of death," we cannot restrict ourselves to the perverse idea of freedom mentioned above. We have to go to the heart of the tragedy being experienced by modern man: the eclipse of the sense of God and of man, typical of a social and cultural climate dominated by secularism, which, with its ubiquitous tentacles, succeeds at times in putting Christian communities themselves to the test. Those who allow themselves to be influenced by this climate easily fall into a sad vicious circle: when the sense of God is lost, there is also a tendency to lose the sense of man, of his dignity and his life; in turn, the systematic violation of the moral law, especially in the serious matter of respect for human life and its dignity, produces a kind of progressive darkening of the capacity to discern God's living and saving presence (EV 21).

20. For more on John Paul II's role in shaping *Gaudium et Spes*, see Dobrzynski and Kijas, *Christ, Church, Mankind*.

In *Evangelium Vitae* John Paul II seeks to make a forceful argument about the immorality of abortion, birth control, and euthanasia. In doing so, he does not begin with doctrine or moral norms, but by echoing and developing *Gaudium et Spes*'s teaching that when the world is drained of mystery and God is eschewed, the mystery and dignity of the human person is also lost. This approach, which had been revolutionary in 1965, seemed quite standard when *Evangelium Vitae* appeared thirty years later in 1995.

The eclipse of the transcendent dimension of human personhood also animates one of Benedict XVI's central concerns: the threat of relativism. Benedict uses a fundamentally anthropological frame to present his argument regarding the loss of truth in modern society. He asserts that the erosion of truth is rooted in the human beings' denial of themselves as God's finite creatures created for a purpose which lies outside of themselves and this world.[21] He asserts that relativistic positions cannot be tolerated because they deny a reality known by human beings at the depth of their being; their relationship to God creates a standard that brings order and meaning to their lives. Benedict argues: "A large portion of contemporary philosophies, in fact, consist of saying that man is not capable of truth. But viewed in this way man would not be capable of ethical values, either. Then he would have no standards. Then he would only have to consider how he arranged things reasonably for himself, and then, at any rate, the only criterion that mattered would be the opinion of the majority . . . That is why we must have the courage to dare to say: Yes, man must seek truth, he is capable of truth."[22] Rather than featuring philosophical proofs for the nature of truth, Benedict typically anchors his rejection of relativism in an instinctive awareness that human beings are capable of truth and ethical values.

Pope Francis' writings also adopt an anthropological starting point. This point of departure is clear in his emphasis on the importance of authentic encounter between individuals and communities and human solidarity. This is evidenced in the fact that Francis has said that his encyclical *Laudato Si': On Care for our Common Home* is not really an environmental document at all; he categorizes it as a text rooted in the notion of human solidarity and the solidarity of all of creation. The real problem with humankind's treatment of the earth, according to Francis, lies in the fact that humans no longer see God as the Creator of all, a reality that orients the human vocation outside of itself to a place of solidarity with others and all created things. Failing to recognize themselves as God's creatures leads to a

21. Benedict conveys this argument very clearly in his essay "God the Creator," 1–18.

22. Benedict XVI, "Dictatorship," 50.

reality where persons see "other living beings as mere objects subjected to arbitrary human domination" and fail to see that "the ultimate purpose of other creatures is not found in us" (LS 82). Recognizing the finite and interdependent nature of human existence by recognizing God as Creator allows people to see the environment not as something apart from themselves or merely the place they inhabit; rather, it reveals the cosmos or created world to be a reality whose flourishing is closely bound up with humanity's own full actualization. The core of *Laudato Si'* therefore advances a very "*Gaudium et Spes-esque*" argument, namely, that recognizing the true nature of human personhood illumines potential paths for advancing contemporary challenges.

John Paul II, Benedict XVI and Francis agree that providing a coherent understanding of the church's teachings depends on its ability to articulate a satisfying answer to the question "what is a human being?" The fact that an anthropological approach is used to address a broad range of questions from moral decisions to the nature of truth to care for the environment does not strike contemporary audiences as innovative because, in fact, this strategy has dominated much of the church's *ad extra* discourse for the past fifty years. *Gaudium et Spes's* bold anthropological turn has become the primary lens through which the church engages the world, demonstrating the decisive impact of the constitution on theological conversation.

Dialogical Style

The decision that *Gaudium et Spes* would address all men and women of goodwill inaugurated a new moment in the church's posture towards the world. This moment has stayed with the church in the papacies of John Paul II, Benedict XVI, and Francis, although it manifests itself in diverse ways. John Paul II pursued dialogue in a consistent and dedicated way among Catholics as well as in both the ecumenical and interreligious spheres. He understood his ministry as one of building common ground and personal relationships to facilitate dialogue. This conviction helped inspire his pioneering travels and efforts to bring people together through such events as World Youth Day and the World Day of Prayer. In his groundbreaking encyclical *Ut Unum Sint,* John Paul II uses the term "dialogue" over a hundred times. In this text he takes the remarkable step of calling for an ecumenical dialogue on the nature of the Petrine ministry. He asks other church leaders and theologians to "engage with me in a patient and fraternal dialogue on this subject, a dialogue in which, leaving useless controversies behind, we would listen to each other, keeping before us only the will of Christ for his

Church and allowing ourselves to be deeply moved by his plea 'that they may all be one . . . so that the world might believe that you have sent me' (Jn 17:21)" (UUS 95). John Paul II also explored the nature of dialogue in his encyclical *Dialogue and Proclamation* (1991). There he reflects on the necessity of interreligious exchange and the dual requirements of proclaiming the gospel and sincerely engaging the followers of other religious traditions. Both *Ut Unum Sint* and *Dialogue and Proclamation* reflect the spirit of reciprocity that lies at the heart of *Gaudium et Spes*; these texts take the constitution's posture towards the world and apply it to the church's ecumenical and interreligious engagement.

Benedict XVI's papacy also affirmed the centrality of dialogue. While he favored a mode of exchange that was distinct from that of his predecessor, he too recognized the importance of engaging other worldviews in a serious way. Benedict's efforts at dialogue focused largely on the relationship among cultures as well as between the church and the secular realm. His style of dialogue begins by addressing difficult and disputed issues rather than highlighting commonalities. In his mind, dialogue can linger too long on common ground so that it risks failing to engage the issues that really divide communities. Benedict believed that dialogue is not about seeking tolerance; it seeks the higher goal of identifying truth. As such, he felt that all parties must be honest and enthusiastic about the truth expressed in their tradition and represent it fully. He expressed this viewpoint clearly in his encyclical *Caritas in Veritate* (2009):

> Today the possibilities of *interaction between cultures* have increased significantly, giving rise to new openings for intercultural dialogue: a dialogue that, if it is to be effective, has to set out from a deep-seated knowledge of the specific identity of the various dialogue partners. Let it not be forgotten that the increased commercialization of cultural exchange today leads to a twofold danger. First, one may observe a *cultural eclecticism* that is often assumed uncritically: cultures are simply placed alongside one another and viewed as substantially equivalent and interchangeable. This easily yields to a relativism that does not serve true intercultural dialogue; on the social plane, cultural relativism has the effect that cultural groups coexist side by side, but remain separate, with no authentic dialogue and therefore with no true integration. (CV 26)

While Benedict has been criticized by some for being less interested in dialogue than John Paul II, there is clear evidence that he sees dialogue as central to the church's life. He embraces a distinctive form of dialogue, but nevertheless affirms engaging the other as essential to human flourishing and the discovery of truth.

A commitment to dialogue on a broad scale is at the center of Francis' pontificate. This is evident in the fact that *Laudato Si'* is addressed to "every person living on the planet" (3), a fact which immediately links this text to *Gaudium et Spes*. Both the content and the style of Francis' teaching illumine the way that he prioritizes authentic engagement with the other. Dialogue for Pope Francis involves not just an exchange of words, but a real encounter between individuals. On this point Francis writes in *Evangelii Gaudium*: "[D]ialogue is much more that the communication of a truth. It arises from the enjoyment of speaking and it enriches those who express their love for one another through the medium of words. This is an enrichment which does not consist in objects but in persons who share themselves in dialogue" (EG 142). Similar to the way that *Gaudium et Spes* communicated the council's theological commitments not just through its content, but also through its style, Pope Francis conveys his dedication to dialogue and the reciprocity essential to dialogue through his actions: washing the feet of women and non-Christians, visiting the poor, marginalized and imprisoned, and traveling to Sweden to partake in the commemoration of the five-hundredth anniversary of the Reformation. Francis sees the church as a community that constantly "goes forth" and is perpetually "in motion" (EG 24). For him, this motion is propelled by dialogue; for it is exchanges between individuals and communities that help shape the church's course through the world. The papacies of John Paul II, Benedict, and Francis are all dialogical in their own distinctive ways. Each seizes on the new moment inaugurated by *Gaudium et Spes* and pursues authentic exchanges with the world.

Attention to Concrete Issues

While there are countless examples of how this feature of *Gaudium et Spes* has become a standard element of the church's post-conciliar life, here we will only focus on the emphasis on the family as a means of *ad extra* outreach. When Suenens originally suggested that the Vatican II's deliberations be ordered in terms of the church *ad intra* and the church *ad extra*, he also suggested particular *ad extra* topics for consideration. First among these was "The Church and Family Society."[23] Suenens recognized that in order to speak meaningfully in the world and spread the Gospel effectively, the church should focus on families as the first teachers of the gospel. The second part of *Gaudium et Spes* engages the topics of marriage and family, yet

23. Suenens, "Plan," 101.

its treatment of these subjects is far from complete and does not rise to the importance ascribed to them by Suenens and John XXIII.

Highlighting the family as a primary means of evangelization has been a critical aspect of the church's work in the last fifty years. The centrality of this theme is reflected in the fact that both John Paul II and Francis chose this topic as the theme for their first synod of bishops. It is noteworthy that both of popes, each of whom had spent a long time as a diocesan bishop and came from a diocese with considerable social and political challenges, chose to dedicate their first synods to considering ways to strengthen families in their efforts to promote the Christian faith. This choice illustrates their understanding that amidst the complexities of the modern world, the church must support families as a vital means of transmitting the gospel. Both popes recognized issues related to the family as "toothing stones" that can help facilitate a dialogue between the church and world.

Not only was the general theme of these synods influenced by *Gaudium et Spes*; the synodal documents draw heavily from the constitution. In the apostolic exhortation that came out of John Paul's first synod, *Familiaris Consortio* (On the Christian Family in the Modern World), the pope makes fifty-two references to Vatican II's documents and almost half of them (twenty-four) come from *Gaudium et Spes*. The *instrumentum laboris* developed for Francis' synod on "The Pastoral Challenges of the Family in the Context of Evangelization" also makes numerous references to *Gaudium et Spes*. The introduction includes six references to Vatican II; five of them are to *Gaudium et Spes*. It notes:

> Over the centuries, especially in modern times to the present, the Church has not failed to continually teach and develop her doctrine on the family and marriage which founded her. One of the highest expressions has been proposed by the Second Vatican Council in the Pastoral Constitution *Gaudium et spes*, which, in treating certain pressing problems, dedicated an entire chapter to the promotion of the dignity of marriage and the family. This document defined marriage as a community of life and love, placing love at the center of the family and manifesting, at the same time, the truth of this love in counter distinction to the various forms of reductionism present in contemporary culture.

John Paul II's and Francis' choice to root a key event in their papacy in the teachings of *Gaudium et Spes* is noteworthy; it reflects an effort to engage some of Vatican II's "unfinished business" and sustain the spirit of the council. It is important that at the outset of their ministry as bishop of Rome, each looks back to *Gaudium et Spes* to help chart a course for the future.

Commemorating the fiftieth anniversary of Vatican II's conclusion invites us to look both backwards and forwards. No area of the church's life remains unaffected by the council's work. Vatican II's teachings exist as an organic whole and, as such, the council's impact in any one area must be seen as a product of all the sixteen documents. While this is true, it is also the case that *Gaudium et Spes* is unique in the way that it initiated conversations and modes of conversation that set the tone for the church's post-conciliar life. Vatican II is lauded by many scholars for starting conversations rather than ending them. *Gaudium et Spes*, in many ways, is "first among equals" as a conversation starter. While *Gaudium et Spes* often serves as the starting point for contemporary conversations, the discussions it initiates rely on Vatican II's overarching theological commitments, including its notion of mystery, the People of God, full and active participation, dynamic view of revelation, and teaching about other religious traditions. Conversations emerging from *Gaudium et Spes* create openings where Vatican II's theology, expressed symphonically in all its texts, may continue to inform and orient the church's life and its conversations with the world. As we anticipate the next fifty years of Vatican II's reception, it is clear that *Gaudium et Spes* and Vatican II remain incredibly fresh and fecund guides for the on-going efforts to speak meaningfully to all men and women.

Bibliography

Alberigo, Giuseppe. "The Announcement of the Council." In *History of Vatican II*, edited by Giuseppe Alberigo and Joseph A. Komonchak, 1:1–54. Maryknoll, NY: Orbis, 1995.

Benedict XVI. "God the Creator." In *"In the Beginning . . ." A Catholic Understanding of the Story of Creation and the Fall*, 1–18. Translated by Boniface Ramsey. Grand Rapids: Eerdmans, 1995.

———. "Dictatorship of Relativism." In *Light of the World: The Pope, the Church and the Signs of the Times*, 50–62. Translated by Michael J. Miller and Adrian J. Walker. San Francisco: Ignatius, 2010.

Congar, Yves. "The Role of the Church in the Modern World." In *Commentary on the Documents of Vatican II*, edited by Herbert Vorgrimler, 5:202–23. New York: Herder & Herder, 1969.

Dobrzynski, Andrzej, and Zdzislaw Jozef Kijas, eds. *Christ, Church, Mankind: The Spirit of Vatican II according to John Paul II*. New York: Paulist, 2012.

Hahnenberg, Edward. *A Concise Guide to the Documents of Vatican II*. Cincinnati: St. Anthony Messenger, 2007.

Hebblethwaite, Peter. *John XXIII: Pope of the Council*. London: Chapman, 1984.

Hollenbach, David. "The Church's Social Mission in a Pluralistic Society." In *Vatican II: The Unfinished Agenda; A Look to the Future,* edited by Lucien Richard, 113–28. New York: Paulist, 1988.

Kasper, Walter. "The Theological Anthropology of *Gaudium et spes." Communio* 23 (1996) 129–38.

Komonchak, Joseph A. "The Struggle for the Council during the Preparation of Vatican II (1960–62)." In *History of Vatican II,* edited by Giuseppe Alberigo and Joseph A. Komonchak, 1:167–356. Maryknoll, NY: Orbis, 1995.

———. "Vatican II as an Event." In *Vatican II: Did Anything Happen?* edited by Joseph Komonchak et al., 24–51. New York: Continuum, 2007.

Moeller, Charles. "History of the Constitution." In *Commentary on the Documents of Vatican II,* edited by Herbert Vorgrimler, 5:1–76. New York: Herder & Herder, 1969.

Ratzinger, Joseph. "The Dignity of the Human Person" In *Commentary on the Documents of Vatican II,* edited by Herbert Vorgrimler, 5:115–63. New York: Herder & Herder, 1969.

Suenens, Leon Joseph. "A Plan for the Whole Council." In *Vatican II Revisited by Those Who Were There,* edited by Alberic Stacpoole, 88–105. Minneapolis: Winston, 1986.

What We Have Seen and Heard in the One Spirit Given to All[1]

—Elizabeth T. Groppe

"**PUSH YOUR LIMITS**" CHALLENGE the bold-face letters on the cover of the magazine that has arrived unsolicited in my mailbox, a free gift from a company from whom I have purchased a pair of shoes. The glossy paper is alluring, and I flip eagerly through *Self* magazine. Lithe women run, bike, swim, and lift weights with such vigor they appear to almost bound off the pages. They glide through color schemes of red, black, and white or sky blue and deep aqua-marine. I discover a sample of men's *eau de toilette* glued to an image of a muscular bare-chested man, and its fragrance bleeds through the packaging. In the center of another page stands a large pink and purple stiletto shoe with thin orange straps, worn by the successful woman engineer who is highlighted in this month's "Self Worth" feature story. "I reward myself," she explains, "with retail therapy." (The stiletto heel is pencil thin—could I walk in those shoes without tipping over, I wonder, even if I were twenty years younger?) An article on soccer programs invites me to

1. Some Scripture quotations in this chapter are taken from the New Revised Standard Version Bible, copyright 1989, Division of Christian Education of the National Council of the Churches of Christ in the United States of America. Used by permission. Some Scripture quotations in this chapter are taken from the *New American Bible, revised edition* © 2010, 1991, 1986, 1970 Confraternity of Christian Doctrine, Washington DC. and are used by permission of the copyright owner. All Rights Reserved. No part of the New American Bible may be reproduced in any form without permission in writing from the copyright owner.

"JOIN THE TEAM" where fitness becomes a party. *Self* holds many promises: "younger-looking skin in just four weeks . . . infinite nude eye looks . . . sipping diet soda . . . be a VIP . . . learn to crave the good stuff . . . sheer bliss . . . skin positively radiant . . . work that core . . . the boyfriend effect . . . a step ahead . . . make a move . . . why a little bit of envy can help you live better—and even have more fun . . . choose your own adventure . . . cocktails, anyone? . . . WATER: grab your paddleboard and make a splash. WATER."

"Ho! Everyone who thirsts, come to the waters" (Is 55:1). I am sitting in darkness and can hear water flowing gently. Its sound is musical, like that of a clear mountain stream cascading across stones. I am sitting in the hushed silence of a chapel, and my son's head is resting in my lap. Around us, people are quietly waiting in the stillness. It is the solemnity of Easter, and we have come in the night to keep vigil. Inside the entrance of the church, beyond the marble baptismal font, an orange flame leaps from a metal urn into the air. "Dear brothers and sisters," a priest in snow-white vestment says solemnly, "on this most sacred night, in which our Lord Jesus Christ passed over from death to life, the church calls upon her sons and daughters, scattered throughout the world, to come together to watch and pray. If we keep the memorial of the Lord's paschal solemnity in this way, listening to his word and celebrating his mysteries, then we shall have the sure hope of sharing his triumph over death and living with him in God." Extending hands over the crackling fire, he continues: "O God who through your Son bestowed upon the faithful the fire of your glory, sanctify this new fire, we pray, and grant that, by these paschal celebrations, we may be so inflamed with heavenly desires, that with minds made pure we may attain festivities of unending splendor."

This "we have seen and heard" (1 John 1:3). The eye and ear that mediate both the glossy images of magazines and the mysteries of the paschal vigil are truly exquisite organs. Our use of the extraordinary capacities that they afford is so integral to our existence that we rarely stop to think about the wonder of vision and sound, jolted into awareness of these senses only when they are lost to us through aging or injury, or when we encounter someone born blind or deaf. Yet neither *that* we can see and hear nor *what* we can see and hear should be taken for granted. Birds, for example, have color vision superior to that of humans and can also see things that are too small for us to perceive.[2] The intricacies of the cell and the vastness of the cosmos were unveiled to us only when we developed powerful microscopes and telescopes to augment our limited human vision as we surveyed and cataloged mitochondria and galaxies. "But," writer Annie Dillard reminds

---

2. Hodos, "What Birds See."

us, "there is another kind of seeing, which involves a letting go. When I see this way I sway transfixed and emptied."[3]

Today, our senses of sight and sound operate in a context that differs from that of most of human history. In the United States, over 80 percent of us live in urban environments where we spend most of our time in cars, cubicles, and buildings with such limited contact with the outdoors that journalist Richard Louv speaks of a "nature deficit disorder."[4] And, at the same time as opportunities to see and hear the beauty of God's creation are attenuated, there has been an explosion of sensory stimuli that lure our attention—radio and movies, TV, and now the Internet and cell phones and iPads. The Kaiser Family Foundation, which has been monitoring media usage by youth in the United States since 1999, found in its most recent study (2005) that 8- to 18-year-olds spend an average of 7 hours and 38 minutes with entertainment media on a typical day, a total of more than 53 hours a week. And because youth spend so much of this time using more than one medium at a time (e.g. listening to music while playing a video game), they receive 10 hours and 45 minutes of media content in those 7½ hours.[5] Teens, on average, process 3,700 texts a month.[6] Even adults have our eyes fixed on screens for 8 hours a day, more time than we spend on any other activity, including sleeping.[7] This media culture is a formative part of the contemporary context in which we are called to give baptismal witness to "what we have heard, what we have seen with our eyes" (1 John 1:1).

In this chapter, I will briefly present the Second Vatican Council's theology of a church in which the one Spirit of Christ is poured out on all the baptized. What, I will then ask, is the relation of this baptismal gift of the Holy Spirit to our exercise of the senses of sight and sound? How can we train our eyes and ears to behold the glory of the Lord? And how might we live our vocation to apostolic witness more visibly?

The One Spirit Given to All:
The Sacramental Ecclesiology of the Second Vatican Council

Vatican II's *Decree on the Apostolate of the Laity* (*Apostolicam Actuositatem*) opens with a reference to a passage in Romans that identifies some of the earliest lay witnesses to the Gospel. These include Phoebe, who is identified

3. Dillard, *Pilgrim*, 306.

4. Louv, *Last Child*.

5. Kaiser Family Foundation, "Generation M2."

6. Dokoupil, "Tweets, Texts?," 27.

7. Ibid.

as a minister in the church at Cenchreae; Prisca and Aquila, who risked their lives for Paul while serving together with him for Jesus Christ; Mary, described as one who worked hard for the community; Andronicus and Junia, both jailed with Paul; Ampliatus; Urbanus; Stachys; Apelles; and the list goes on (Rom 16:1–16; AA 1). This recovery of the biblical witness to the missionary discipleship of all those baptized in the Spirit of Christ is one legacy of the Second Vatican Council. When Cardinal Fernando Cento presented a draft of *Apostolicam Actuositatem* to the bishops assembled in Saint Peter's, he explained that the desire of the drafting commission was to make it clear that all Christians by virtue of baptism are to be apostles. If this truth were to be lived out, he noted, it would be the council's greatest triumph.[8]

It is a truth that had been obscured. Prior to the council, it was commonly assumed that the mission of the church is the responsibility primarily of the ordained and those in religious life. Even Catholic Action, the umbrella name for lay organizations including the Catholic Family Movement, the Legion of Decency, and the National Councils of Catholic Men and Women, was defined by proponent Pius XI (1922–1939) not as a lay apostolate but as "the participation of the laity in the apostolate of the Church's hierarchy."[9]

It is no coincidence that, in this same period of time, the theology of the Spirit's action in the church had been attenuated. In the aftermath of Pope Leo XIII's encyclical *Aeterni Patris* (1879), which made Thomism the norm of Catholic theology, seminarians preparing for the priesthood learned theology through neoscholastic manuals written in Latin and systematically organized into a series of tracts on an array of doctrinal topics: God, Christ, grace, and so forth. Sulpician Adolphe Tanquerey's *Brevior synopsis theologiae dogmaticae* is one of the manuals that was widely used, and its chapters on grace (*De Gratia*) explain that the Holy Spirit dwells within the hearts of all the justified, bestows spiritual gifts, illumines the intellect, and makes us adopted children of God. There is, however, no development of the implications of this indwelling of the Holy Spirit for the life, structure, and mission of the church. One might expect to find this elaborated in Tanquerey's chapters on the church (*De Ecclesia*), but there he mentions the Holy Spirit only as the guarantor of the Roman Catholic Church's preeminence over other Christian denominations and the infallibility of the pontiff and the apostolic college. In some neoscholastic theological manuals,

---

8. Hahnenberg, *Concise Guide*, 102.

9. Pius XI to Cardinal Bertam, 31. For further discussion, see Congar, *Lay People*.

Dominican theologian Yves Congar observed, the tract on the church did not even mention the Holy Spirit at all.[10]

The same lack of development of the ecclesiological implications of the gift of the Holy Spirit was true of books written for a readership beyond than that of seminarians and clergy. Cardinal Henry Edward Manning's *Internal Mission of the Holy Ghost* (1895), Hugh Francis Blunt's *Life with the Holy Ghost: Thoughts on the Gifts of the Holy Ghost* (1943), and *El Espiritu Santo* by Luis M. Martinez (1939) were intended for a broad audience. These books reflected on the indwelling of the Holy Spirit in the souls of the just, but it was assumed that this had no implications for the organization and mission of the church, constituted through the transfer of power from Christ to the ordained. "Spiritual anthropology," Congar lamented "now seems to have been drawn off from ecclesiology; the legal structure is all sufficient with its guaranteed administrative charisms."[11]

Congar is one of many theologians whose *ressourcement* (retrieval) of biblical, patristic, and medieval sources enabled the bishops gathered at the Second Vatican Council to articulate a much richer ecclesiology. Ecumenical engagement with the Eastern Orthodox tradition also contributed to the council's expression of what Congar termed a "pneumatological ecclesiology"—an ecclesiology that emphasizes the church's absolute dependence on the Spirit of Christ, the universal vocation to holiness, and the constitutive role of the gifts of the Holy Spirit in the life of the ecclesial body. The *Dogmatic Constitution on the Church* (*Lumen Gentium*) opens with a chapter on the mystery of the church that describes the *ecclesia* as a sacrament of communion in the triune God. God the Father created the universe, predestined us to adoption in the Son, and sends the Holy Spirit:

> This is the Spirit of life, the fountain of water springing up to eternal life [see John 4:14; 7:38–39], through whom the Father gives life to human beings dead in sin, until the day when, in Christ, he raises to life their mortal bodies [see Rom 8:10–11]. The Spirit dwells in the church and in the hearts of the faithful as a temple [see 1 Cor 3:16; 6:19], prays and bears witness in them that they are his adopted children [see Gal 4:6; Rom 8:15–16 and 26]. He guides the church in the way of all truth [see John 16:13] and uniting it in fellowship and ministry, bestows upon it different hierarchic and charismatic gifts, and in this way directs it and adorns it with his fruits [see Eph 4:11–12; 1 Cor 12:4; Gal 5:22] (LG 1.4).

10. Congar, "*Council* as an Assembly," 45.

11. Congar, *Tradition*, 397.

It is notable in this passage that the church is "directed and adorned" through both hierarchic gifts of the ordained *and* the charismatic gifts of all the baptized.

Reborn in the waters of the baptismal font and sealed with the chrism of the Holy Spirit, the baptized are a kingdom of priests and prophets who participate in the offering of the Eucharistic sacrifice, receive holy Communion, and manifest in a concrete way the communion of the people of God (LG 11) which "prefigures and promotes universal peace" (LG 13). In a world torn by sin and divided by injustice, ethnic discrimination, sexual violence, and warfare, God has gathered together people from every nation in a church that is intended to be "the visible sacrament of this saving unity" (LG 9).

It is in this context that *Apostolicam Actuositatem* speaks not with Pope Pius XI of "the participation of the laity in the apostolate of the hierarchy" but of a genuine lay apostolate. Indeed, the *Decree on the Apostolate of the Laity* affirms that this apostolate "is something that derives from the lay person's very vocation as a Christian," and present circumstances require its exercise in a manner "more extensive and more vigorous" than that of the first century (AA 1). "A sign of this urgent and many-faceted need," the decree continues, "is the manifest action of the Holy Spirit making lay people nowadays increasingly aware of their responsibility and encouraging them everywhere to serve Christ and the church" (AA 1).

No member of the living body of Christ, the decree emphasizes, is purely passive (AA 2). Our human agency is not abrogated or overpowered by the Spirit in baptism but rather healed of sin so that we may exercise our will in holiness. The Holy Spirit bestows charisms—gifts of nature elevated by grace to serve the mission of the church—to all members of the body of Christ, and the laity are to be good stewards of these varied gifts (1 Pet 4:10), using them in charity for the building up of the whole body (Eph 4:16). Just as every organ in the human body has a purpose, so too in the body of Christ each part works together to "promote the body's growth" (Eph 4:16). If some members fail to do their part, all will suffer the loss, like a body that is missing an organ or a limb.

In the communion of the Spirit, all the baptized participate in the priestly, prophetic, and kingly office of Christ and share with the ordained the apostolate of evangelization and sanctification, proclaiming the Gospel both in word and in the witness of their lives. There is also an apostolate particular to the laity: the renewal and revitalization of the temporal world, which is inherently good by virtue of its creation by God, but fallen. It is the distinctive task and charism of the laity to draw this temporal order—including the family, trades and professions, economic relations, government, and culture—closer to the perfection of the love and justice of the reign of God (AA 7). In exercising the apostolate, the laity are to attract people to Christ by the witness of their lives. Doing good to everyone, they are to live in humility, put aside ill will, deceit, hypocrisy, envy, and slander; and do that which pleases and serves God, even if this means suffering persecution. That they can witness to Christ in this manner is possible through the love of the Holy Spirit, who is poured into our hearts (Rom 5:5, AA 4).

Training Eye and Ear on the Glory of God

"Dear friends," the presider declares in one of the rites of Christian initiation of Adults, "the church joyfully welcomes today those who will be received into the order of catechumens. In the months to come they will prepare for their initiation into the Christian faith by baptism, confirmation, and Eucharist" (RCIA, para. 508). With these words, the women and men who desire baptism or reception and full communion and their sponsors are greeted by the liturgical assembly. After a series of questions in which the catechumens share their names and intentions, the presider states:

> God is our Creator and in him all living things have their exis-
> tence. He enlightens our minds, so that we may come to know
> and worship him. He has sent his faithful witness, Jesus Christ,
> to announce to us what he has seen and heard, the mysteries of
> heaven and earth (RCIA, para. 511; also 52.B).

The sponsors affirm that they are ready to help the catechumens to follow Christ and the presider marks the foreheads of those seeking baptism with the sign of the cross. Then, in an optional rite of signing of the senses, the sponsors mark the sense organs as the celebrant prays: "Receive the sign of the cross on your ears, that you may hear the voice of the Lord" and "Receive the sign of the cross on your eyes, that you may see the glory of God." The intense spiritual formation that will follow in the weeks ahead prepares the catechumens for the Easter Vigil in which they will hear the Word of God proclaimed and behold the paschal candle lighting up the darkness. "You have been enlightened by Christ," the celebrant will affirm after they pass through the waters of baptism: "Walk always as children of the light and keep the flame of faith alive in your hearts. When the Lord comes, may you go out to meet him with all the saints in the heavenly kingdom."

The sacraments of baptism and confirmation conferred so beautifully in the *Rite of Christian Initiation of Adults* (RCIA) are the beginning of a pilgrimage of faith, not the end. They do not automatically or magically

us for participation in the apostolate of the church. For this, rig-
\ing religious formation is necessary. The concluding chapter of
, *stolicam Actuositatem* on "Training for the Apostolate" highlights the
importance of the education of children and youth and the ongoing formation of adults.

From a pneumatological perspective, this formation is essential. The
Holy Spirit graces us with participation in the very love of God, but the
indwelling of the Spirit in the human heart transpires in a manner that does
not eclipse the activity of our own human faculties and freedom. "When
we cry, 'Abba! Father!'" St. Paul wrote, "it is that very Spirit bearing witness
with our spirit that we are children of God" (Rom 8:15–16, NRSV). And yet,
Congar comments, "it is *we* who cry." The Spirit is given in our hearts with
such subtlety, intimacy, and interiority that the action of the Spirit is almost
indistinguishable from our own. God "is so deeply within us, because he
has been sent 'into our hearts' and, as the Holy Spirit, he is so pure, subtle
and penetrating (Wis 7:22) that he is able to be in all of us and in each one
of us without doing violence to the person, indiscernible in his spontaneous movement."[12] Our sinful deeds are not the work of the Spirit, but if
our actions are truly rooted in goodness and love, they are acts of both our
human faculties and the indwelling Spirit of God. Thomas Aquinas wrote
of a created *habitus* or principle of action that accompanies the uncreated
charity that is the Spirit of God, and the Eastern Orthodox tradition speaks
of human cooperation with grace as synergy, a principle that combines a
strong sense of God's initiative with an equally strong emphasis on human
agency and freedom.

Human cooperation with grace does not mean that God and creature
operate on the same level or that we earn our own salvation. Our human
faculties—even when exercised rightly—are incommensurate with our destiny to share in the eternal life of God. "Merit" in regard to salvation, Congar
explains, exists only because of grace. "The Holy Spirit as uncreated grace
takes the initiative and provides the dynamism until the ultimate victory
is reached in which God is merely crowning his own gifts when he awards
us a crown for our 'merits.'"[13] Adoption as daughters and sons of God and
deification in Christ are not something that we can earn.

And yet the crown of eternal communion with God is something for
which we must prepare ourselves with at least the same degree of discipline
as the Greek athlete training in the first century for the laurel wreath that
was the Olympic victor's crown. The magazine that was in my mailbox urges

12. Congar, *I Believe*, 114.
13. Ibid., 108.

me to run, swim, take up yoga and karate, surf, paddleboard, and work my abs and arms. Caring for health and wellness is indeed an important discipline, but the apostolate of the church requires additional training. "Every athlete," Paul wrote "exercises discipline (*ascesis*) in every way. They do it to win a perishable crown, but we an imperishable one. Thus I do not run aimlessly; I do not fight as if I were shadowboxing. No, I drive my body and train it, for fear that, after having preached to others, I myself should be disqualified" (1 Cor 9:25–27, NAB). Persons who enter the priesthood or religious life commit themselves to a life-long process of spiritual formation, and the council's inclusion of all the baptized in the apostolic mission of the church requires a comparable formation process appropriate to each person's state of life. The universal call to holiness requires a universal practice of spiritual disciplines.

Author and theology professor David Fagerberg describes this discipline as a "liturgical asceticism," a form of asceticism that originates not in a spirit-flesh dualism disdainful of the world but in the sacraments that affirm the goodness of creation and elevate matter to participation in divine life. The paschal candle illuminating the darkness at the Easter Vigil and the harmony of voices intoning "Veni Sancte Spiritus" as men and women in white garments with hair still wet from the baptismal font are anointed with fragrant oil kindle our desire for eternal communion with God. The prophet Isaiah invites us to "come to the water" and to come "without money" and "without cost" (Is 55:1, NAB)—but the invitation requires the equivalent of allowing a seraph to touch our lips with a burning ember (Is 6:1–6). "Every Christian," Fagerberg writes, "should feel liturgy awaken and command asceticism."[14]

A multiplicity of time-tested forms of asceticism can be found in the Christian spiritual tradition: fasting, abstinence, almsgiving, praying the divine office, practicing *lectio divina*, contemplative prayer, adoration of the Blessed Sacrament, making a daily *examen* of conscience and participating in the sacrament of reconciliation, working with a spiritual director, and so forth. With good reason, Fagerberg notes, the narratives of the *abbas* and *ammas* of the Egyptian desert come to us as a book of stories—*The Sayings of the Desert Fathers*—not the rule of the one and only way to practice a spiritual life.[15] Different forms of asceticism will be more helpful or more appropriate for people in different circumstances. Monks and cloistered nuns, for example, practice an asceticism distinct from that of parents with children, and spiritual formation in our twenty-first century culture may well require

---

14. Fagerberg, *On Liturgical Asceticism*, xiii.
15. Ibid., 86.

not only periodic fasting from food but also fasting from media exposure. "A sort of 'interiorized monasticism,'" Fagerberg writes, "is incumbent on every baptized Christian."[16] The goal of the monastic life, fourth-century monk and theologian John Cassian explains in his *Institutes*, is purity of heart,[17] and those who are pure of heart "shall see God" (Matt 5:8, NAB).

A fundamental obstacle to the purity of heart that can open our eyes to a vision of the glory of God is the human ego, which filters all that we see and hear through a lens in which I myself am the center of the world. So distinctive from our ordinary vision is the perception necessary to behold God's glory that there is a tradition of reflection in Christianity on an array of five spiritual senses analogous to the corporeal senses of sight, hearing, taste, touch, and smell, which enable us to behold spiritual realities. A theology of the spiritual senses was first articulated by Origen (ca. 185–232) and this tradition has been retrieved in our own era by Karl Rahner and Hans Urs von Balthasar.[18] To see and hear with a spiritual sense requires, Origen explains, a spiritual *gymnasia*, or training. Just as an art historian must train her eyes to observe in paintings things that the unschooled cannot see, or a radiologist must be trained to see abnormalities in X-rays, so too we must be trained to see and hear in the Holy Spirit. Without this training, lay persons exercising the apostolate may be like blind men and women teaching sight to others (Matt 15:4).

Spiritual exercises enable a shedding of the callous layers of the ego that cover our eyes and ears. "If we consider deeply what faith in God or faith in Jesus means," reflects Carmelite Ruth Burrows:

> We sense, though perhaps dimly, that it involves a total dying to self . . . By faith we "die." (1 Cor 15:31) This means renouncing myself as my own base, my own centre, my own end. It means so casting myself on another, so making that other my *raison d'etre* that it is in truth, a death to the ego.

The spiritual perception that Christian asceticism cultivates does not train the eye or ear to disdain the things of the earth. "We do not detach ourselves from things in order to attach ourselves to God," wrote Trappist monk Thomas Merton from his hermitage in the woods of Gethsemane, "but rather we become detached from ourselves in order to see and use all things in and for God."[19]

16. Ibid., xvii.

17. Cassian, *The Institutes*.

18. Gavrilyuk and Coakley, *Spiritual Senses*; McInroy, *Balthasar*; Rahner, "'Spiritual Senses.'"

19. Merton, *New Seeds*, 21.

My own need to cultivate such a detachment was evident last spring when I participated in a guided walk through a small surviving patch of old growth forest on land preserved by the Sisters of Charity on the west side of Cincinnati. The sister who was leading the walk put her hand to the deep grey bark of a magnificent tree and explained that this was a cherry. I immediately thought: "What a beautiful desk that would make! Or a chest of drawers!" My perception of the magnificence of the tree was filtered through an egocentric vision that saw the tree first and foremost as something that could potentially serve my own desires. Merton, in contrast, testifies that "a tree gives glory to God by being a tree."[20] In *Laudato Si'*, Pope Francis invites us all to become mystics who see creation with the gaze of Jesus and the sacramental vision of St. Francis,[21] and the authentic joy that Pope Francis himself radiates would not be possible, theologian Jana Bennett reflects, without his own disciplined practice of simplicity of life.[22]

Outside the forest, I often see men and women standing on street corners holding signs made of cardboard asking for work or food: "Anything will help. Thank you and God bless!" My first instinctive reaction is to turn my head so as not to see or hear their need. My ego does not want to take time from a busy day to stop to talk, nor to consider the moral questions that this situation poses. "*I have a home and food and work,*" I tell myself, "Doesn't this woman on the corner of Oak and Main realize that she is disturbing my peace?"

Merton writes of another kind of vision. He entered the monastery to get away from the world, and then, one day, while running errands for his Trappist community, he had an experience at the corner of Fourth and Walnut Streets in Louisville, Kentucky, at a site now so well known that it is marked by a placard that says "Revelation." He explains:

> I was suddenly overwhelmed with the realization that I loved all those people, that they were mine and I theirs, that we could not be alien to one another even though we were total strangers. It was like waking from a dream of separateness, of spurious self-isolation in a special world, the world of renunciation and supposed holiness . . . This sense of liberation from an illusory difference was such a relief and such a joy to me that I almost laughed out loud . . . I have the immense joy of being man, a member of a race in which God Himself became incarnate . . . And if only everybody could realize this! But it cannot be

20. Ibid.

21. Francis, *Laudato Si'*, 96–100 and 10–12.

22. Bennett, "Everyday Ascetic."

> explained. There is no way of telling people that they are all walking around shining like the sun . . . At the center of our being is a point of pure truth, a point or spark which belongs entirely to God . . . This little point . . . is the pure glory of God in us . . . It is like a pure diamond, blazing with the invisible light of heaven. It is in everybody.[23]

Merton's Trappist spiritual discipline wore away at the ego-self that separated him from others and opened space for a revelation of the glory of God.

Discipline is a recurring theme of the articles in the magazine I found in my mailbox, which idealizes physical exercise, fitness, and sports. These are indeed important disciplines and they have the potential to be spiritually as well as physically transformative.[24] The magazine, however, presents the resculpting of my aging mortal body as an end in itself. Craving and envy are upheld as virtues, retail purchasing is the implicit measure of my self-worth, beauty is equated with a physique that no regimen of pushing my limits will ever produce, and infinity is construed as an eye cosmetic that can attract a man's sexual attention. Studies by cognitive scientists indicate that the imagery that we behold in our environs can change the brain's chemistry and neural circuitry. For young women, the American Psychological Association has found, the consequences of contemporary media imagery include the undermining of confidence, eating disorders, depression, and a sense of oneself as having value only as a sexual object.[25]

"God made me," writes Ruth Burrows from the monastery where she practices the contemplative disciplines of the Carmelite life, "in order to give himself to me, and he wants nothing of me, literally nothing, other than to let him love me, let him pour himself out upon me in everlasting joy."[26] The fruit of Christian asceticism is not the reward of retail therapy nor the prize of a sexual gaze but the knowledge of God's infinite and tender love for each and every creature. According to Orthodox theologian Oliver Clement, the purpose of spiritual disciplines is "to dissolve in the waters of baptism, in the waters of tears, all the hardness of the heart, so that [the heart] may become an antenna of infinite sensitivity, infinitely vulnerable to the beauty of the world and to the sufferings of human beings, and to God who is Love, who has conquered by the wood of the cross."[27]

23. Merton, *Conjectures*, 156.

24. Kelly, *Catholic Perspectives*.

25. American Psychological Association, "Report of the APA Task Force."

26. Burrows, *Guidelines*, 62.

27. Clement, *Roots*, 126.

Baptismal Witness in the World

"You went, you washed," Bishop Ambrose said to the newly baptized of Milan in the fourth century, "you came to the altar, you began to see what you did not see before."[28] And then the baptized, with this new power of sight, are sent forth to witness to that which they have seen and heard. The *Decree on the Apostolate of the Laity* emphasizes that all the baptized are called to missionary discipleship and that "the mission of the Church is not only to bring the message and grace of Christ to men but also to penetrate and perfect the temporal order with the spirit of the Gospel" (AA 5). In the fifty years since the conclusion of the council, the church has been invigorated by laity who have lived the vocation to missionary discipleship through a wide array of lay ecclesial ministries and through witness in the temporal order of family, farm, workplace, and public square.

The *Decree on the Apostolate of the Laity* distinguishes two forms of temporal witness: that of groups and individuals (AA 15–22). Catholic organizations such as the Catholic Campaign for Human Development, People of Life, Catholic Rural Life, and the Catholic Climate Covenant witness to the God of Jesus Christ through corporate, public action. Brother Andrew, for example, serves with Catholic Charity's migrant ministry as part of an international team.[29] He is a prayerful presence at the side of undocumented workers when they find themselves in court for driving without a license, domestic violence, or other violations of the law. Andrew is a lawyer, but in most cases there is no basis for objection to the charges, and he is simply a presence of compassion for people who often don't speak the language of the courtroom and who live in the awareness that they could be deported at any time. "I always speak respectfully about my clients," he explains, "giving them the dignity that they are due. In the back rooms with the prosecutors, police officers, and the other lawyers . . . this is not often the case—especially for undocumented immigrants . . . It can get pretty raunchy in these rooms—with lots of stories, gossip, and a bunch of four letter words (i.e. not—HOLY, LOVE). On several occasions, after a lawyer would let out a curse word, the prosecutor would stop the conversation, look at me, and say, 'Sorry, Brother'—he allowed my quiet witnessing—and then became a witness himself. Maybe it wasn't much . . . but there turned out to be a witness there that just may have had some impact and spoke of God's unconditional love."

---

28. Ambrose, *De sacramentis* 3.15 (SC 25bis:164; FOTC 44:295), cited in Frank, "'Taste and See,'" 619.

29. Andrew is a pseudonym. This story is used with permission.

The second form of apostolic action in the temporal order is the ongoing witness "everywhere and always" of each baptized member of the body of Christ as she or he goes about daily life and routines (AA 16). Virtuous actions enabled by the grace of the Spirit quietly imbue the home, the workplace, and the public square with a witness to the God of Jesus Christ. Sister Anna, for example, was working as a social worker with a non-profit organization in California serving youth at risk of entering the penal system.[30] Through home and school visits, counseling referrals, family mediation and victim offender restitution, the organization has been successful in nurturing a supportive community that has enabled many youth to avoid actions that would have led them into the criminal justice system. One morning, Anna asked a young woman in the program how she was doing. Although the organization in which Anna is working is not religiously affiliated, the young woman sensed a compassionate presence and poured out her heart, sharing her difficulties, her anger, and the challenges she faces in her relationship to God. In response, Anna affirmed, "you are a good person." The young woman's reaction, Anna shares, "was quite moving. I was seeing the hunger of people for God, a desire to be recognized, to be listened to as a human being and to be respected."

In both of these stories, the apostolic witnesses were clearly recognizable as Catholic Christians by symbols on their clothing and their names. Brother Andrew and Sister Anna are both members of religious orders. They make the apostolate of the church and the love of the Holy Spirit visible and audible through their consecrated lives and their legal and social work. They are publically identifiable through the symbols they bear on their bodies (necklaces or rings of their orders) as baptized and consecrated men and women who "bear witness to Christ all the world over," making manifest the charity that "is given to them and nourished in them by the sacraments, and especially by the Eucharist" (AA 3).

Most of the baptized, however, bear no visible sign of their immersion in the paschal waters once baptismal garments have been laid aside. Those who work in Catholic parishes and schools or formal Catholic organizations are recognizable through these affiliations. However, the quiet witness of Christians in their daily activities in the domestic household, the community, the economic arena, and the public sphere is less clearly identifiable. How will others hear and see in them a sign of Christ? How will it be manifest that they are acting not strictly as individuals but as members of Christ's body through the grace of the Holy Spirit? As we reflect together on baptismal witness to "what we have seen and heard," I invite readers to

---

30. Anna is a pseudonym. This story is used with permission.

think creatively about ways to make this daily apostolate of the baptized more visible. This is particularly important in a media culture that saturates our perceptions and imaginations with many images that are antithetical to the baptismal vocation.

In order to make lay witness in the temporal world more evident, for example, the church could institute a tangible symbol of some kind. A ring, perhaps, or a pin—something variable enough to be suitable to the wide variety of circumstances in which the laity live and work, but uniform enough that it is easily recognizable. We live, writes religion professor Tom Beaudoin, in a "branded culture" in which young people immediately recognize a hundred different logos and purchase branded clothing not only to cover their bodies but to express their identity.[31] Baptism is not a "brand." It is, however, a mystery whose witness must be publically seen and heard.

The institution of a visible sign of baptism would present a variety of dangers, including the real possibility of ostentation, hypocrisy, and the reduction of a spiritual witness to a culture of branding and marketing. It is also possible, however, that this visible symbolism could enable the laity to exercise their baptismal witness more effectively. A man who is a secular Franciscan, for example, told me that he has for many years worn the ring that he received after his profession of the Rule. He doesn't know if the youth whom he teaches ever notice it—but he, at least, is aware of the presence of the ring on his body. Often, he told me, it catches his eye, or he becomes suddenly aware of its presence, and this sensory experience strengthens his resolve to live the commitment that he has made. Dianne (not her real name), an associate of the Dominican Sisters of Peace, wears a pin on her clothing. "What's that?" she is regularly asked, and the question provides an evangelical opportunity for her to articulate in words the witness that she is offering with her life.

The ordained, those vowed to the consecrated life, associates of religious orders, and those persons whose profession of faith is simply that of baptism each witness to the Gospel in complementary manners appropriate to their respective vocations. Distinct visible signs of their varied forms of witness could make the public apostolate of all the baptized more tangible. "The church on earth is by its very nature missionary," *Ad Gentes* affirms, and "all Christians by the example of their lives and the witness of the world, wherever they live, have an obligation to manifest the new person which they put on in baptism" (AG 2, 11).

"Ho! Everyone who thirsts, come to the waters" (Is 55:1). The chapel that we entered in the darkness on Holy Saturday is now illuminated. The

31. Beaudoin, *Consuming Faith*, 3–13.

flame of the paschal candle was passed from one small white hand-held candle to another, person to person, light from light. The pool of running water was blessed with a prayer invoking the Holy Spirit, baptismal promises were renewed by the entire assembly, and in a joyous procession encircling the entire chapel the priest sprinkled everyone with its moist drops. Catechumens who have prepared intensively for this holy night for forty days now stand before the altar in white garments, awaiting the Holy Spirit's seal. "My dear candidates for confirmation," the priest says solemnly, "by your baptism you have been born again in Christ and you have become members of Christ and of his priestly people. Now you are to share in the outpouring of the Holy Spirit among us, the Spirit sent by the Lord upon his apostles at Pentecost and given by them and their successors to the baptized. The promised strength of the Holy Spirit, which you are to receive, will make you more like Christ and help you to be witnesses to his suffering, death, and resurrection. It will strengthen you to be active members of the Church and to build up the Body of Christ in faith and in love."

Bibliography

American Psychological Association. *Report of the APA Task Force on the Sexualization of Girls*. 2007. www.apa.org/pi/women/programs/girls/report.aspx.

Beaudoin, Tom. *Consuming Faith: Integrating Who We Are with What We Buy*. Lanham, MD: Sheed & Ward, 2003.

Bennett, Jana. "The Everyday Ascetic: Thoughts on *Laudato si*." *Catholic Moral Theology*. June 23, 2015. catholicmoraltheology.com/the-everyday-ascetic-thoughts-on-laudato-si/.

Burrows, Ruth. *Guidelines for Mystical Prayer*. New Jersey, Dimension, 1976.

Cassian, John. *The Institutes*. Translated by Boniface Ramsey. New York: Newman, 2000.

Clement, Olivier. *The Roots of Christian Mysticism*. New York: New City, 1996.

Congar, Yves. "The *Council* as an Assembly and the Church as Essentially Conciliar." In *One, Holy, Catholic and Apostolic. Studies on the Nature and Role of the Church in the Modern World*, edited by Herbert Vorgrimler, 44–88. London: Sheed & Ward, 1968.

———. *I Believe in the Holy Spirit*. Vol. 2. Translated by David Smith. New York: Seabury, 1983.

———. *Lay People in the Church: A Study for a Theology of the Laity*. Translated by Donald Attwater. Westminster, MD: Newman, 1957.

———. *Tradition and Traditions: A Historical and Theological Essay*. Translated by Michael Naseby and Thomas Rainborough. London: Burns & Oates, 1966.

Dillard, Annie. *Pilgrim at Tinker Creek*. In *The Annie Dillard Reader*, 279–424. New York: Harper, 1994.

Dokoupil, Tony. "Tweets, Texts, Email, Posts: Is the Onslaught Making Us Crazy?" *Newsweek* 160 (July 9, 2012) 24–30.

Fagerberg, David W. *On Liturgical Asceticism*. Washington, DC: Catholic University of America, 2013.

Francis. *Laudato Si'*. May 24, 2015. w2.vatican.va/content/francesco/en/encyclicals/documents/papa-francesco_20150524_enciclica-laudato-si.html.

Frank, Georgia. "'Taste and See': The Eucharist and the Eyes of Faith in the Fourth Century." *Church History* 70 (2001) 619–43.

Gavrilyuk, Paul L., and Sarah Coakley, eds. *The Spiritual Senses: Perceiving God in Western Christianity*. Cambridge: Cambridge University Press, 2012.

Hahnenberg, Edward. *A Concise Guide to the Documents of Vatican II*. Cincinnati: St. Anthony Messenger, 2007.

Hodos, William. "What Birds See and What They Don't." In *How Animals See the World: Comparative Behavior, Biology, and Evolution of Vision*, edited by Olga F. Lazareva et al., 5–24. New York: Oxford University Press, 2012.

Kaiser Family Foundation. "Generation M2: Media in the Lives of 8- to 18-Year Olds: A Kaiser Family Foundation Study." 2010. kaiserfamilyfoundation.files.wordpress.com/2010/01/mh012010presentl.pdf.

Kelly, Patrick,. *Catholic Perspectives on Sports: From Medieval to Modern Times*. New York: Paulist, 2012.

Louv, Richard. *Last Child in the Woods: Saving Our Children from Nature-Deficit Disorder*. New York: Algonquin, 2005.

McInroy, Mark. *Balthasar on the Spiritual Senses: Perceiving Splendour*. Changing Paradigms in Historical and Systematic Theology. Oxford University Press, 2014.

Merton, Thomas. *Conjectures of a Guilty Bystander*. Garden City, NY: Doubleday, 1966.
———. *New Seeds of Contemplation*. New York: New Directions, 2007.

Pius XI to Cardinal Bertam. November 13, 1928. Cited in *Clergy and Laity: Official Catholic Teachings*, edited by Odile M. Liebard, 30–34. Official Catholic Teachings. Wilmington, NC: McGrath, 1981.

Rahner, Karl. "The 'Spiritual Senses' according to Origen." Translated by David Morland. In *Theological Investigations*, 16:81–103. New York: Seabury, 1979.

Rite of Christian Initiation of Adults: Study Edition. Chicago: Liturgy Training Publications, 1988.

6

From "Missions" to "Mission"

Trinity, World Christianity,
and Baptismal Witness[1]

—Stephen Bevans, S.V.D.

> The pilgrim church is missionary by its very nature, since it is from
> the mission of the Son and the mission of the Holy Spirit that it
> draws its origin, in accordance with the decree of God the Father.[2]

OVER THE LAST SEVERAL years I have become more and more convinced
that this lapidary phrase, found in *Ad Gentes*, is one of the most radical
and fundamental statements of the Second Vatican Council. Unfortunately,
the statement came late in the council (*Ad Gentes* was one of the last documents to be approved in 1965), and so has not been a major influence in
subsequent interpretations of conciliar ecclesiology. It only appears with
such clarity here. What became the key to interpreting the council's understanding of the church was the *Dogmatic Constitution on the Church's*

---

1. Some Scripture texts in this chapter are taken from the New Revised Standard
Version Bible: Catholic Edition, copyright 1989, 1993, Division of Christian Education
of the National Council of the Churches of Christ in the United States of America.
Used by permission. All rights reserved. Some scripture texts in this chapter are taken
from the *New American Bible, revised edition* © 2010, 1991, 1986, 1970 Confraternity
of Christian Doctrine, Washington DC and are used by permission of the copyright
owner. All Rights Reserved. No part of the New American Bible may be reproduced in
any form without permission in writing from the copyright owner.

2. Second Vatican Council, *Ad Gentes*, 2.

breakthrough from a basic *institutional* and *hierarchical* understanding of the church to a more biblically and patristically anchored understanding of it as Mystery and its communal nature as the People of God.[3]

The mission dynamic expressed so clearly in *Ad Gentes* was subtly at work throughout the entire council, as well. It was signaled by an understanding of the church as *sacrament* (*Lumen Gentium*, LG 1, 48)—both *sign* and *instrument* of salvation, its distinction—however cautious—between itself and the Reign of God (LG 5), the vision of the *Pastoral Constitution on the Church in the Modern World* (*Gaudium et Spes*), and by the missionary tenor of the opening paragraphs of each of the four main constitutions.[4] The conviction was also clear, it seems, in the Council Fathers' understanding of *Lumen Gentium* during the council. In the rather tumultuous debate on the council floor in October, 1964, over the reduced schema on The Missions (*De Missionibus*), an objection was raised by Cardinals Josef Frings and Bernard Alfrink among others that the proposed schema was inadequate in the context of the council's understanding of the church's missionary nature. In a famous speech, Bishop Donal (the text says Daniel) Lamont of (then) Rhodesia spoke of the reduced schema in terms of Ezekiel's vision of the Valley of the Dry Bones and called for a document that would have real nerves and flesh.[5]

Why do I think that *Ad Gentes*'s statement of the missionary nature of the church rooted in the Trinity is so fundamental and radical? For three reasons, all of which I hope explain the title of these reflections: "From 'Missions' to 'Mission': Trinity, World Christianity, and Baptismal Witness."[6] The first reason is that the statement *relativizes* the mission of the church because it locates it within the wider and all-embracing mission of God. The second reason is that it locates the church's missionary activity not in exotic locations that have been baptized with the "mystical doctrine of salt water,"[7] but in every place and among every people in which the church finds itself. In the same way, in the third place, *Ad Gentes* 2 locates the subjects or protagonists of mission not just among a special, often highly trained group,

---

3. Second Vatican Council, *Lumen Gentium*.

4. See Bevans, "Revisiting Mission"; "Mission as the Nature of the Church: Development in Catholic Ecclesiology"; "Mission as the Nature of the Church in Roman Catholic Contexts"; "Beyond the New Evangelization."

5. See the discussion at the Third Session of Vatican II, November 7, 1964, in *Acta Synodalia acrosancti Concilii Vaticani II*, 3.6. Bishop Lamont's speech is found on 392–94.

6. This chapter was published in part in Kavunkal and Tauchner, *Mission beyond*.

7. See Bridston, *Mission, Myth*, 32.

but calls all Christians to witness to and proclaim what they have seen and heard in faithful baptismal witness.

These three reasons will serve to structure these reflections. A first section will reflect on the shift from "missions to mission" in terms of the basic understanding of missionary activity as participation in the *missio Dei* or Mission of God. A second section will reflect on the shift from understanding that activity as one of several vital activities of the church to understanding the church itself as constituted by mission, becoming itself, in Pope Francis' challenging phrase, "A Community of Missionary Disciples."[8] A third section will connect this one mission to the one basic vocation of all Christians who called to baptismal witness. The complexity involved in that baptismal witness will be sketched in a fourth and final section.

From Missions to Mission

In his commentary on *Ad Gentes*, theologian Yves Congar notes that the document's statement about the church's missionary nature rooted in the Trinity has deep roots in Catholic theology, going back to Augustine, Alexander of Hales, Bonaventure, Aquinas and the thought of the seventeenth century founder of the French School of Spirituality, Cardinal Pierre de Bérulle. It has roots as well, he also acknowledges, in twentieth-century Protestant thought.[9] Congar only alludes to this, saying that the influence is of a more general type, but I'm not so sure of that.

Although he is generally acknowledged as the principal author of this section of *Ad Gentes*, Congar may have understated the Protestant influence. To understand it fully, I believe, the Trinitarian turn in Catholic mission theology needs to be understood from the work of Protestants Karl Barth and Karl Hartenstein in the 1930s, and in the groundbreaking conference of the International Mission Council held in Willingen, Germany, in 1952.

At the Brandenburg Mission Conference in 1932, Barth rejected the idea of mission as a human activity of witness and service, the work of the church, and insisted that it was primarily *God* who engages in mission by sending God's self in the mission of the Son and the Spirit. It is not primarily the church that sends women and men to the "missions," but God who sends the church into the world. "The church can be in mission authentically only in obedience to God as *mission*."[10] There is only one mission, in other words, not a plurality of missions organized by the church.

8. Francis, *Evangelii Gaudium*, 24.

9. Congar, "Principes doctrinaux," 186.

10. I am following closely here Schroeder's and my development of the *Missio Dei*

This perspective was taken up by Karl Hartenstein, who in 1934 coined the term *missio Dei* and distinguished it from the *missio ecclesiae*, the mission of the church that takes its existence from its participation in God's Trinitarian mission. Even though the term *missio Dei* was not used explicitly, it became the key idea at the 1952 meeting in Willingen, Germany. Mission, said the final document, "comes from the love of God in His active relationship with [humanity]."[11] The great South African missiologist David Bosch summarizes Willingen's message eloquently:

> The classical doctrine of the *missio Dei* as God the Father sending the Son, and God the Father and the Son sending the Holy Spirit was expanded to include yet another "movement": Father, Son, and Holy Spirit sending the church into the world . . . Willingen's image of mission was mission as participating in the sending of God. Our mission has no life of its own: only in the hands of the sending God can it truly be called mission, not least since missionary initiative comes from God alone.[12]

Ad Gentes has certainly embraced this perspective and develops it in its first five paragraphs, where we see a continuity between the overflowing love of God the Father as Creator and the mission of the Son in Incarnation and Redemption (AG 2–3), between the Son and the vivifying and inspiring mission of the Spirit, and between the Spirit and the mission of the church (AG 4), which "is fulfilled by that activity which makes it fully present to all peoples and nations. It undertakes this activity in obedience to Christ's command and in response to the grace and love of the Holy Spirit (AG 5).

Following along the lines of some contemporary Trinitarian theologies, however—notably those of Bernard Lonergan, Frederick E. Crowe, Elizabeth Johnson and, most recently, Sarah Coakley[13]—I have tried to develop in my own teaching and writing an understanding of the *missio Dei* from the more "incorporative" perspective that would posit the mission of the Spirit as "prior" (at least, as Crowe says, in the *ordo essendi*, or as Johnson would say, in the order of experience).[14] In this approach, the Spirit "incorporates" believers into faith in Jesus as Christ, who in turn leads them

---

in *Constants in Context*, 348–98. See the excerpt from Barth in Thomas, ed., *Classic Texts*, 104.

11. Ibid., 103.

12. Bosch, *Transforming Mission*, 390.

13. Lonergan, "Mission and the Spirit," 253–59; Crowe, "Son of God,"; Johnson, *She Who Is*; Coakley, *God, Sexuality*.

14. See Coakley, *God, Sexuality*, 112; and Johnson, *She Who Is*, 121–23.

into the dynamic life of Holy Mystery at reality's heart who in turn sends them in the same way as the Spirit and Jesus were sent.

The advantage of this approach is that it highlights a real continuity between God's mission from the first moment of creation and the mission of the Spirit and the Son in that work, which culminates in the Incarnation. It also highlights the continuity between God's mission and that of the church, emphasizing even more that from a Trinitarian perspective there is *only* one mission—that of God, who incorporates women and men into that mission by making them adopted daughters and sons, sharers of the divine nature, and so true partners in the divine work. The one mission of God is reflected in communal and corporate activity of the church. It is, then, in the words of *Ad Gentes*, "nothing else and nothing less than a manifestation or epiphany of God's will and the fulfillment of that will in the world and in world history" (AG 9).

It may be helpful here to sketch out briefly this more Spirit-centered perspective.[15] It begins with the conviction that God's act of creation, the consequence of the "fountain of love" that is what tradition has called "the Father," in whom is "the origin without origin" of the Trinity (see AG 2), is the first act of mission. From the first nanosecond of that creation—what contemporary scientists have called the "Big Bang"—God has been totally present within it, although not as a manipulative, coercive presence, but through the gentle, whispering, persuasive presence of the Spirit. This active presence of the Spirit was guiding, persuading, inspiring the evolution of the gasses, the formation of molecules, the development of the galaxies and their billions of planets, calling forth life in all its abundance, committing itself to healing and reconciling what has been broken by selfishness and sin as self-conscious, free-willed humans emerge, living (as AG 9 puts it) as "secret presence" among all cultures and religions.[16]

Focusing in on our own Judeo-Christian tradition, this always and everywhere presence of God is described in images of a rushing wind (Gen 1:2), a life-giving stream of water or gentle breath (Ezek 47:1–12; Gen 2:8), of commissioning oil (Is 61:1–4), wisdom (Sophia) that dances in the God's presence and roams the city streets preaching repentance (Proverbs 8:22–30; 1:20), an active Word (*logos*) that never returns empty and unfulfilled (Is 10:11). God's mission continues in Israel, giving and restoring life, healing, and anointing prophets to offer hope and to call God's people to fidelity.

15. A fuller sketch of this more "incorporative" approach can be found in Bevans, "Missiology as Practical Theology," 253–74.

16. See Edwards, *Breath of Life*, 171–72.

In the "fullness of time" (Gal 4:4) this all-pervasive, life-giving, heal-ing, insistent presence takes on concrete existence and a human face in Jesus of Nazareth, upon whom the Spirit is poured (Luke 4:18–20), in whom the Word became flesh (John 1:14). Jesus embodies God's active presence in Israel and in all creation. He is "God's body language."[17] His speech was filled with parables about God's all-embracing and merciful love—God's "no-matter-whatness," as Jesuit activist Gregory Boyle has described it.[18] His healings and exorcisms were signs of the wholeness of salvation and God's work for liberating creation from all that holds it captive. His meals with sinners and other marginalized women and men are signs of God's passion to include all in the world that God continues to create and renew. Jesus's vision, as Gregory Boyle puts it powerfully, is that while God's "ways aren't our ways, but they sure could be."[19]

Jesus's message and behavior constantly got him in trouble with the powers that be in his day. As U.S. Latino theologian Virgilio Elizondo ob-served astutely, it was especially Jesus's practice of not being scandalized by anything or anyone that was most scandalous to the religious leaders of his day, and was probably the biggest reason why they began quite early in his ministry to plot his death.[20]

But Jesus's death was not the end. Several days after his horrible death by crucifixion his disciples began to experience his presence among them and at Pentecost that Spirit that had anointed Jesus at his baptism was lavished upon them, an anointing that they gradually came to recognize as commissioning them to continue Jesus's liberating, healing, life-giving work. It was in that gradual realization as well that they realized they were the church, vitally linked but nevertheless discrete from Judaism, that was called to share God's mission to the ends of the earth and the end of time.

Thus the church is truly "missionary by its very nature," called into being to share and continue the mission of God. Mission is not just one thing among several that the church had been called to do in the world. It is the foundation of its very being. All the church's activity—its "missions"—is grounded in the one mission of God, active from the first moment of cre-ation, active in Israel's history, active in Jesus, now active and formative in its own life. As the saying goes, the church does not have a mission. The mission—of God—has a church.

17. Oakley, *The Collage of God*, 26–27.

18. Boyle, *Tattoos on the Heart*, 52. Boyle repeats the phrase throughout the book.

19. Ibid., 155.

20. Elizondo, "Miracle," 205.

It is this powerful understanding of *missio Dei* that has developed since *Ad Gentes* was published in November of 1965. It helps us clearly negotiate the path from "missions" to "mission."

Mission in the Context of World Christianity

Ad Gentes's embrace of the *missio Dei* has also had another consequence that further explains and enriches the shift from missions to mission. It points to the fact that mission can no longer be understood in strictly geographical terms—resulting in the idea of "missions"—but in terms of particular contexts that need the illumination and healing presence of the gospel and the communal presence of the Christian community. Even though the term "missions" is explicitly used in *Ad Gentes* 6, the word is defined as "the term usually given to those particular undertakings by which the heralds of the gospel are sent out by the Church and go forth into the whole world to carry out the task of preaching the gospel and planting the Church among peoples or groups who do not yet believe in Christ." What is to be noted here is that this definition does not refer exclusively to particular territories, or to a "sending church" and a "receiving church," but to "peoples or groups." Further on in the paragraph, *Ad Gentes* speaks of the close connection between this work "among the nations" and "pastoral activity exercised among the faithful" and works that aim "at restoring unity among Christians," although these latter two are clearly different.

Under the influence of the *missio Dei*, however, these differences have become more and more to be regarded as less and less important, especially in the light of the globalization of the world in which we now live fifty years after *Ad Gentes*, and because of the position of the church in that world. Pope John Paul II in *Redemptoris Missio* also speaks of the close connection among the various "fields" of mission, adding the field that he developed throughout his pontificate, the "New Evangelization," and not mentioning ecumenical activity as did *Ad Gentes*.[21] He emphasizes the fact that the mission "*ad gentes*" is mission in the proper sense of the word, but then he blurs the lines of this field when he speaks of "new worlds and social phenomena" and "new Areopagi" of mega-cities, migration, science, the arts, and communication.[22] In *Evangelii Gaudium* Pope Francis also connects these same fields of mission together, although interestingly he does not mention

21. John Paul II, *Redemptoris Missio* (RM), 31, 33. Ecumenical activity, I would suggest, becomes part of the basic dialogical stance of the church in terms of other religions, those who share the Christian faith, and those who have no faith at all.

22. John Paul II, *Redemptoris Missio*, 37.

the term New Evangelization in this context. He says that the mission "*ad gentes*" is what mission ("evangelization") is all about, although he does not use that term either.[23]

Francis makes another crucial move, however. He calls for the entire church to "go forth," a church that is to be "in a permanent state of mission," and speaks of the church as a "community of missionary disciples," where one cannot say simply "disciples" or "missionary," but only both in the same breath.[24] This move toward a totally missionary church is perhaps most clearly articulated in a passage where he speaks of his dream for a "missionary option":

> That is, a missionary impulse capable of transforming every-
> thing, so that the Church's customs, ways of doing things, times
> and schedules, language and structures can be suitably chan-
> neled for the evangelization of today's world rather than for
> her self-preservation. The renewal of structures demanded by
> pastoral conversion can only be understood in this light: as part
> of an effort to make them more mission-oriented, to make ordi-
> nary pastoral activity on every level more inclusive and open, to
> inspire in pastoral workers a constant desire to go forth and in
> this way to elicit a positive response from all those whom Jesus
> summons to friendship with himself.[25]

While there are different *ways* of doing mission, there is only one mission, not "missions." This is a consequence of *Ad Gentes*'s insistence that the church is "missionary by its very nature."

More than Theology

Francis' move, along the lines implied by *Ad Gentes* 2, a move very much in tune with a good deal of contemporary missiological thinking,[26] is not simply a theological, theoretical one. It is based on a real shift in the shape of the twenty-first century world that is quite different from the world in

23. Francis, *Evangelii Gaudium*, 14. In a presentation at a mission congress at Rome's Pontifical Urbaniana University in April 2015, Cardinal Fernando Filoni, pre-fect of the Congregation for the Evangelization of Peoples, remarked that Pope Francis avoids using the terms New Evangelization and *ad gentes* and presses for the widest possible understanding of mission.

24. Francis, *Evangelii Gaudium*, 24, 25, 120.

25. Ibid., 27.

26. See Bosch, *Transforming Mission*; Hanciles, *Beyond Christendom*; Walls, *The Missionary Movement* and "Missions or Mission"; Shenk, *Enlarging the Story*; Sanneh, *Whose Religion*; Irvin, *Christian Histories*.

which the concept of "missions" emerged. Francis' call for a truly missionary church comes out of a totally different context, and reflects not the interests of a Western, more affluent world but that of the poorer and today more
Christian-majority world. His community of missionary disciples calls to
mind a church that is always and everywhere aware of its minority status,
always and everywhere ready to listen, always and everywhere eager to get
its shoes "soiled by the mud of the street."[27]

A missionary church recognizes that the world has profoundly
changed in the wake of two devastating wars in the twentieth century, the
demise of the communist vision in almost every place in which it once had
a stranglehold, and the renaissance of the world's major religions and in particular the ascendancy of Islam as the world's fastest-growing religion and
menacing radical parties within it. The face of the world has changed, with
what many claim is the greatest movement of peoples in the world's history. The amazing development of communications media in the last several
decades, with computers, e-mail, mobile phones, Skype, texting, Facebook,
and Twitter has made time and space almost irrelevant in today's world.
Anyone can virtually be any place at any time. This is the world in which
the church must witness in its life and service, and proclaim a relevant and
challenging gospel message. Such a world calls for a thorough renewal of the
church in every aspect of its life and mission. The world of "missions" does
not reflect this reality; the world of "mission" does.

While we can still speak of the distinctiveness of pastoral work, work
among people who have ceased practicing religion, and primary evangelization among people who have not yet accepted the gospel, we can no longer
divide up the world into places that are evangelized and places that are
not, places that require "missions" and those that send missionaries. Every
church exists in a "missionary situation." Today, as Francis suggests, there is
only a missionary church. The center of gravity of Christianity has shifted
to the "Global South," and yet these vital churches in places that were once
considered "the missions" are often without adequate resources of personnel. Members of those "mission churches" have migrated to lands where
there exist what were formerly considered "sending churches." With those
migrants have also come women and men of other religious ways, and so
countries that have been traditionally Christian are no longer overwhelm-
ingly so. Missionaries need not cross oceans to engage in primary evangelization; they need only walk down the streets of their home cities. In those
countries as well, missionaries from former mission churches now arrive to
care for those who have migrated there, to engage in primary evangelization,

27. Francis, *Evangelii Gaudium*, 45.

or to evangelize or re-evangelize their former evangelizers. As the Western Christians find themselves in numerical decline, they have come to recognize the need to witness to and preach the gospel in new ways and with new urgency in the pluralist and secularist societies in which they live. Mission is everywhere, on six continents as the 1963 Mexico assembly of the World Council of Churches' Commission on World Mission and Evangelism put it.[28] As Anglican Bishop Stephen Neill expressed it at the end of that conference, "the age of missions is at an end. The age of Mission has begun."[29]

Call to Baptismal Witness

To say that the church is missionary by its very nature by virtue of its origin in Trinitarian mission is to say something as well about the missionary privilege and duty of every Christian. *Ad Gentes* was written in the context of the great shift in ecclesiology signaled by the move in *Lumen Gentium* to place the chapter on the people of God before any discussion of church structure or church office, and by the equally important shift in the theology of the laity. This was a shift from an understanding of the lay faithful—at least 99.9 percent of all Christians—as auxiliaries to the hierarchy to participants in their own right in the mission of the church as such.[30] These shifts emphasized that every member of the church in her or his own way participates in the threefold office of Christ as priest, prophet, and king, and that "all share a true equality with regard to the dignity and to the activity common to all the faithful for the building up of the Body of Christ."[31]

Every Christian, therefore, is called upon to bear missionary witness in the world. This may vary according to a person's state of life, natural inclinations, or gifts, but as Pope Francis puts it, "in virtue of their baptism, all the members of the People of God have become missionary disciples (cf. Matt 28:19). All the baptized, whatever their position in the church or their level of instruction in the faith, are agents of evangelization, and it would be insufficient to envisage a plan of evangelization to be carried out by professionals while the rest of the faithful would simply be passive recipients."[32] Mission is to be engaged in everywhere the church is, therefore, by everyone

---

28. See Orchard, *Witness in Six Continents*.

29. Neill, *History of Christian Missions*, 572.

30. In regard to LG's chapter on the People of God, see, e.g., O'Malley, *What Happened at Vatican II*, 177–78. Regarding the shift in the theology of the laity, see LG 31 and Vatican Council II, *Apostolicam Actuositatem* (AA), 2.

31. Second Vatican Council, *Lumen Gentium*, 32.

32. Francis, *Evangelii Gaudium*, 120.

who is in the church. Baptismal witness is not simply an ideal, but a genuine goal of pastoral ministry and formation. It constitutes every Christian's fundamental ordination to the service of the world in partnership with the work of the Triune God in mission.

"Single, but Complex Reality"

This one mission of God, however, in which every member of the church participates wherever she or he is, is in the words of Pope John Paul II, a "single, but complex reality."[33] I think this is true in several senses. In the first place, as Roger Schroeder and I have interpreted it in our book *Constants in Context*, mission today is constituted by several components.[34] First of all, missionary practice is one of embodied witness to the gospel and, when appropriate, humble, vulnerable, and yet clear and relevant proclamation of the gospel message. Second, mission is constituted by liturgical celebration and the practice of prayer and contemplation. Third, as the 1971 Synod of Bishops has said famously, it has justice (and we could add peacemaking and ecological commitment) as constitutive elements. Fourth, Christians engage in mission through the practice of secular, interreligious, and ecumenical dialogue. Fifth, efforts of the contextualization and inculturation of the faith are an essential part of mission, as is, sixth, the practice of reconciliation.

Mission as Prophetic Dialogue

A second sense of the unity and complexity of God's mission shared by the church is that it is carried out in what can be described as "prophetic dialogue."[35] On the one hand, mission must be carried out with a deep dialogical spirit, rooted in openness to the context within and the people among whom one works, marked at all times by a spirit of deep listening and respect, carried out with a sense of God's presence in every context and among every people—in the words of Orthodox missiologist Michael

---

33. John Paul II, *Redemptoris Missio*, 41.

34. See Bevans and Schroeder, *Constants in Context*, 348–95.

35. The term "prophetic dialogue" was first used by the 2000 General Chapter of my missionary congregation, the Society of the Divine Word, and has been developed in various documents published by the Society. Schroeder and I have taken this term as a key to missionary thinking and practice in *Constants and Context* and in our subsequent book *Prophetic Dialogue*. See also Bevans, "Mission as Prophetic Dialogue: A Roman Catholic Approach." See also Ross and Bevans, *Mission on the Road to Emmaus*.

Oleksa, we never know where God is not.[36] Contemporary missiology expresses this basic attitude of dialogue in terms of a shift from speaking of mission *ad gentes* (*to* the nations) to mission *inter gentes* (*among* the nations).[37] On the other hand, in a kind of a dialogical/dialectical way, mission must be carried out as a practice of prophecy, understood in manifold ways. Prophecy can be practiced either in the silent embodied witness or in explicit annunciation or denunciation. It can consist of witnessing to or expressing hope, speaking a clear, inculturated message, or speaking out against sin and injustice in particular situations. The first task of mission in the light of the practice of prophetic dialogue is discernment as to whether a context or situation calls for patient and respectful dialogue or for clear and outspoken prophecy—or a mixture of both. I imagine missionary practice being discerned along the lines of a continuum, which is constantly being evaluated and revised.

Three "Fields," One Mission

A third level of complexity in the practice of mission today involves the mutual interaction among what have emerged as the three "fields" of missionary practice: pastoral work, "New Evangelization," and mission among those who have not yet come to believe in the gospel. As I have observed previously, every situation of the church today needs to be conscious that it is in a missionary situation. In this regard, although pastoral work has its own integrity, it can deeply profit from the thinking and practice of classical "cross-cultural" mission work, particularly as it is carried out in contexts that are multicultural, multi-generational, multi-religious, and highly globalized and technologized. Not all pastoral work is of this nature, just like not all work in a missionary church is missionary. Much of it is, however, and pastors will do well to see themselves in pastoral situations that demand the skills of what was once attributed exclusively to the cross-cultural missionary.

The same needs to be said for those who work in situations in which many baptized have ceased to practice their faith. A real contextual sensitivity needs to be developed, a real sense of discernment needs to be engaged in that can find the grace operative in secular, youth, and young adult cultures, and this demands pastoral skill that might be learned from cross-cultural missionary practice, as well.

---

36. Oleksa, "Orthodox Missiological Education," 86.

37. See Tan, *Christian Mission*, 1–2.

In a truly Catholic church, the need for women and men who leave their homelands or home cultures to work temporarily or permanently in other places and among other peoples is still necessary. The foreign missionary vocation is still, and perhaps more than ever with contemporary globalization, a valid one. Consider the importance of foreign mission personnel among AIDS victims in Thailand, in South Sudan, among migrants in Europe and Australia, in universities in Asia and Africa, working with gangs and street children in Latin America.[38]

Of course, it is no longer a simple matter of "the West going to the Rest." This still should happen, certainly, but today we recognize missionaries from all parts of the world working in all areas of need. We see as well missionaries from Asia and Africa coming to the West to work among migrants from their own countries or to help with the pastoral care and re-evangelization of places like the United States and Canada, Europe, Australia, or New Zealand. Foreign missionaries, of course, whether from the West or from the Global South, still need to commit themselves to language and culture learning as an integral part of missionary service.

Conclusion

The church is "missionary by its very nature," because it is rooted in the Trinity's life, which is a life poured out in a mission of healing, reconciliation, lifegiving, and joy. Like Pope Francis' dream of a "missionary option" for the church, recognizing the reality of God's life of missionary service "changes everything."[39] It makes mission not just one of several activities of the church, but grounds the church's identity, calling it forth, guiding it and challenging it. It makes God's mission primary for the church, while recognizing that women and men are partners in this mission, and—both amazingly and scarily—co-responsible for it. It in no way denies the validity of cross-cultural or foreign missionary activity, but while it is not everything the church does, it serves as the basic lens from which it carries out all of its ministry. It recognizes that mission takes place wherever the church is, and calls every Christian to a clear and faithful baptismal witness in the world. All of this is what we are called to recognize and put into practice as

38. These places of work have faces, e.g., SVD confrere Anthony Duc Le and Brothers Ron Fratzke, Damien Lunders, and Berndt Rüffing in Thailand; SVD confrere Andrzej Dzida in South Sudan; David Burrell, CSC, at the University of Notre Dame in Bangladesh; lay missionaries from the ecumenical community InnerChange and Nate and Jenny Bacon in Guatemala.

39. Francis, *Evangelii Gaudium*, 27.

we make the switch, implied by those powerful, profound, and radical lines from *Ad Gentes* 2, from "Missions" to "Mission."

Bibliography

Bevans, Stephen B. "Beyond the New Evangelization: Towards a Missionary Ecclesiology for the Twenty-first Century." In *A Church with Open Doors*, edited by Richard R. Gaillardetz and Edward J. Hahnenberg, 1–22. Collegeville, MN: Liturgical, 2015.

———. "*Missio Dei* and *Missio Ecclesiae*: Trinitarian Mission, *Theosis*, and the Missionary Nature of the Church." In *Mission beyond* Ad Gentes, edited by Jacob Kavunkal and Christian Tauchner, 17–30. Siegburg, Germany: Schmitt, 2016.

———. "Missiology as Practical Theology: Understanding and Embodying Mission as Trinitarian Practice." In *Invitation to Practical Theology: Catholic Voices and Visions*, edited by Claire Wolfteich, 253–74. New York: Paulist, 2014.

———. "A Prophetic Dialogue Approach." In *The Mission of the Church: Five Views in Conversation*, edited by Craig Ott, 3–20. Grand Rapids: Baker Academic, 2016.

———. "Mission as the Nature of the Church: Development in Catholic Ecclesiology," *Australian eJournal of Theology* 21 (2014) 184–96. aejt.com.au/__data/assets/pdf_file/0011/694298/AEJT_Mission_as_the_Nature_of_the_Church_Developments_in_Catholic_Ecclesiology_Bevans.pdf?utm_source=AEJT&utm_medium=email_html&utm_campaign=eJournal&utm_content=Vol_21_No_3_2014&utm_term=Mission_as_the_Nature_of_the_Church.

———. "Mission as the Nature of the Church in Roman Catholic Contexts." In *Called to Unity for the Sake of Mission*, edited by John Gibaut and Knud Jorgensen, 128–40. Oxford: Regnum, 2015.

———. "Revisiting Mission at Vatican II: Theology and Practice for Today's Missionary Church." *Theological Studies* 74 (2013) 261–83.

Bevans, Stephen B., and Cathy Ross, eds. *Mission on the Road to Emmaus: Constants, Context, and Prophetic Dialogue*. London: SCM, 2015.

Bevans, Stephen B., and Roger Schroeder. *Constants in Context: A Theology of Mission for Today*. American Society of Missiology Series 30. Maryknoll, NY: Orbis, 2004.

———. *Prophetic Dialogue: Reflections on Christian Mission Today*. Maryknoll, NY: Orbis, 2011.

Bosch, David J. *Transforming Mission: Paradigm Shifts in Theology of Mission*. Maryknoll, NY: Orbis, 1991.

Boyle, Gregory. *Tattoos on the Heart: The Power of Boundless Compassion*. New York: Free, 2010.

Bridston, Keith. *Mission, Myth and Reality*. New York: Friendship, 1965.

Coakley, Sarah. *God, Sexuality, and the Self: An Essay on the Trinity*. Cambridge University Press, 2013.

Congar, Yves. "Principes doctrinaux." In *Vatican II: L'activité Missionnaire de L'Église*, edited by Johannes Schütte, 186. Unam Sanctam 67. Paris: Cerf, 1967.

Crowe, Frederick E. "Son of God, Holy Spirit, and World Religions: The Contribution of Bernard Lonergan to the Wider Ecumenism." Chancellor's Address II. Toronto: Regis College, 1985.

Edwards, Denis. *Breath of Life: A Theology of the Creator Spirit*. Maryknoll, NY: Orbis, 2004.

Elizondo, Virgilio. "The Miracle of Conversion." *Give Us This Day* 3.1 (2013) 205.

Hanciles, Jehu J. *Beyond Christendom: Globalization, African Migration, and the Transformation of the West.* Maryknoll, NY: Orbis, 2008.

Irvin, Dale T. *Christian Histories, Christian Traditioning: Rendering Accounts.* Maryknoll, NY: Orbis, 1998.

John Paul II. *Redemptoris Missio.* December 7, 1990. w2.vatican.va/content/john-paul-ii/en/encyclicals/documents/hf_jp-ii_enc_07121990_redemptoris-missio.html.

Johnson, Elizabeth A. *She Who Is: The Mystery of God in Feminist Discourse.* New York: Crossroad, 1992.

Lonergan, Bernard J. F. "Mission and the Spirit." In *A Third Collection: Papers by Bernard J. F. Lonergan, SJ,* edited by Frederick E. Crowe, 253–59. New York: Paulist, 1985.

Neill, Stephen. *A History of Christian Missions.* London: Penguin, 1964.

Oakley, Mark. *The Collage of God.* London: Canterbury House, 2012.

Oleksa, Michael James. "Orthodox Missiological Education for the Twenty-First Century." In *Missiological Education for the Twenty-first Century: The Book, the Circle and the Sandals. Essays in Honor of Paul E. Pierson,* edited by J. Dudley Woodbury et al., 83–90. American Society of Missiology Series 23. Maryknoll, NY: Orbis, 1996.

O'Malley, John W. *What Happened at Vatican II.* Cambridge, MA: Belknap, 2008.

Orchard, Ronald K., ed. *Witness in Six Continents: Records of the Meeting of the Commission on World Mission and Evangelism of the World Council of Churches Held in Mexico City December 8 to 19, 1963.* London: Edinburgh House, 1963.

Sanneh, Lamin. *Whose Religion Is Christianity? The Gospel beyond the West.* Grand Rapids: Eerdmans, 2003.

Second Vatican Council. *Acta Synodalia Sacrosancti Concilii Vaticani.* Vatican City: Vatican Polyglot, 1970.

———. *Ad Gentes.* December 7, 1965. www.vatican.va/archive/hist_councils/ii_vatican_council/documents/vat-ii_decree_19651207_ad-gentes_en.html.

———. *Apostolicam Actuositatem.* November 18, 1965. www.vatican.va/archive/hist_councils/ii_vatican_council/documents/vat-ii_decree_19651118_apostolicam-actuositatem_en.html.

———. *Lumen Gentium.* November 24, 1964. www.vatican.va/archive/hist_councils/ii_vatican_council/documents/vat-ii_const_19641121_lumen-gentium_en.html.

Shenk, Wilbert R., ed. *Enlarging the Story: Perspectives on Writing World Christian History.* Maryknoll, NY: Orbis, 2002.

Tan, Jonathan. *Christian Mission among the Peoples of Asia.* American Society of Missiology Series 50. Maryknoll, NY: Orbis, 2014.

Thomas, Norman E., ed. *Classic Texts in Mission and World Christianity.* American Society of Missiology Series 20. Maryknoll, NY: Orbis, 1994.

Walls, Andrew F. *The Missionary Movement in Christian History: Studies in the Transmission of Faith.* Maryknoll, NY: Orbis, 1996.

———. "Missions or Mission: The IRM after 75 Years." *International Review of Mission* 100.2 (2011) 181–88.

7

A Baptismal Faith That Does Justice

—Jack Jezreel

I HAVE SPENT THE last thirty years trying to communicate the intrinsic relationship between a Catholic faith and the commitment to be about the care for the poor and vulnerable and the healing of the world's wounds; this effort has expressed itself in membership in a Catholic Worker community, a full-time position in parish social ministry, workshops, lectures, programs, a nonprofit organization, parish missions, keynote addresses, clergy trainings, preaching workshops, retreats, articles and, soon, a book. Of course, most of this work has happened in parishes, which, of course, is where most homilies happen.

I mention my background partly to warn you that my style has been crafted with an eye toward **popular education**. As a popular educator, I deliver my message in phrasings and images that are meant to be easy to remember and easy to speak, all of which is useful in a homily. I know that many would like to "up your game" when it comes to preaching the church's social mission. I am hoping that you will not only find something helpful in the specific advice I will offer near the end of this chapter but also in the deliberate crafting of language in an accessible style that I have found to be most effective in inviting and prompting interest and engagement in the work and dream of the church's social mission.

My work as a teacher has been substantially informed and made possible by the excellent education I received while I was at Notre Dame as a master of divinity student in the early 1980s. Let me be sure to mention two of my instructors: first, my homiletics instructor, Marianist Father John Melloh, who was a spectacular teacher and who died in 2014. His death, even while I had not seen him in twenty years, made me weep, so important was his teaching and impact on my life. And I want to also mention that I came to Notre Dame as a first-year master's student in 1979, the year Fr. Richard McBrien arrived. I had him—and I suppose he had me—the first semester we were both here for a class in ecclesiology. Much of what I have to say today has its roots in that class. Richard McBrien died in early 2015, less than a month after John Melloh. I held both of them in high regard and now I miss them. May they rest in peace.

What I would like to do is to give you a cursory snapshot of the last fifty years to provide understanding of the context and challenge of our topic and, in so doing, also provide thoughts on how to preach social mission, given this context and historical moment. The title for this chapter is "A Baptismal Faith that Does Justice," and this title has within it all of the challenge I will now try to describe.

Many, if not most, theologically informed religion writers and reporters covering the still young papacy of Pope Francis rightly identify him as a Vatican II product and flag bearer. Pope Francis has made this clear with frequent references to the vision and interests of the Second Vatican Council. He has also made clear his opinion that the work of Vatican II is still not complete. In 2013, a month after being elected pope, Francis offered a homily in which he said about Vatican II, "The council was a beautiful work of the Holy Spirit. But after 50 years, have we done everything the Holy Spirit in the council told us to do?" The pope asked if Catholics have opened themselves to "that continuity of the church's growth" that the council signified. The answer, he said, is "no."[1]

My thesis is that, indeed, the vision of Vatican II is yet to be completed, that this incompleteness has everything to do with the church's commitment to its social mission, and that Pope Francis is indeed pushing for the completion of Vatican II. Recognizing this and the skillful manner of Pope Francis

---

1. Homily on April 16 at an early morning Mass in the chapel of his residence, the Domus Sanctae Marthae.

provides us with an important backdrop for the preaching of social mission, charity, and justice in the twenty-first century U.S. Catholic parish.

In the spirit of giving you something you can take with you back to your parish to preach with, I want to describe, evocatively and provocatively I hope, a snapshot about where we are mid-decade. I want to agree with Pope Francis that the Holy Spirit is constantly nudging and drawing the church and the world into a holy evolution, a becoming, that is not yet complete. And that Vatican II represents part of that evolutionary call.

I do a lot of speaking and traveling, and when I am speaking at a parish on the weekend, it's my habit to attend liturgy. I am always very deliberate about picking up a bulletin, because the bulletin is essentially the parish's weekly autobiography. One look through the bulletin—even a quick one—and you can usually make a lot of accurate observations. Occasionally, when I pick up a bulletin, it will say this: "St. Mary's Catholic Church, a Vatican II parish." I read that line again, "A Vatican II parish," and then begin eagerly and excitedly to turn the pages of what, in some cases, is a very thick document. And after completing my survey through the bulletin, I sadly conclude, "Not a Vatican II parish. This is a Vatican 1½ parish!" And I mean that in a literal way.

Now, I think it's reasonable to posit that Vatican II occurred because there was a perceived, to use Pope Francis' words, urging from the Holy Spirit for the church to continue to evolve and grow. I suppose another way to say this is that Pope John XXIII and others were convinced that the church *needed* to evolve, to change, partly because some felt it had become stagnant and stale. So, it comes as no surprise that there are significant adjustments in the theology and documents of Vatican II that reflect a change in course, a change in vision.

To make my point, let me draw from the experience of most Catholics growing up in this country just prior to the Second Vatican Council. The religious or theological education of most Catholic adults in the early 1960s came by way of the most ubiquitous religious education tool used at that time, the *Baltimore Catechism*. From the 1880s to the 1960s, it was the default option of nearly every Catholic parish to educate young and/or new Catholics. And since there was little in the way of adult religious education during this same period of time, most Catholic adults drew from their memory of the *Baltimore Catechism* for their understanding of Catholicism and their place in it.

I'd like to draw a sample from the *Baltimore Catechism*, which reflects a theme that permeates the assumptions of the entire tool. Question #508 asks, "Why Did Christ Found the Church?" In other words, what is the church's role, purpose, and work? It's one of the big questions about the nature of church. The answer given is, "Christ founded the Church to teach, govern, sanctify, and save all men."[2]

I want to look closely at this three-infinitive phrase, "to teach, govern and sanctify," because hovering around these words are assumptions that form the challenge and opportunity facing the twenty-first century American Catholic Parish.

I want to argue that Vatican II essentially asks two critical questions about this phrase and comes up with very different answers than the Vatican I church with which it was in dialogue. And the answers that Vatican II comes up with form the very heart of Vatican II. The first question that Vatican II asks about the phrase "to teach, govern and sanctify" was a "who" question. That is, *who* teaches, governs, and sanctifies? *Who* are the ministers? To put it another way, *who* are the active agents of the church's purpose and work?

Of course, the answer was "clergy." Clergy taught, governed, and sanctified. Clergy were the agents of ministry. And, it must be insisted, clergy in many, many cases have done this well. But one of the problems with this answer is that if clergy, who represent less than 1 percent of the community called Catholic, are the only active agents of ministry, that means that the other 99 percent—the laity sitting in the pews—is defined essentially as the ones being ministered *to*. Again, there is no sin in being ministered to; we all need to be ministered to. But the negative consequence of defining the role of the laity as primarily being ministered to is that their role is essentially a passive one. Catholics were trained to think of themselves as the ones being tended to and they assumed—because this is what they experienced—that the work of church was the work of priests, with an assist from women religious.

Now, in stark contrast, the message and vision of Vatican II is that active ministry is not just associated with ordination—the sacrament of Holy Orders—but the sacrament of baptism. In other words, in response to the question, "Who is called to be active agents of the Church's work?" the answer is "Everyone," or all of the baptized. To draw from the title of this presentation, a "baptismal faith" means that I and you and all who are baptized are called to minister. Everyone is called not just to Mass but to ministry.

And as we consider the transition from Vatican I to Vatican II, we can say that this part of the transition is well on its way. As one kind of evidence, referring back to the parish bulletin as the telltale evidence of the state of the parish, you will find parishes all over the country whose bulletins are filled weekly with descriptions of 146 parish-based ministries (these

2. See http://sacred-texts.com/chr/balt/balt02.htm.

are *fat* bulletins). And these 146 ministries are typically started by, led by, and populated with the baptized. If you were to look at the parish bulletins from fifty years ago, June of 1965, you would have seen nothing resembling today's bulletins, which often describe a veritable beehive of lay activity.

Again, let me repeat, this transition from Vatican I to Vatican II, executed over the last fifty years, has really been quite successful. "A baptismal faith," to draw from this chapter's title, means we are *all* called to the work, to the ministry, to an active faith.

However, not all transitions have gone so well.

The second question that Vatican II asked about the description, "to teach, govern and sanctify," was not "Who?" but "Where?" That is, if active ministry is defined by "teaching, governing, and sanctifying," *where* did this ministry mostly take place? And the answer was that it happened on the parish block.

As a young Catholic attending Catholic grade school and attending the only Catholic church in my hometown of Clearwater, Florida, prior to Vatican II, I remember well the routine of getting in the station wagon on a Sunday morning with my brothers and sister and experiencing the usual raucous back seat chaos of too many kids in too little space. Past the grade school we would go, arguing, laughing, and wrestling. Past the Dairy Kurl we would go, teasing, complaining, and joking. Past the high school we would go, with all manner of tumult and playground happening in the back of that car . . .

. . . Until the right front tire of the car touched the church parking lot. And, suddenly, because all of us kids were students at St. Cecelia's Catholic school and because all of us were taught by nuns and because all of us knew exactly what we were supposed to do, our voices went silent, all teasing and tickling stopped, all smiles (mostly) disappeared. And we quietly got out of the car and walked silently into church, into a building with its mysterious stained glass windows, into a space where a language was spoken that none of us knew (I just assumed it was God's language), and into a space where smoke from incense would drift up from the altar. Here on the parish block, holy men wore black, and holy women wore black and high, holy headwear. Here my parents and my siblings and I saw and did things we never did anywhere else—we kneeled, we prayed, we worshipped God. And then we would walk back to the car and the minute the left front tire touched the road that would return us to our home, it was back to the monkey farm. And we would live our lives another week in normal time.

And the impression I came away with as a young boy was that this block is where the action is. This is the block where God lives, where church is, where faith is lived out. And, indeed, the faith of my mother and father for most of the years of their lives was a faith that was dedicated to the block called parish property. This "Sanctuary Catholicism" defined a loyal faith in terms that mostly highlighted what was going on at the sanctuary. The logic of "Sanctuary Catholicism" went thus: The more time you spent at the sanctuary, the holier you were. The more times you went to Mass, the holier you were. The more times you went to "confession," the holier you were. The more you washed the sanctuary linens, the more meetings you went to on sanctuary property, the more time you spent praying in the adoration sanctuary, the more money you gave to build or to maintain the sanctuary, the more Catholic you were. To teach, govern and sanctify were activities that happened on church property. They did not happen anywhere else. And church property is where I assumed the work of God happened. As a boy who thought he was going to be a priest, I was pretty sure I knew where I was going to spend most of my time.

But Vatican II, in sharp contrast, insists that ministry is not limited to parish property; ministry is to happen *everywhere*. The vision of Vatican II is that all the world is the geography of faith and the place where faith goes. That world—its joys, horrors, wonder, wounds, celebration and lamentation—is the world that God is interested in, that Jesus was interested in, that faith is interested in. The language of "peace" is not limited to the peace we know deep inside after we receive communion and kneel silently in prayer, but also the peace that seeks to end warfare, violence and hate. The language of "love" is not limited to caring for our children and friends, but requires a broad embrace of all and therefore will not tolerate hunger and homelessness, oppression and exploitation, and the dehumanization of widows, orphans and strangers. And the language of ministry is not limited to ecclesial ministry (sanctuary ministry); the language of ministry is only limited by the time and space of this world. The "Reign of God," we learn, has to do with all earthly matters under the sun.

One of the best expressions of the expansiveness of ministry happens near the end of liturgy. There is this theologically sublime, pastorally powerful word that gets spoken near the end of Mass and that word is "Go." "Go in peace to love and serve the Lord and one another" or some variation on the theme. It is a part of the sending rite, and its meaning is that, having broken bread and shared a cup, having experienced the presence of the living God yet again, there is but one thing to do and that is to be about the world's care.

So, for the hour or so that we have been gathered for Eucharist, our touchstones for behavior are the customs, responses, and ritual that are all part of the experience of the Mass. We know when to sit, kneel and stand; we know the responses; we know how and when to get in the communion line, and so on. And this kind of shared familiarity is part of what makes a rich communal prayer experience. Then we are told to "Go," and as we turn our gaze from altar to the exit doors at the back of the church and make our way out of the church, we realize that where we are "Go-ing" is back to the station wagon. It's a world of family and neighborhood and workplaces. As we gaze out of church doors to world around, it's also a world of politics and economics, it's a world of odd weather patterns, as the pope insisted recently, that are threatening and destructive. The world we go to is a world in which almost half of the human population lives in poverty on less than $2.50 a day and over a billion people live in extreme poverty. The world we go to is a world where human trafficking is one of the largest industries and growing fast. The world we go it is the richest country in the world where one in five children live in poverty and with food insecurity. The world we go to is a world preoccupied with accumulation, status, and power and the violence required to maintain such.

And as we pass through the exit door to the world outside the church walls, we realize that knowing when to sit, kneel and stand is not going to help us figure out how to address the problem of homelessness in our community. The touchstones of faith now move from the assumptions of common prayer to the assumptions of faith in action—what we call Catholic social teaching or, even better, Catholic social witness. It is a rich tradition.

But here is the problem. Remember those parishes with 146 ministries in their bulletin? Guess where 144 of those ministries meet? Parish property. And guess what their focus is? The business of the parish property and the people who gather there. The truth of it is that the parish is still pretty much a self-preoccupied reality. One massive piece of evidence of this self-preoccupation is the attention we give, the staff we hire, the budget we create, for example, to prepare our members for sacraments—sanctuary activities—versus the attention we give, the staff we hire, and the budget we provide for preparing people to care for the poor and vulnerable. The sad fact that I observe in my too robust travel for the last twenty years is that most parishes don't even understand that an important part of their task is to prepare—spiritually and functionally—its members for the off-parish-property work of compassion, mercy, and justice.

So, when Pope Francis speaks of Vatican II still needing to be completed, he has this off campus mission in mind. So, the challenge before us is not just how we preach social mission. Those who try to preach social mission to a community that otherwise has not been catechized, formed, educated, or commissioned for mission will come across as a stranger from a strange land—often misunderstood and unwelcome. The challenge before us is how to change the geography of being parish.

What Pope Francis is hoping for I think is indeed, to quote our title for this chapter, "a baptismal faith"—*everyone engaged in ministry*—"that does justice"—that is, *engaged in ministry everywhere*. In the context of a truly Vatican II community—where everybody is ministering everywhere—the preaching of social mission will not only come across as familiar but critical, relevant, and celebrated. So, for example, in U.S. parishes that have been attempting to engage in a deliberate and loving way the injustice and violence of racism, the recent events in Charleston, South Carolina, will invite and require a homily that reassures and re-inspires a community already committed to the human dignity of all people. The people of that kind of parish will beg for such a homily.

In *Evangelii Gaudium*, his apostolic exhortation released in November 2013, Pope Francis makes some remarkable statements about the parish that speak to this paradigm shift from a community whose focus is the parish block to a community whose focus is also beyond the parish block to the wounded places. Here are five extraordinary quotes with a few words bolded in each for emphasis:

> I want to emphasize that what I am trying to express here has a programmatic significance and important consequences. I hope that all communities will devote the necessary effort to advancing along the path of a **pastoral and missionary conversion which cannot leave things as they presently are.** (EG 25)

The pope's words suggest that he is interested in something tangibly different happening on the level of the parish. There is something new—a conversion even!—that needs to alter the status quo.

> I dream of a "missionary option," that is, **a missionary impulse capable of transforming everything,** so that the Church's customs, ways of doing things, times and schedules, language and structures can be suitably channeled for the evangelization of today's world rather than for her self-preservation. (EG 27)

The language of "missionary" speaks to movement and what some call "voluntary displacement," which requires of us that we physically move ourselves in order to build relationships in places that have been wounded of abandoned. It is the way of many we call saints: Mother Teresa, who displaced herself in the streets of Kolkata; Dorothy Day, who displaced herself in the New York neighborhoods of the poor and homeless; Damien of Molokai, who displaced himself in the camps of the lepers; and Greg Boyle, who displaced himself in the world of gangs. Most saints spend their saintly lives with those who have been abandoned.

> The **renewal of structures** demanded by pastoral conversion can only be understood in this light: as part of an effort to **make them more mission-oriented**, to make ordinary pastoral activity on every level more inclusive and open, to inspire in pastoral workers **a constant desire to go forth** and in this way to elicit a positive response from all those whom Jesus summons to friendship with him. As John Paul II once said to the Bishops of Oceania: "All renewal in the Church must have mission as its goal if it is not to fall prey to a kind of ecclesial introversion." (EG 27)

Both here and in the previous quote, the pope seems concerned about a church that has become self-preoccupied. But there is an antidote and the antidote is mission. Many U.S. parishes risk this self-preoccupation, not because they are selfish or mean-spirited but because they are not structured for mission, not even self-aware of the responsibility and opportunity of sending people on mission.

> The parish is not an outdated institution; precisely because it possesses great flexibility, it can assume quite different contours **depending on the openness and missionary creativity of the pastor and the community** . . . [I]f it proves capable of self-renewal and constant adaptivity, it continues to be "the Church living in the midst of the homes of her sons and daughters." This presumes that it really is in contact with the homes and the lives of its people, and does not become a useless structure out of touch with people or a self-absorbed cluster made up of a chosen few. (EG 28)

Notice these words in the quote above: "flexibility," "openness," "creativity," "self-renewal," and "adaptivity." These are words that suggest the opportunity and invitation to change. Parishes can change, says the pope. For those of you who are pastors, I hope you might see that there's an exciting opportunity on the horizon.

> We must admit, though, that the call to review and renew our parishes has not yet sufficed to bring them nearer to people, to make them environments of living communion and participation, and to make them **completely mission-oriented**. (EG 28)

The pattern that runs through these quotes is: 1) language inviting a new paradigm for parish life, and 2) that paradigm is connected to mission.

So, I'd like to offer some of my own observations about the opportunities the pope's vision might invite. These are some of the transitions I offer for your imagination:

From how to equip people to be part of Sanctuary *to* how to *also* equip people to heal and make holy the world.

1. From religious education focused on life in the church ***to also*** religious education focused on the human reality and the church's response in the light and hope of faith

2. From a place of pastoral care of the members of the parish ***to also*** a place of prophetic urgency for the poor who may not be part of the parish

3. From sacraments emphasizing belonging ***to also*** sacraments emphasizing empowerment

4. From evangelization as a way of getting people to the sanctuary ***to also*** evangelization as a way of engaging people in the meaning and missional geography and care of Jesus

5. From "church going" being about going to the sanctuary ***to also*** "church going" as actually going from the church to the world

6. From tithing and parish budget primarily focused on church-building and sanctuary activities ***to also*** tithing and parish budget focused on addressing scarcity and need and ministry in the world

7. From membership ***to also*** discipleship

8. From leadership as dock manager and caretaker of people in the sanctuary ***to also*** leadership as lifeboat captain and caretaker of God's World and leader of the crew that saves

9. From parish as hang-out ***to also*** parish as launching pad

Each of these transitions is intended both as a prompt for re-imagining but also as a metric for parish focus. Notice that in each of the propositions, I have italicized and bolded the two-word phrase, "to also," suggesting that there needs not to be a wholesale dismissal of the parish as most of us have known it, but a partnership between the internal nurture of the community and its responsibility to be a vessel of hope, healing, light and leaven to the world.

I would like to propose, again for your imaginations, that this partnership be considered a 50/50 proposition. Here's what I have in mind in snapshot form: fifty percent of the parish's resources should go to the work of community nurture—the activities of worship, prayer, education, formation, sacramental preparation, celebration. And fifty percent of the parish's resources should go to the work of social mission—charity, advocacy, community building and organizing, global mission and solidarity, volunteer placement, attention to poverty, climate change, human trafficking, homelessness, abortion, and peacemaking. That means fifty percent of the parish staff is dedicated to the work of gathering people on parish property for education, sacrament, worship and celebration, and fifty percent of the parish staff dedicated to the work of preparing and engaging people in the world of social mission and accompaniment. That means that fifty percent of the budget will be dedicated to the work within the parish block, and fifty percent of the budget will be dedicated to the work outside the parish block. Fifty percent of the parish's buildings will be on the parish block and used for education and prayer and fifty percent of the parish's buildings will be somewhere else, used to address human crisis and social need.

Finally, what does all of this mean for the homilist? I have six suggestions.

First, preach the geography of a faith in Jesus Christ. Jesus was a road guy, not a sanctuary guy. Yes, he has a proper appreciation of the gathering place of prayer as holy, but he spends most of his time on the road going to where he is needed. This is not just the characteristic of the messiah, it's also a characteristic of the disciple, the one who follows Jesus, a characteristic of "baptismal faith." So, in this regard, I think Pope Francis is brilliant: "Get smelly, like the sheep." Don't go directly to issues, go to relationships. We must, as a matter of faith, build relationships with those who have been left behind: the stranger, the foreigner, the poor ones, the discarded, and the abandoned. And, then, out of the logic of friendship and familiarity, we can move to charity and justice because we have experienced what they have experienced. We can now move forward on solutions and responses that are well informed and not just good intentioned. If you start with issues, people will just argue. But if you start with discipleship—missionary discipleship—it will be a big challenge but one that invites and intrigues.

Second, do not presume your preaching, regardless how good it is, will be enough to engage people into social mission. Your preaching must be a part of a larger orientation within the parish that makes social mission a priority. I have known too many pastors with great hearts, a fine education in Catholic social teaching, and excellent homiletic skills find themselves alienated from their parishioners because nothing else in the parish was preparing them for what they would hear on Sunday morning. You will not preach your parish into submission. Make sure people have lots of opportunities at your parish to study Catholic social teaching. Make sure there are lots of opportunities for people to cross the tracks and to get involved in the lives of the poor. Make sure there are lots of retreats that support and encourage social mission. Then—and maybe only then—will your sermons nourish and challenge.

Third, tell stories. Do not cite statistics, at least not at first. Tell stories of generosity, and stories of vulnerability, and stories of courage, and stories of hurt. Tell stories of heroes and saints, people who loved large. Theologize and comment around the stories. Theology is mostly boring. Stories are always interesting. Jesus tells stories. After telling stories, then invite the community to their best selves. And give them something tangible to do.

Fourth, the invitation to be involved in social mission is, more often than not, portrayed as or presumed to be something that we don't really want to do or, if we do it, something we do out of a sense of unpleasant obligation. But those who work with vulnerable people say something very different. Abundant life—a life rich in meaning and Spirit—is understood to be a consequence of discovering, via our faith, that pouring ourselves out on behalf of neighbor transforms and makes holy our lives. It is a privilege to be invited—via the Gospel—to be a vessel of God's healing, restoring love in this world. It's a privilege and, we're all invited.

Fifth—and this is critical—your preaching will be doubly potent if you are engaged. If you can speak from your experience at the prison or the soup kitchen or at the homeless shelter, your listeners will assume you have the authority and integrity to preach on your topic. Your experiences in these places will change you and give you insight and experience from which to speak. This will make all the difference. On the occasion of being back on the Notre Dame campus for the first time since Fr. Theodore Hesburgh's passing in 2015, I have wondered if his death would have stirred so many of us had he not been a man who was so engaged in the wounds and causes of the world. He was certainly a Notre Dame man, but he was a man who saw the church and this university as a launching pad, not a hangout. People will forgive us our stumbling words and imperfect oratory if we are people of integrity and compassion.

Finally, smile. In *Evangelii Gaudium*, Pope Francis uses a word that had never been used before in papal statements. In so many words, the pope says that those who follow Christ may *not* be—and the word he uses is— "sourpusses." Do not preach social mission with a scowl. No one will be interested or attracted except other sourpusses. Joy anchored in faith is our starting point.

8

Religious Witness in the Struggle against Apartheid

—Peter-John Pearson

MICHAEL MAYNE, THE ONE-TIME dean of Westminster Abbey in London, tells of how Nelson Mandela on a state visit to the U.K. toured the abbey. As the dean led him through the cloisters, Mayne recalls: "he places a hand on my arm and says 'I never cease to be grateful to the church: without it I should have had no education and I should not be here.'"[1]

Sakhela Buhlungu, the academic and chronicler of the trade union movement in South Africa, in particular of the era when union activity was brutally outlawed by the apartheid regime, commenting on the movement's role in the anti-apartheid struggle and its resilience and ability to function and to inspire and educate its members despite the repression, says: "Religion imbued many [trade unionists] with a sense of justice and provided them with a rationale for challenging oppressive and exploitative relations in society."[2]

A close reading of these random quotes or cameos provides a powerful insight into the role of religion in contributing to the emergence of credible witnesses whose leadership is critically and creatively informed by faith values as seen in Mandela. Religion also can be credited with creating, on the other hand, a sense of hope and solidarity among one of the most

---

1. Mayne, *Pray, Love,* 122.
2. Buhlungu, *Paradox,* 1–2.

exploited, vulnerable and marginalized groupings in South African society under apartheid.

This quest for informing the public space and for articulating hopes and dreams in practical ways was and indeed remains a key task of the faith community in the service of humanity. Albert Nolan, the Dominican theologian, holds with others that in a society of such rampant inequality and unfulfilled aspirations, "solidarity and love for one another cannot remain an abstract idea or a warm feeling. In practice it will have to become however gradually an economic reality."[3]

Nolan understands the power of the word, especially the spoken or articulated word, to hold the aspirations of people, its power to inspire and to keep hope alive in the public domain. He also understands and warns that until the word is translated into powerful practical expressions it remains a partial word, a word that is unfulfilled.

These comments, however, also bear eloquent testimony to the role of churches and faith-based communities as a significant source, not only of inspiration, but of practical engagement, an account of the hope that is in us and indeed of providing or "growing" leadership, a role that faith communities played most significantly in the overthrow of the iniquitous system of apartheid. It is also clear that this testimony, if I read my notes from my homiletic class correctly, is also an accurate description of what should be the outcome of all preaching. In the light of this assertion, I want to propose that as the fiftieth anniversary of the close of the Second Vatican Council has passed, at a time when it is opportune to assess the impact of the council in specific contexts, and in a celebration and examination of the preaching ministry in the light of that council, it is appropriate to look at the reception of the council through the lens of the leadership offered by the bishops of South Africa and to understand that commitment to the struggle against apartheid as a sermon preached to the people of South Africa as an exercise of "faith seeking understanding." Put somewhat differently, I would argue that the bold, prophetic engagement in the struggle for justice was in effect a creation of a contested public sermon.

It is thus my contention that the reception of Vatican II into the conflicted reality of apartheid South Africa and the witness of church leadership were as much acts of political resistance as they were bold, prolonged, prophetic, public sermons in very dark days seeking at a broad level to fulfill what all sermons are meant to accomplish. These two expressions, in as far as they were separable, shared remarkably similar characteristics that

---

3. Nolan, *Jesus Today*, 203.

are worth revisiting as we harvest the lessons for the ongoing challenge of preaching in contested, public domains.

The council, in a profound sense, framed the bishops' engagement and prophetic homily. In a special way Pope Paul VI's remarkable sermon on December 8, 1965, at the closing Mass of the council provided the impetus for such a daunting task. The pope said:

> This is a unique moment, a moment of incomparable signifi-cance and riches. In this universal assembly, in this privileged point of time and space, there converge together the past, the present and the future—the past: for here, gathered in this spot, we have the Church of Christ with her tradition, her history, her councils, her doctors, her saints; the present: for we are taking leave of one another to go out towards the world of today with its miseries, its sufferings, its sins, but also with its prodigious accomplishment, its values, its virtues; and lastly the future is here in the urgent appeal of the peoples of the world for more justice, in their will for peace, in their conscious or unconscious thirst for a higher life, that life precisely which the Church of Christ can and wishes to live them.

"The urgent appeal of the peoples of the world for more justice, in their will for peace" remains a profound hermeneutic for interpreting the reception of the council in South Africa as indeed it also provided the content of the public sermon. Those words constitute the very core of the witness of the church in South Africa.

As a footnote, I want to suggest that we understand these insights as fit-ting quite comfortably into Joseph Komonchak's observation that: "In three respects at least, the Council posed major threats to the self-articulation of modern Catholicism: by its far more positive assessment of modernity in its political and cultural features, by its call for an updating and reform of church practice in the light of modernity, and by its appeal to particular and local churches to assume responsibility for culturally distinct realizations of Catholic Christianity."[4]

One of the key fruits of the reception of the council in South Africa (and indeed in line with Komonchak's observation) was to grapple with its specific context. In 1987, as the fires of resistance grew ever fiercer in towns and villages across South Africa, the Southern African Catholic Bishops Conference (SACBC) committed themselves to "take into account the sin-gular situation and resultant tensions in the Church in South Africa where 80% of the laity are black and 80% of the clergy are white, and to investigate

4. Komonchak, "Ecclesial," 56–82.

as a matter of extreme urgency the feasibility of a pastoral Consultation in which lay people, religious and priests, in large majority black, may participate with the bishops, in arriving at policy on Church life and apostolate (in an apartheid society) but not on doctrinal or canonical matters."[5]

Mervyn Abrahams remarks that it was a process of consultation aimed "to present practical ways of accomplishing the Church's mission in the South African context in the spirit of the Second Vatican Council. The Theme Paper for the Pastoral Plan (1987) put it as follows: 'As the council pointed out each local church, each local community has its own character, its own culture, its own special talents (LG 13). The special character of each local church also implies that it can have its own special problems. For these reasons it is desirable that the church in a particular region should have a pastoral plan designed for it."[6] The church leaders understood that mere words, generalities, platitudes, devoid of context, would remain unconvincing. As with preaching generally, so too in this specific situation, context is both critical and persuasive.

The response of the church in South Africa, as bidden by the council, to its particular context was indeed abundantly clear. Archbishop Denis Hurley, O.M.I., arguably the most outspoken Catholic leader in the struggle against apartheid, emphasized this point. In his response to the questionnaire for the special Synod of Bishops in 1985 called by Pope John Paul II to reflect on the reception of the council, he wrote: "The pursuit of justice in South Africa and the dismantling of apartheid must become priority number one for the churches, the chief concern of their spiritual, pastoral and evangelising effort."[7]

The point is clear that the reception of the council had to be context-specific as indeed good preaching must necessarily be "embodied, concrete and context specific if it is not to hang nebulously over our lived realities."[8]

Three years earlier Archbishop Hurley had already pointed to a significant paradigm shift in the political or struggle consciousness of the SACBC. He said that the "evolution of the church towards an ever increasing concern for the social, economic, political and cultural dimensions of human life, is a fact of our time . . . The evolution is slow. The process of moving from declarations, resolutions, findings and recommendations to implementation and action is painful and precarious and at times scarcely perceptible."[9]

5. SACBC, Interdiocesan Pastoral, 4.

6. Abrahams, "Denis Hurley," 246–47.

7. Ibid., 246.

8. Le Bruyns, "Transforming?," 118.

9. Borer, *Challenging*, 54.

It is probably universally true that the same could be said for the impact of formal preaching! Its reception is slow and partial. The value of the pondering on the word lies more deeply in it being an expression of conviction. Hence I argue that both the appreciation of context and the uncompromised convictions were key to the bishops' leadership being noticed, if not always appreciated and acted upon.

Thus what South Africans began to see and hear, as a fruit of the council, was an early realization of that famous passage flowing from the 1971 Synod of Bishops on justice "Action on behalf of justice and participation in transformation of the world fully appears to us as a constitutive dimension of the preaching of the gospel or, in other words, of the church's mission for the redemption of the human race and its liberation from every oppressive structure."[10]

Three conciliar approaches are already clearly evident, approaches that would continue to frame the praxis of the Southern African Catholic Bishops Conference and which for the homilist remain necessary preparatory work; namely, a more dialogical approach with an emphasis on listening to the aspirations and questions of those who suffer; a more historically conscious approach, reading the signs of the times and seeking to discern the meaning of the emergent history and, especially from *Gaudium et Spes*, urged on by the impulse to "associate the light of revelation with the experience of humanity" (GS 33); the shift from a stance of neutrality to practical participation, and indeed as repression intensified, leadership in actions on behalf of justice. The shift to practical participation also provided an edge to the sermon preached by the bishops in the public domain! It is interesting to note the echo of the homiletic principle, that a good sermon only carries if it is backed by the preacher's own integrity, by the preacher's own experience, by the depth of solidarity or sharing in the plight of the hearers. It is a question of publicly testifying to one's concrete convictions. So aware of the fact that solidarity required more than sentiment, powerfully the bishops entered into a very vulnerable space, opened themselves to considerable risk and danger, moved out of their comfort zones, and thus shared in the extreme vulnerability and dangers of the people whom they dared to inspire. Let me spell this out specifically.

10. *1971 Synod of Bishops*, "Justice."

A 1986 pastoral letter from the bishops declared "Let there be no mistake—we are not neutral in the current conflict in South Africa. We fully support the demands of the majority of the people for justice."[11] In the same year the bishops took the decision to allow church buildings to be used by resistance organizations, stating quite categorically that "making church buildings available is an opportunity for the church to identify itself with the peoples struggle for liberation."[12] As draconian legislation and the armed forces' brutality closed the few remaining spaces for protest activity, the church was forced to take up the slack and in 1987 the SACBC sponsored a newspaper, *New Nation*, which became the first of the alternative newspapers publishing news that the commercial press was afraid to publish, committed "to telling the truth about reality." It was unashamedly a mouthpiece for voices excluded or silenced by the state and a platform for the spread of various ideological positions. The next year the headquarters of the SACBC was bombed and destroyed, churches were burnt on the Vaal Triangle, in the informal settlements on the outskirts of Cape Town, church personnel were banned or detained, as torture became more commonplace, as did disappearances and deaths in detention. In Tristan Anne Borer's words, the church was forced into a "spiral of involvement"[13] as repression intensified on the one hand and resistance to apartheid grew more radical on the other hand.

Using the hermeneutic of participation in action for justice, this practical action became the most pronounced witness of the institutional church. Stronger than words, it carried into the public domain the insight attributed to Francis of Assisi: "preach always and if necessary use words." It is an acknowledgement of different ways and differing forms of preaching, of the power of the word spoken formally and informally to challenge people.

Albert Nolan understands this solidarity with the oppressed as an expression of preaching. He understands these actions as a promotion of structures of grace that are in truth the social embodiments of the personal experience of the saving power of God which in a deep way is the subject matter of all preaching. Preaching is really any form, verbal or otherwise, of reflection upon this relationship. Nolan describes the characteristics of such structures of grace. Such structures "embody the right use of power: the power of service, the power of sharing, the power of solidarity and love, the power of faith and commitment, the power of hope. In the name of

---

11. SACBC, Pastoral Letter, 1.

12. SACBC Justice and Reconciliation, "Use of Church," 1–2.

13. Borer, *Challenging*, 51.

justice and freedom, it is these embodiments of God's saving power that will confront sin and evil."[14]

There is no question that this justice commitment, this paradigm shift was rooted to a very significant degree in the Second Vatican Council. John de Gruchy, a theologian from the Reformed tradition writing on the topic of political landmarks and the response of churches in South Africa, noted: "Two other major ecumenical events of the 1960s had important consequences for the church situation in South Africa. The first was the Second Vatican Council; the second was the Geneva Conference on Church and Society sponsored by the World Council of Churches in 1966. Vatican II brought the Roman Catholic Church in South Africa into much more direct contact with other churches and the Christian Council. Moreover the Roman Catholic hierarchy encouraged a far stronger commitment to social justice than before."[15]

John de Gruchy in another article sees 1957 as a critical year for church opposition to apartheid. The government had decided to legislate the infamous "church clause," which would force segregation of churches at worship and in pastoral activities in the same way as public amenities were racially segregated. He writes: "Indeed, 1957 marked a significant change in the Roman Catholic approach to the state and to apartheid . . . during that year Catholic Archbishop Whelan of Bloemfontein declared that apartheid was nothing less than a heresy. The 'Statement on Apartheid' issued by the hierarchy indicated that the more progressive bishops had finally taken the lead."[16]

Two points are worth noting at this juncture. One is that it is clear that the Southern African Catholic Bishops Conference's public witness was not, solely, the result of the Second Vatican Council. Public criticism of apartheid has had a long tradition. Like good formal preaching, the spoken words are always the result of a much longer and deeper spiritual gestation. In 1948 the same year as the Nationalist Party came into power, Bishop Hennemann of Cape Town wrote: "In recent years it (segregation) has reappeared in the guise and under the name of apartheid. A beginning has already been made to put into practice this noxious, unchristian and destructive policy."[17] In 1952 on the tercentenary of the white colonization of the Cape, the bishops issued a strong condemnation of racial superiority. This was followed by seven letters solely on the subject of race and social justice.

14. Muyebe, "Experience," 300.

15. De Gruchy, "Political," 12.

16. Ibid., 10.

17. De Gruchy, *Church Struggle*, 98.

In 1957 the SACBC issued a prophetic and courageous "Statement on Apartheid" which was one of the first outright denunciations of apartheid issued by a body of leaders rather than an individual church leader, thus carrying the weight of a type of *imprimatur*. The statement spoke of apartheid as a "fundamental evil and blasphemous."[18] In a profound way this opened the way for the declaration of apartheid as a heresy, a judgment that would be taken up with vigor in the 1980s.

In 1962, on the eve of the opening of the council, the bishops stated: "We dare not remain silent and passive in the face of the injustices inflicted on members of the unprivileged racial groups especially where they are denied the elementary right to organise in defence of their legitimate interests."[19] Pope Paul VI's farewell remarks at the close of the council would have not so much begun the public protest against apartheid as it would have inspired the bishops and strengthened their resolve to fight injustices and apartheid specifically, more boldly and uncompromisingly. It would also have offered them the theological categories and vocabulary to bring their actions in line with official church teaching. The documents of Vatican II, from 1962 on, however added a profound edge to the church's response to apartheid. Pope Paul VI had reminded the participants at the council that the decrees are not so much a destination but departure points for new goals.[20]

It must be noted that the inspiration and ideas birthed by the council were global in their outreach and later became a source of further inspiration and strength across boundaries as the translation of theological ideas were worked out in practice. Writing in the U.S.A. context, Kristin Heyer and Brian Massingale capture the transformative effect of the council. "The dialogical engagement with the wider society, central to *Gaudium et spes*, is evident in the theological, pastoral and social movements in subsequent decades across the globe—from liberation to feminist theologies to renewed commitments to justice on the part of educational institutions and Catholic involvement in the civil rights movement."[21]

In an important analysis of the political consequences of conciliar teaching, Tristan Anne Borer says, "Perhaps the most well known document of the Council was *Gaudium et Spes*, which held that Catholics has a Christian

---

18. Abraham, *Catholic Church*, 116.

19. SACBC, "Lawful Means," 38.

20. Abraham, *Catholic Church*, 241.

21. Heyer and Brian Massingale, "Impact," 86.

responsibility to learn from the world, involve themselves in the problems of society and work to overcome them. Fulfilling one's Christian responsibility meant serving the world in a never ending effort to bring God's Kingdom on earth."[22] *Gaudium et Spes* spoke of the need to engage in social action wherever the rights of people were at stake, the duty to pass moral judgment even in matters relating to politics and the idea that action was necessary and legitimate. The document opened up a new religious paradigm. It also introduced Justice and Peace Commissions and in so doing narrowed the gap between people on the ground and church leadership. These commissions provided a sounding board for ideas but also a very close contact with the realities on the ground. *Gaudium et Spes* further began to introduce key concepts for theological interrogation and for use in responding to the signs of the times. It further offered a much more common language which allowed for deeper ecumenical and interfaith joint action. For the SACBC it provided insights which were used profitably to forcefully resist the increasing repression which coincided with the years of the most active reception of the council across the world. Words such as liberation, social sin, the gap between rich and poor, the legitimacy of opposition to tyranny, the attainment of the various human and social rights contained in particular documents widened the legitimate topics for theological interrogation and application by church leadership in consultation with those who suffered most. The quest for social justice was in the process normalized as an ordinary part of church life.

Borer makes the very important point that "Churches become overt political actors under the influence of a specific set of circumstances, when three distinct factors coalesce to produce a very highly politicized outcome. At a bare minimum, three factors influence the adoption of an explicitly politicized model of church. A changing political context characterized simultaneously by increasing repression and increasingly militant opposition; a changing religious context whereby the rise of a new universe of religious discourse forms the bases for a new agenda for organizations, allowing issues that were formerly not considered legitimate for theological debate to now become so; and the character of the institutional contexts of political debates." She adds, "new religious ideas originating in Vatican II and further developed in the Latin American context were to have a profound influence

---

22. Borer, *Challenging*, 86.

in South African theological circles as well."[23] This discovery of a vocabulary and categories of theology that underpinned the urgent pastoral tasks of the times might well be one of the most enduring fruits of the council for the church in South Africa.

I would argue that without these post-conciliar reflections and insights, without the commitment to resistance, to challenging the state, to mutual cooperation with a range of civil society players, the church's witness would have been seriously diminished, if not rendered impossible since participation in the struggle needed a new hopeful imagination and a different universe of discourse which the council and the post-conciliar theologies provided. *Gaudium et Spes* also provided a shared discourse with other Christian churches and opened up powerful platforms for shared activities. It offered people of faith a shared analysis and a common bases for action.

Borer provides instances of the mechanics of this process and teases out the theological and practical implications of the paradigm shift:

> One major outcome of the Council was a revised self-identity. The church minimized its traditional model of an unchanging and hierarchically ordered institution in favour of a new model: the Pilgrim People of God. Several ideas resulted from the adoption of this model, perhaps the most important of which was the acceptance of temporal, historical change both as a fact and as a source for new and valid ideas, this understanding that the church should learn from the world, grew form the Council's stress on the need to read the signs of the times. This emphasis which underpins a position that is open to change, has implications for the long term interaction of religion and politics.
>
> The modest idea of accepting change as normal had far reaching and unexpected implications for the Catholic Church. First it allowed the church to potentially free itself from identification with existing structures and social arrangements under the notion that if all situations and institutional arrangements are historically determined, then no particular arrangement is necessarily the correct one. The idea of change was important for a second reason as well—it led to concern for how societies developed as they did. If no particular societal arrangement was predetermined by God, by what was it determined? The question opened the floodgate, for in seeking an answer to it the church turned to other disciplines for explanation, especially the social sciences. A final consequence of accepting the idea of change is that it led to new ideas about Catholic activism. With the

23. Ibid., xvii and 11.

recognition that societies can be changed by human will, a new emphasis on praxis became important. Action towards change was necessary and legitimate. In fact for some theologians action became a necessary consequence for authentic faith: a kind of validation of the reality of that faith. When the implications of religious faith were expanded in this way to encompass action, spirituality became linked to politics.[24]

A further expansion of the conciliar teaching emerged also in the growth of support for change from below for the nurture of agency in the people most affected by the injustices so that they became the interlocutors of their own destiny, and as it were, spoke for themselves.

Success, it has often been observed, at local level demands a recognition of a shared humanity, the need to act together and a belief in the possibility of change, these values help stimulate a "deeper kind of politics." From very early on the bishops knew that it was not enough to publish denunciations of apartheid, ordinary people needed to be empowered so as to be able to carve their own destinies and to cast off the shackles of oppression. Pope Paul VI had already in *Populorum Progressio* (81) reminded lay people that without waiting passively for orders or directives, they should freely take the initiative to infuse a Christian spirit into the mentality, customs, laws and structures of the communities in which they live. In the immediate period after the Council spurred on by the concerns of the bishops over the issue of migratory labor, much of the practical focus of their pastoral efforts leaned in this direction.

It is interesting that John de Gruchy makes mention of the SACBC especially with regard to empowering workers and addressing the inequalities found in the work place. He says: "It is also noteworthy that Catholic analysis of the situation have paid considerable attention to labour and other economic factors."[25]

In the context of our exploration of various aspects of preaching it is worth noting the obvious point, that sermons remain incomplete. What is preached is always only the beginning. It is completed in the myriad of ways in which it inspires personal or local action, prompts new thoughts, and enriches the imagination. Albert Nolan makes the same point in that earlier insight which I referred to.

Clint Le Bruyns, drawing from Buhlungu's study, cited above, points to six areas where church witness and leadership impacted even more directly in the more secular and often most exploited sector and indeed amongst the

24. Ibid., 11–12.
25. De Gruchy, *Church Struggle*, 99.

most contentious areas, namely that of trade unionism. Here in a sense we see a practical application of the many words spoken.

Firstly he points to the institutional contribution of religion towards organizational building. He points to the work of the Young Christian Workers born of Cardinal Joseph Cardijn's spirituality, which painstakingly over decades educated young workers with organizational skills, built capacity, equipped workers with progressive ideas in the political and economic domain and in constructing what Le Bruyns describes as a "democratic ethos."[26] Members were accompanied by chaplains who provided a theological support system when all of these activities were illegal. Secondly there was what could be called the paradigmatic contribution where explicit links were made between the Bible, church teaching and liturgy so that religious ideas strengthened and informed political activity. Bible studies, discussion groups, Lenten groups were key vehicles for this kind of instruction. One memorable convergence of this aspect was the Good Friday morning Stations of the Cross through the streets of Durban led by Archbishop Hurley carrying a life sized cross, to the prison where young workers were being held by the police. Enroute Biblical exegesis was held and the crowd was given an opportunity for some to reflect on the significance of the day, the event and to unpack the political and spiritual significance of this procession. The third area is what Le Bruyns calls the ecumenical contribution, which he understands as a shared collection of religious rituals and activities that serve as a "unifying force" in an often ideologically diverse environment and across sundry divisions such as traditional and geographic affiliations. He writes that religious actions can be seen in many situations bringing workers together while attributing "legitimacy and respectability to the struggle."[27]

Closely linked to the above is the way in which adaptation was absorbed by the struggle, especially hymns that had widespread currency across denominational lines and were often a powerful emotional means of mobilizing the masses. Academic literature shows an increasing awareness of the transforming power and educational possibilities of song in the process of helping to understand the realities around people and building their confidence in facing various challenges. Corneille Nkurunziza writes, "The role of songs in contextualization of the Christian faith is widely recognized. Like Steve de Gruchy, various scholars have insisted on the importance of songs in contextualising the gospel in a manner which resonates with people. Among others Kwame Bediako saw the implicit theology expressed through

26. Le Bruyns, "Religion and the Economy?," 96.

27. Ibid., 97

songs as a liberating force."[28] What is said in this quote of the Christian faith and the gospel bodes equally well for politics and political education. Next he refers to the leadership contribution. He writes that many union leaders attest to the leadership capital attained previously in different religious organizations, including that of "public speaking, negotiating and organising skills."[29] What should also be noted is that this was and is true across various classes and in the formal and informal sense of leadership. A sixth contribution lies in what Le Bruyns calls the communicational or networking contribution. He speaks here of the "extensive national and international network of people, facilities and resource bases which play strategic roles."

The long road to freedom was walked bravely even if sometimes hesitantly by many in the church inspired by the hope offered by their leaders. But this project, like the unfolding of the reign of God, is indeed a work in progress.

President Nelson Mandela, whom I quoted as I embarked on my reflections on the influence of the council on the struggle for justice in South Africa, pointed prophetically to the ongoing role of the church in the burgeoning democracy. Speaking at the Methodist Church's Triennial Conference, Mandela said: "Religious communities have a vital role to play. Just as you took a leading role in the struggle against apartheid, so too you should be at the forefront of helping to deliver a better life for all people. Amongst other things you are well placed to assist in building capacity within communities for effective delivery of a better life."[30]

In asking this of the church, he was indeed close to the heart of the hopes and dreams of the council, which Paul VI closed with this ringing affirmation: "We exhort you to open your hearts to the dimensions of the world, to heed the appeal of your brothers, to place your youthful energies at their service. Fight against all egoism. Refuse to give free course to the instincts of violence and hatred which beget wars and all their train of miseries. Be generous, pure, respectful and sincere, and build in enthusiasm a better world than your elders had."[31]

Therein lies the road map for all our future endeavors, for our ongoing reception of the council whose lofty aims have yet to be realized and therein, to a greater or lesser degree, lies the still beckoning content of our preaching!

28. Nkurunziza, "Locally?," 61.
29. Le Bruyns, "Religion?," 97.
30. Nelson Mandela, address at the first Triennial Conference.
31. Paul VI, Second Vatican Council closing Mass.

Bibliography

Abraham, Garth. *The Catholic Church and Apartheid*. Johannesburg: Ravan, 1989.

Abrahams, Mervyn. "Denis Hurley and the Reception of Vatican II." In *Vatican II: Keeping the Dream Alive*. Pietermaritzburg: Cluster, 2005.

Borer, Tristan Anne. *Challenging the State*. Notre Dame: University of Notre Dame Press 1998.

Buhlungu, Sakhela. *A Paradox of Victory: COSATU and the Democratic Transformation in South Africa*. Pietermaritzburg: University of Kwa Zulu-Natal, 2010.

De Gruchy, John. "Political Landmarks and the response of Churches in South Africa, 1936–1994." *Journal of Theology for Southern Africa* 118 (2004) 3–26.

———. *The Church Struggle in South Africa*. Cape Town: Phillip, 1979.

Heyer, Kristin and Brian Massingale. "*Gaudium et spes* and the Call to Justice: The U.S. Experience." In *From Vatican II to Pope Francis*, edited by Paul Crowley, 81–100. New York: Orbis, 2014.

Komonchak, Joseph. "The Ecclesial and Cultural Roles of Theology." *Proceedings of the Catholic Theological Society of America* 40 (1985) 56–82.

Le Bruyns, Clint. "Religion and the Economy? On Public Responsibility through Prophetic Intelligence, Theology and Solidarity." *Journal of Theology for Southern Africa* 142 (2012) 80–97.

———. "Transforming Hope? A Theological-Ethical Vision, Virtue and Practice for the Common Good." *Journal of Theology for Southern Africa* 146 (2015) 118.

Mandela, Nelson. Address at the first Triennial Conference of the Methodist Church of Southern Africa, Durban. July 17 1998. www.sahistory.org.za/article/address-president-nelson-mandela-first-triennial-conference-methodist-church-south-africa.

Mayne, Michael. *Pray, Love, Remember*. London: Darton, Longman & Todd, 1998.

Muyebe, Stanislaus. "The Experience of those Sinned Against: Albert Nolan." In *Preaching Justice*, edited by Francesco Compagnoni and Helen Alford, 287–304. Dublin: Dominican. 2007.

Nolan, Albert. *Jesus Today: A Spirituality of Radical Freedom*. New York: Orbis, 2006.

Nkurunziza, Corneille. "Locally Composed Songs: An Expression of Genuine Contextual theology?" *Journal of Theology for Southern Africa* 142 (2012) 58–79.

Paul VI. Second Vatican Council closing Mass. December 8, 1965. www.papalencyclicals.net/Paul06/p6closin.htm.

SACBC. Interdiocesan Pastoral Consultation 1980 Report. Pastoral Action Series no. 22. 1981. Pretoria: SACBC.

———. Pastoral Letter of the SACBC on Christian Hope in the Current Crisis. The Bishops' Speak, vol. 4, 1986–1987. www.sacbc.org.za/the-bishops-speak/.

———. "Lawful Means Must be Used to Resist Apartheid." The Bishops' Speak, vol. 1, 1952–1966. No URL.

SACBC Commission for Justice and Reconciliation. "Use of Church Buildings and Facilities." 1986 plenary session report.

1971 Synod of Bishops. "Justice in the World." www.shc.edu/theolibrary/resources/synodjw.htm.

9

Spiritualities of Lay Witness in the World[1]

—Ann Astell and Danielle Peters

Ann Astell

CHAPTER 4 OF *LUMEN Gentium,* the *Dogmatic Constitution on the Church,* calls special attention to the "situation and mission" of the laity (LG 30), who "by their very vocation, seek the kingdom of God by engaging in temporal affairs and by ordering them according to the plan of God," sanctifying "the world from within, in the manner of leaven" (LG 31). In that same chapter we read, "The lay apostolate . . . is a participation in the saving mission of the Church . . . Thus every layman, by virtue of the very gifts bestowed on him, is at the same time a witness and a living instrument of the mission of the Church herself" (LG 33).[2]

In the few lines I have quoted from *Lumen Gentium* we find already some of the key terms in this chapter's title: "lay," "witness," "world." Each of these words, taken separately, is rich in significance, but what governs their conjoined meanings in the present context is the still missing word

1. Scripture quotations in this chapter are taken from the *New American Bible, revised edition* © 2010, 1991, 1986, 1970 Confraternity of Christian Doctrine, Washington DC and are used by permission of the copyright owner. All Rights Reserved. No part of the New American Bible may be reproduced in any form without permission in writing from the copyright owner.

2. Throughout this chapter, we quote from Abbott, *Documents of Vatican II.*

"spiritualities." Rare in the documents of Vatican II, the term *spirituality* (sometimes translated as "form of spiritual life") appears once and only once, in chapter 6 of the *Decree on the Apostolate of the Laity (Apostolicam Actuositatem)*. Entitled "Formation for the Apostolate," chapter 6 is "directed toward the [apostolic] formation of the laity and not of religious and priests."[3] The document's editor notes, "The length and completeness of this full chapter on formation clearly indicate where the bishops wished to place their greatest emphasis."[4] That chapter includes the following statement: "Since laymen share in their own way in the mission of the Church, their apostolic formation takes its special flavor from the distinctively secular quality of the lay state and *from its own form of spirituality*" (AA 29). What does it mean to speak of a lay spirituality? How might such a spirituality give a distinctive form to, and impulse for, a lay witness in the world?

In his *Introduction to the Devout Life* (1608), Saint Francis de Sales advised the laity under his spiritual direction not to "conduct themselves like monks," but to devote themselves to the fulfillment of their everyday duties, to doing ordinary things extraordinarily well. He distinguished between the "purely contemplative, monastic, and religious devotion" that cannot be exercised while "living under the pressure of worldly affairs," and the devotion "adapted to bring perfection to those living in the secular state," whether in the "regiment of soldiers, the mechanic's shop, the court of princes, or the home of married people."[5]

This early modern Salesian distinction stands behind Vatican II's understanding of "the distinctively secular quality of the lay state" and its spirituality, but the separation of church and state in modern Europe, the rise of anti-clericalism there and elsewhere, the declining influence of Christianity upon culture, and the reality of Christian persecution have added to the church's understanding of lay spirituality. Lay spirituality is now increasingly understood not simply from the perspective of its secular setting, tasks, and responsibilities, but also from the perspective of baptismal grace and of charisms, spiritual gifts given both to the individual for the good of the church and to the groups, families, associations, and movements within which lay saints can be formed.

"Spirituality" is a word that is notoriously difficult to define and there is no generally accepted definition among scholars. Viewed "from the perspective of the human pole," forms of spirituality are understood "within the context of socio-cultural reality and [its] anthropological implications,"

---

3. Second Vatican Council, *Apostolicam Actuositatem*, 71.

4. Ibid.

5. De Sales, *Introduction to the Devout Life*, 44, 34.

writes Kees Waaijman, O.Carm., editor of *Studies in Spirituality*. Seen "from the perspective of the divine pole," however, "what matters in actually lived spirituality is the divine Reality [experienced] in the life of every day"—a reality that gradually transforms a person and "leaves its imprint upon his or her concrete conduct of life."[6] Both perspectives need to be combined, according to Waaijman. "God is Spirit" (John 4:24), and "The Spirit itself bears witness with our spirit that we are children of God, and if children, then heirs, heirs of God and joint heirs with Christ, if only we suffer with him so that we may also be glorified with him" (Rom 8:16-17).

A Christian spirituality results when "The Spirit itself bears witness with our spirit"—when the human heart, mind, and will find themselves borne up by the Spirit of God to recognize and accept revealed truth and when the human spirit is moved to testify to the truths of the faith in concrete circumstances and through a definite style of life and practical apostolate. In Waaijman's words, "Spirituality is characterized by a certain style: of believing . . . of living and working."[7] In Christian history, various spiritualities have arisen at key junctures in time and through particular persons and religious experiences. One thinks, for example, of the spiritualities of the desert fathers, the Benedictines, the Carmelites, the Franciscans, the Dominicans, the Jesuits, the Salesians, the Vincentians, the Redemptorists, the family of Holy Cross, etc.—each representing an enduring, tested way of Christian holiness, characterized by a distinctive charism and virtue; a definite theological emphasis; a saintly founding narrative; a recognizable idiom of expression; a particular mission; and a customary sphere of charitable activity.

When these enduring spiritualities of religious orders and congregations are set beside the laity's "form of spirituality"—so called in paragraph 29 of *Apostolicam Actuositatem*—one understands the council fathers' emphasis on the need for a proper spiritual formation of the laity both to equip them for their apostolate in the world and to enable them to attain "to the fullness of the Christian life and to the perfection of charity" (LG 40). As I have argued elsewhere, the council's bold enunciation of a universal call to holiness, inclusive of the laity, in chapter 5 of *Lumen Gentium*, brought with it the recognition of the pressing need for definite schools of holiness for the laity, who had often previously felt excluded from the possibility of a Christian perfection seemingly reserved for priests and religious and apparently attainable only through withdrawal from the world.[8]

6. Waaijman, "Toward a Phenomenological Definition," 44.

7. Ibid., 46.

8. See Astell, *Lay Sanctity, Medieval and Modern: A Search for Models*; "All Saints:

The chapter in *Apostolicam Actuositatem* on the laity's formation for the apostolate is disappointing, from this perspective, in its generality. It declares that the layperson should "base his life on belief in the divine mystery of creation and redemption," "be sensitive to the movement of the Holy Spirit," receive "doctrinal instruction in theology, ethics, and philosophy," acquire the "practical and technical training" necessary for professional leadership, and foster the "truly human values" that facilitate "good human relations," cooperation, and conversation with others (AA 29).

Echoing the formulaic language ("see-judge-act") of Joseph Cardinal Cardijn (1882–1967), the Belgian founder of the Young Christian Workers (*Jeunesse Ouvrière Chrétienne* [JOC], perhaps the most famous of the Catholic Action organizations), chapter 6 of the decree goes on to state: "The laity should gradually and prudently learn how to view, judge, and do all things in the light of faith as well as to develop and to improve themselves and others through action, thereby entering into the energetic service of the Church" (AA 29). This learning should take place in the home and family, starting in earliest childhood; in Catholic schools and universities; and within the framework of "lay groups and associations" (AA 30). Calling these groups "the ordinary vehicle of harmonious formation for the apostolate," the document envisions the laity's regular meetings "in small groups with . . . associates or friends" to "examine the methods and results of their apostolic activity and measure their daily way of life against the gospel" (AA 30). One significant fruit of this sort of group work is said to be the "better self-knowledge" of the individual person who has grown "to evaluate more accurately . . . and to exercise more effectively *those charismatic gifts* which the Holy Spirit has bestowed on him for the good of his brothers (and sisters)" (AA 30).

In keeping, then, with the then-dominant model of Catholic Action, the chapter on the spiritual formation of the laity recognizes the value of associations of the laity for the individual's spiritual growth, the existence of charisms given to individual persons for the common good, the urgency for laypeople to give "the witness of an evangelical life" in secular settings increasingly permeated by materialistic values, and the pragmatic power of groups in performing "the works of charity and mercy" that "afford the most striking testimony of the Christian life" (AA 31).

The Universal Call to Holiness," unpublished talk given at the University of Notre Dame, January 19, 2008: "What remained at issue at the conclusion of the council, however, were the means of spiritual formation and the necessary theological understandings that would enable the laity to achieve an officially recognizable (that is, canonizable) holiness."

The website of the Pontifical Council for the Laity lists 122 international associations of the faithful, many of them for specific professions and age groups, some of them open to a general membership. Gathered together, these associations reflect the broad goals of a lay apostolate exercised *in* the modern period of church/state separation on the one hand, and *for* what Vatican II calls "the consecration of the world" (*consecratio mundi;* cf. LG 34), on the other. Because they are chiefly but not exclusively lay in their membership, the modern ecclesial movements—the Catholic Charismatic Renewal, L'Arche, the Focolare Movement, Communion and Liberation, the Sant'Egidio Community, Regnum Christi, Teams of Our Lady, Worldwide Marriage Encounter, Schoenstatt, and the Neocatechumenal Way (approved in 2008)—are now recognized as international associations of the faithful. In 1998, Pope St. John Paul II hailed the rise of these movements as "one of the most significant fruits of that springtime in the Church which was foretold by the Second Vatican Council."[9]

These largely lay movements are known not only for the growth of personal holiness in their members, but also for their effective evangelical works in the spheres of apostolate the council's documents especially ascribe to the laity: marriage and family, cultural development, socio-economic life, political life, ecumenism, and the fostering of peace.[10] Modern schools of holiness for the laity, these ecclesial movements claim for themselves elements of spiritual formation once typically associated only (or almost only) with religious orders and congregations: saintly exemplars, saintly founding narratives, charisms, ascetical practices, biblical illumination, rites of consecration, and mission zeal for a new evangelization.

In the spiritualities of these largely lay movements, what Kees Waaijman calls the "divine pole" of spirituality comes to the fore, but in balance with the "human" pole of culture, work, and striving. This creative bipolarity suggests that every Christian spirituality has a covenantal character, "the Spirit itself bear[ing] witness with our spirit" (Rom 8:16). This divine-human relation is reflected, *mutatis mutandis*, in what *Apostolicam Actuositatem* names as the double responsibility of the lay apostle—namely, "bringing the gospel and holiness to men" and "perfecting the temporal sphere of things through the spirit of the gospel" (AA 2). "Let there be no false opposition between professional and social activities, on the one part, and religious life, on the other," we are instructed in *Gaudium et Spes* (GS 43). "Laymen are not only bound to penetrate the world with a Christian spirit," we read,

---

9. John Paul II, "Message to the World Congress of Ecclesial Movements, 1998," 222.

10. This list reflects the chapters in the second part of *Gaudium et Spes*.

"they are also called to be witnesses to Christ in all things in the midst of human society" (GS 43).

In *Apostolicam Actuositatem*, the *Decree on the Apostolate of the Laity*, the Holy Spirit who sanctifies is also said to give "to the faithful special . . . charisms or gifts, including those which are less dramatic"—gifts and charisms that bring with them "the right and duty to use them in the Church and in the world" (AA 3). Addressing the members of ecclesial movements in Rome on May 30, 1998, Pope John Paul II explained, "By their nature, charisms are communicative and give rise to that 'spiritual affinity between persons' and friendship in Christ which is the origin of 'movements.'" I offer here a brief sketch of three of the largest ecclesial movements—the Work of Mary (also known as the Focolare), the Neocatechumenal Way, and Schoenstatt—showing how their members offer a manifold witness in the world that is imbued with a distinctive spirituality. In each case, the particular apostolic works of the members can be traced back to the founding charism of the movement. These works give expression to the charism, provide a practical means for the members' individual and communal growth in that imparted grace, and secure the communication of the specific charism to the church and world.

Focolare's Witness of Unity

Focolare, the popular name for the international Work of Mary, means "hearth" or "family fireside." It suggests the warmth that beckons an intimate gathering of people, but also the flames of Pentecost, which appeared above the heads of the disciples, gathered in the Upper Room, who had a communal experience of the descent of the Holy Spirit. As philosopher Donald Mitchell writes, "The interplay between this communal fire and the inner fire of the Spirit has formed the spiritual life of Chiara Lubich and that of the whole Focolare movement."[11] Here, too, a dialogic and covenantal relationship obtains: "The Spirit bears witness with our spirit" (Rom 8:16).

Chiara Lubich (1920–2008) is said to have founded the Focolare Movement on December 7, 1943, when she consecrated her life to God in a private moment of personal surrender, sealing her "choice" of God as her ideal and embracing an adventurous vocation: a life of lay consecration, to be lived in the midst of a spiritual family that was not a religious order. A small group of young women friends between the ages of fifteen and twenty-five soon joined her in this consecration. In May of 1944, when the allies heavily bombed Trent, Italy, this circle of friends met repeatedly in the

11. Mitchell, "A Life between Two Fires," 174.

bomb shelters, where they read and reflected on the scriptures, hungry for guidance as to how to live their great common ideal of God-Love. Ready to die with and for each other, they experienced a unity that illumined for them the key biblical passages that have become the watchwords of the movement; in particular, the prayer of Jesus before his death "that they may all be one; even as thou, Father, art in me, and I in thee, that they also may be in us, so that the world may believe that thou hast sent me" (John 17:21), and "for where two or three are gathered in my name, there am I in the midst of them" (Matt 18:20).

For the sake of a oneness with God and each other that would be a convincing witness to the Trinity and to Christ, experienced as "Jesus-in-the-midst," the first Focolare members renounced anything that would violate or impair their unity. In practical terms, this meant a community of goods to be shared with each other and the needy in the war-ravaged city; an asceticism joyfully heroic in overcoming selfishness, moodiness, hurts, and prejudice; and a regular praxis of shared biblical reflection and striving that later developed into monthly "Word of Life" meetings, during which Focolare members meditate upon chosen scriptural passages and individuals' experiences in trying to live them. Since its first founding in 1943, the Focolare Movement, inspired by the ideal of unity, has entered into an ever-widening practice of dialogues and charitable works, aimed at transcending the divisions between Christians, Catholic, Protestant, and Orthodox; among believers of different religions; and between believers and non-believers, in whom Christ is also to be found, often under the particular aspect of "Jesus Forsaken": "God, my God, why have you abandoned me?" (Matt 27:46). In this way, the Focolare have given a remarkable response to the following exhortation from the decree on the Apostolate of the Laity: "Among the phenomena of our times worthy of special mention is the growing and inevitable sense of solidarity of all peoples. Lay people in their apostolate should earnestly promote this sense of solidarity and transform it into a sincere and genuine fraternal love" (AA 10).

In 2000 Chiara Lubich reported that "a thousand or so projects in the charitable and welfare fields" had already been accomplished by Focolare members, including the building of entire towns and the establishment of more than 650 businesses worldwide that operate according to an "economy of communion in freedom" (EOC) that makes workers shareholders in owning and developing the company, allocates a regular percentage of profits (1/3) to the relief of the poor, and uses additional profits (1/3) to stimulate an "evangelical culture of *giving* in opposition to that of *having*."[12] Initiated

12. Lubich, "Focolare Movement," 149–50.

in Brazil in 1991, the "economy of communion" is now operative in at least 750 businesses. Pope Benedict XVI cited this economy with approbation in *Caritas in Veritate* (46). Through it, the Focolare Movement has given a powerful lay witness in the world to the Gospel, consciously inspired by the early Christian ideal of a society where goods were held in common and no one suffered need (Acts 4:34).

Reporting an estimated membership of five million persons in 182 countries, the Focolare includes "18 branches with the most varied vocations."[13] The effectiveness of its wide-ranging apostolates stems from its founding charism of unity, which has manifested itself clearly also in holiness of life—the Movement having brought forth thirteen Servants of God, sixteen seminarians considered martyrs, Blessed Chiara "Luce" Badano (1971–1990), aged 18 at the time of her death (beatified in 2010), and Venerable Maria Orsola Bussone (1954–1970), another Focolare youth, declared venerable in 2015. Chiara Lubich's own cause of beatification was opened in Rome on Jan. 27, 2015.

Kerygma of the Neocatechumenal Way

Like many of the modern ecclesial movements, the Neocatechumenal Way defies classification as a discrete movement or association,[14] not only because of its mixed membership, which is lay and clerical, but also because it exists to enable and to safeguard a profound process of conversion centered on baptism, the sacrament of initiation that gives persons membership in the church itself, not in any organization apart from the church. The foundation of the Neocatechumenal Way in 1964 coincides with Vatican Council II, however, and the charismatic experience of its lay co-founders, Kiko Argüello and Carmen Hernández (1930–2016), accords with the council's close association of evangelization with baptismal commitment.

In *Ad Gentes*, the *Decree on the Mission Activity of the Church* (1965), the council fathers called "the catechumenate . . . not a mere expounding of doctrines and precepts, but a training period for the whole Christian life"; petitioned for a restoration of the solemn ancient liturgies for Lent and Easter; and gave "the entire community of the faithful" an apostolic

---

13. Ibid., 152.

14. As Hanna points out, Kiko Argüello repeatedly denies the nomenclature of "movement" and "association," but he nonetheless accepts papal invitations to meetings of the ecclesial movements, and he addressed the large gathering at the historic, international congress of ecclesial movements held in Rome on Pentecost, 1998. See *New Ecclesial Movements*, 54–56.

responsibility for the catechumenate as a period of individual and communal preparation for missionary activity (AG 15). The catechetical experience of Kiko Argüello and Carmen Hernández in 1964 in the slums of Madrid—an extraordinary experience that evangelized the slum's residents, many of them illiterate prostitutes, alcoholics and thieves who had been baptized as infants, but insufficiently instructed in the faith—established an important prototype for what later became the R.C.I.A. (Rite of Christian Initiation for Adults).[15] Much longer than the R.C.I.A., however, the Neocatechumenal Way guides a life-long process of adult conversion aimed at the renewal of baptismal vows by the already baptized—an itinerary in stages of personal and communal spiritual formation that can be adapted for missions *ad gentes,* to the unbaptized.

In the throes of an existential crisis, the young Argüello—a talented painter and a musician who had made a *cursillo*—followed the example of Charles de Foucauld and moved into the urban desert of the shantytown with only a crucifix, a Bible, and his guitar, there to seek Christ crucified, whose presence he sensed in "the most deprived and impoverished people on earth."[16] Argüello inspired the curiosity of the unchurched slum-dwellers, who began to come to him to converse with him about God and to ask him questions. These questions, in turn, led to catechesis, to an awakening of Christian faith, and to the establishment of vibrant Christian communities in the slums. These communities of the poor evangelized, in turn, the archbishop of Madrid, Casimiro Morcillo, who recognized in them good news for the church as a whole, a "fulfillment of the Council."[17] With the help of Hernández, Argüello sketched the stages that had occurred in the process of post-baptismal evangelization and conversion. A "kerygmatic, theological, and catechetical synthesis" was the result—a "synthesis between word (*kerygma*), liturgy, and morality."[18] Reflecting on his experience, Argüello confesses, "We have always felt ourselves to be part and parcel of the reality of evangelization entrusted by Jesus to the apostles: 'Go therefore and make disciples of all nations . . . and lo, I am with you always, to the close of the age' (cf. Matt 28:19–20)."[19]

With the encouragement of four popes—Paul VI, John Paul II, Benedict XVI, and Francis—and local acceptance by many bishops and pastors, the Neocatechumenal Way has established an estimated 25,000 communities

---

15. See Hanna, *New Ecclesial Movements*, 50.

16. Argüello, "Neocatechumenal Way," 159.

17. Hanna, *New Ecclesial Movements*, 50.

18. Ibid., 48; Argüello, "Neocatechumenal Way," 161.

19. Argüello, "Neocatechumenal Way," 160.

in 800 dioceses and 6,000 parishes in 124 nations. Striking is the large number of vocations to the priesthood (2,000 men already ordained and 2,000 seminarians currently in formation) that have been awakened through the Way, which has inaugurated a hundred Redemptoris Mater seminaries worldwide for the New Evangelization.

Original, too, in the movement is the phenomenon of family missions. About 1,000 Neocat families have been sent out in groups of families to settle in targeted areas, often in slums on the peripheries of cities, in order to form nuclei for evangelization. A bishop in Germany, for example, envisioned "a personal parish with a mission for the non-baptized, formed of . . . Christian families that have already completed the Neocatechumenal Way, often with more than ten children."[20] The implantation of such a community of families in a totally de-Christianized urban neighborhood, Argüello asserts, awakens a wonderment in non-believers akin to that of witnessing a physical miracle, and it opens the way for *kerygma,* the announcing of the Gospel. "What most surprises non-Christians," he writes, "are our interpersonal relations, the beauty of our way of relating to each other . . . the miracle of love."[21]

On fire for a new evangelization, the members of the Way organized a "Great Mission" that involved Christian witness through songs, testimony, and catechesis in over 10,000 public squares in 120 countries during the five Sundays of Easter in the Year of Faith. On February 1, 2014, Pope Francis sent out 450 Neocat families on mission and blessed 42 new missions *ad gentes,* each of these involving a group of four or five families and a priest, sent together to bring Christian life to a de-Christianized or non-Christian area.

These missions give an obvious response to the call issued in the Vatican II decree *Ad Gentes,* which attaches "the greatest importance" to lay witness, to the planting and replanting of the church in secular surroundings, and to organized efforts by the laity to "announce Christ to their non-Christian fellow-citizens by word and deed" (AG 15). As Kiko Argüello explains with conviction, Christ himself proclaims the Kingdom of God in and through the catechist. "What happens when someone proclaims the *kerygma?*" Argüello asks. "St. Paul says: 'The Spirit himself [bears] witness with our spirit' (Rom 8:16–17). There is an encounter in the spirit of man with this Holy Spirit that is given to him *freely.* And this encounter with a living person who is Christ, through the Spirit, changes that person's life,

---

20. Argüello, "Small Christian communities," 99–105, at 101.

21. Ibid., 101, 104.

gives him the chance to abandon sin, and he discovers 'new things' within him: he is a creature born anew."[22]

Schoenstatt's Apostolate of Pilgrimage

Among the oldest and largest of the modern ecclesial movements, Schoenstatt was first founded on October 18, 1914, at the outbreak of World War I, and experienced a second founding as an international movement in 1944 in the concentration camp at Dachau during the founder's imprisonment there. All that has developed in and through the vast Schoenstatt work—which now includes six different secular institutes, an apostolic federation, apostolic leagues, youth branches, and a pilgrims' movement—can be traced back to what Schoenstatters call the "Covenant of Love," which was sealed on October 18, 1914, between Father Joseph Kentenich (1885–1968), a Pallottine priest, the young members of a Marian sodality under his spiritual direction, and the Mother of God, whom they honored with the title "Mother Thrice Admirable."

Meeting with a group of teenaged boys in a small, recently renovated chapel, Father Kentenich proposed to them the idea of converting the chapel in Schoenstatt into a place of pilgrimage, a new Tabor, where Mary would reveal her glories as the educator of Christians, the former of modern saints. "Undoubtedly, we could not accomplish a greater apostolic deed nor leave our successors a more precious legacy," he said, "than to urge our Lady and Queen to erect her throne here in a special way, to distribute her treasures, and to work miracles of grace." The condition for Mary's activity from the shrine would be the ardent longing of the boys for her intercessory presence there, a longing given concrete expression through their offerings of prayers, sacrifices, works of charity, and zealous efforts at self-sanctification for the sake of others. The model of free human cooperation with graces freely and generously mediated by Mary is covenantal—a structure of mutual relationship later expressed in the motto "Nothing without you, Nothing without Us" but already articulated in the founding document in a quotation from Proverbs, placed on the lips of Mary: "I love those who love me" (Prov 8:17).

Father Kentenich, the child of a single mother, had spent years in an over-crowded urban orphanage before gaining acceptance to seminary training. His biological mother fostered his attachment to the Mother of God, even as his own lack of fatherly care and acknowledgement inspired in him a desire to be a fatherly educator for those entrusted to his care as teacher and spiritual director. His childhood experience of homelessness in

22. Argüello, "Neocatechumenal Way," 165.

the orphanage made him sensitive to what he later diagnosed as a modern disease, "a whirlpool of inner and outer nomadism,"[23] of uprootedness, of weak and broken attachments to persons, places, and things. To this disease he was inspired to offer the remedy of a Marian pilgrimage place, a spiritual home, a Shrine for the Pilgrim People of God—*Lumen Gentium*'s favorite title for the church *in via,* on its earthly way to the heavenly Jerusalem (cf. LG, chapter 7).[24]

The Original Shrine in Schoenstatt, Germany, has been replicated worldwide in 200 daughter shrines in 30 different countries on six continents, in countless homeshrines (citadels for the domestic church), and heartshrines. Pilgrimages to the daughter shrines, which are regularly built in proximity to centers for meetings and retreats, have proven to be a powerful means of evangelization. From the Schoenstatt shrines, moreover, images of the Pilgrim Mother Thrice Admirable are sent out, carried by lay apostles, to travel to homes, hospitals, businesses, classrooms, and prisons, thus renewing the mystery of the Virgin Mary's visitation of her cousin Elizabeth in an estimated 110 countries.

The married layman John Pozzobon, who began the travels of the Pilgrim Mother during the Holy Year 1950, walked over 87,000 miles in southern Brazil between 1950 and 1985, the year of his death, carrying an image of our Lady of Schoenstatt weighing twenty-five pounds from home to home, praying with the people, and caring for their needs. His cause for beatification opened in 1994. He is one of five officially recognized Servants of God from the Schoenstatt work, which also claims Venerable Emilie Engel (1893–1955) and Blessed Karl Leisner (1915–1945), a martyr of Dachau beatified by Pope John Paul II on June 23, 1996.

In each of the movements I have briefly sketched here, the founding charism is clearly evident in the particular apostolic works taken up by the members—unity in a bomb shelter in Trent leading to ecumenical and inter-religious dialogue and to an innovative commerce (in the case of the Focolare), *kerygma* in a slum in Madrid leading to catechetical formation and global mission (in the case of the Neocatechumenal Way), and the Covenant of Love in a small chapel in Germany leading to a vast network of stationary and mobile shrines in the Schoenstatt family. In each case, the Holy Spirit bore witness with something crying out in the human spirit, bringing it to its fulfillment. In this experienced descent of the Holy Spirit, the human protagonists find themselves to be "other Marys," bearing the Word. All three movements cherish Mary as the ideal apostle and Queen of

23. See Niehaus, *Brushstrokes of a Father,* 246–47.

24. See Astell and Peters, "Schoenstatt's Shrine," 68–84.

Apostles, the best guarantee for what Pope Francis in *Evangelii Gaudium* has called the merciful Marian style of evangelization needed today. Fifty years ago, however, the documents whose anniversaries we celebrate acknowledged Mary to be the Queen of Apostles, who "cooperated in the work of the Savior in a manner altogether special" (AA 4), who continues to do so through her intercession (cf. AG 42), and who provides, as we read in the *Decree on the Apostolate of the Laity*, "the perfect example of this [lay] type of spiritual and apostolic life" (AA 4).

Danielle Peters

In his last words directed to the Council Fathers of the Second Vatican Council, Paul VI reminisced:

> It is necessary to remember the time in which it [the council] was realized . . . it took place at a time which everyone admits is oriented toward the conquest of the kingdom of earth rather than that of heaven; a time in which forgetfulness of God has become habitual, and seems, quite wrongly, to be prompted by the progress of science; a time in which the fundamental act of the human person, more conscious now of himself and of his freedom, tends to pronounce in favor of his own absolute autonomy, in emancipation from every transcendent law."[25]

Evidently, the pontiff sensed that the signs of the time pointed in the first place to a crisis of culture with serious anthropological consequences, identified in *Gaudium et Spes* (GS 55) as "the birth of a new humanism."[26] Like every birth, the new humanism will be a gift, yet—as we already know from hindsight—it was, is and will not be exempt from birth pangs and related challenges.

Vatican II's universal call to holiness explicitly or implicitly includes a call to give witness to Christ in the world and thereby to engage in and combat these challenges. *Gaudium et Spes* emphasizes that ecclesial offices and states of life, as central and decisive they may be for the church and the individual, are secondary compared to the supernatural vocation to communion with God of all the faithful.[27] Notwithstanding the special dignity and model character of religious life, this universal call valid for

25. Paul VI, address during the last general meeting of the Second Vatican Council.

26. According *to Gaudium et Spes* (GS 54), Vatican II's *Pastoral Constitution on the Church in the Modern World*, this new humanism is necessary due to the profound social and cultural changes of post modernity.

27. Cf. *Gaudium et Spes*, 19.

all Christians without distinction of age, state of life, profession, race and language underlines that perfection consists in Christian love rather than a commitment to religious life and/or the evangelical counsels for example.[28] Practically all ecclesial movements present a proposal of how this high ideal, hitherto thought to be answered only by "fleeing the world"—*fuga mundi*— can be implemented *in* the world! Their pedagogical and spiritual formation aims at the critical juncture between salvation and secular reality endured with all its tensions and conflicts. The polarity between communion with God and a life in the world cannot simply mean to give a pious touch to everything one does. Rather, it is a form of existence, a manner of being by virtue of which the profane is sanctified. *Gaudium et Spes 13* refers to the polarity of such a "divided person" with a "high calling" and a simultaneous experience of "deep misery." This tension needs to be endured in the everyday circumstances and made fruitful.

Just as Christ could not be contained in the world, a Christian—by virtue of his or her intimate union with Him—may not be absorbed by the world either. Baptism, in a way, de-secularizes a Christian; it influences his or her interior attitude towards the realities of this world, and it bestows on him or her the responsibility to serve the world and to make it more human. Baptismal grace, in a way, forges a friendship between the Christian and Christ that is not directed by duties, laws and restrictions, but by generosity that offers and asks always for what pleases the Father. In virtue of baptism,

28. On the other hand, many members of ecclesial movements, especially their inner circle, strive toward the perfection of charity through the observation of the evangelical counsels assumed with the obligations laid down by the statutes. This is in conformity with CIC canon 298.1, which makes provision for associations that strive by common effort to promote a more perfect life based on *Lumen Gentium* 39, the universal call for holiness, which is expressed in various forms among the faithful. Cf. LG V. Cf. Ihnatowicz, "Consecrated Life," 15. The apparent dichotomy throughout history between religious life as the state of perfection and the lay state is at least partially due to a view that equals holiness to adherence to the three evangelical counsels. See Aquinas, *Summa Theologica*, 2.2, q. 186.2, ad 3; 2.2, q. 184.3; 1.1, q. 108.4c. While there may be an intimate link between Christian perfection and the counsels, already St. Thomas offered a salutary counterbalance in claiming that Christian perfection consists in the perfection of love and is thus not a matter of counsels but of a Christian precept that needs to be pursued by every Christian. Cf. *ST* 2.2, q. 184.1, 4. St. Francis de Sales, sometimes referred to as "the first theologian of the laity," stated that it is an error, or rather a heresy to wish to exclude those in the world from Christ's call to become holy as the Heavenly Father is holy. Cf. de Sales, *Introduction to the Devout Life* 1.3. Perhaps the strongest appeal to this teaching prior to Vatican II comes from Pius XI, encyclical letter *Rerum Omnium*, 3: "We cannot accept the belief that this command of Christ (cf. Matt 5:48) concerns only a select and privileged group of souls and that all others may consider themselves pleasing to Him if they have attained a lower degree of holiness. Quite the contrary is true, as appears from the very generality of His words. The law of holiness embraces all men and admits of no exception."

the Christian takes on a manner of life that brings to perfection his or her witnessing in word and deed. This charge comes from Christ himself, who summons us to be his witnesses, providing us with the "understanding of the faith" and the "attractiveness in speech," for a truly ecclesial and apostolic purpose (*Lumen Gentium* 35; cf. Catechism of the Catholic Church 904). "This evangelization, that is, this announcing of Christ by a living testimony as well as by the spoken word, takes on a specific quality and a special force in that it is carried out in the ordinary surroundings of the world" (LG 35; CCC 905). Christians must show that there is no opposition between following Christ and fulfilling the tasks that they must carry out in their "secular" condition, and that fidelity to the Gospel actually helps to enhance and improve earthly structures and institutions. Pope Francis in his encyclical *Laudato Si'* (LS 216) notes that "The rich heritage of Christian spirituality, the fruit of twenty centuries of personal and communal experience, has a precious contribution to make to the renewal of humanity." He wonders "how such a spirituality can motivate us to a more passionate concern for the protection of our world" since "a commitment this lofty cannot be sustained by doctrine alone . . . without an interior impulse which encourages, motivates, nourishes and gives meaning to our individual and communal activity."[29]

The movements apparently are an answer to these challenges. Their charism and evolving spirituality specialize, so to speak, in providing a corresponding formation for this high standard of ordinary Christian existence which does not dissociate the spirit "from nature or from worldly realities, but live[s] in and with them, in communion with all that surrounds us."[30]

So far we have seen that the movements are a gift of the Holy Spirit in answer to the needs of our time. Given that the action of the Spirit in the history of salvation and in the church finds its full and archetypal realization in Mary, it should not come as a surprise that the ecclesial movements turn to Mary, the lay witness *par excellence!*[31] The *Decree on the Apostolate of the Laity*,

29. Francis, *Evangelii Gaudium*, 261. Cited in Francis, *Laudato Si'*, 215.

30. Ibid.

31. Cf. *Catechism of the Catholic Church*, art. 485. Also see Coda, "Ecclesial Movements," 103. Coda argues that since ecclesial movements are an authentic gift of the Spirit, i.e., a charism in their own right, their birth and existence have to have a Marian dimension. He cites Louis de Montfort, who said: "Two alone are capable of giving birth together, in synergy, to the Son of God in the flesh and, in Him, to us too as children of the Father: namely the Holy Spirit and Mary."

Apostolicam Actuositatem, affirms the Blessed Virgin Mary as the perfect example of the spiritual and apostolic person since she "while leading the life common to all here on earth, one filled with family concerns and labors, was always intimately united with her Son and in an entirely unique way co-operated in the work of the Savior" (AA 4). "She is the perfect Christian, fiancée, spouse, mother, widow, virgin, the model of every Christian, one like us laity,"[32] notes Chiara Lubich. Through her immaculate and unconditional *fiat* she becomes the first and the most perfect of Christ's lay witnesses. From crib to cross her witnessing consists in unswervingly directing us towards *Him* to the point of "the shocking mystery of [her] self-emptying" which Saint John Paul II considered to be "perhaps the deepest 'kenosis' of faith in human history" (*Redemptoris Mater* 18). This supreme form of witnessing is aptly described by Hans Urs von Balthasar: "Progressively every shade of personal intimacy is taken from her, to be increasingly applied to the good of the Church and of Christians."[33] Precisely in this stage of giving witness she became abundantly fruitful.

Pentecost as the archetypal event of birthing in the church captures best this unique encounter with Mary, which implies the idea of model but also that of mediation.[34] By accepting the second dimension of her maternity, Mary cooperates with the Holy Spirit in the birth of all who receive supernatural life at baptism (cf. John 3:7)—at least in the objective plan of redemption.[35] As a consequence, authentic Christian witness in the world "is transmitted from her to us by osmosis, less by imitation than by generation," due to her effective mediation that is the work of the Holy Spirit.[36] Continuing in this vein argues Notre Dame Lutheran theologian Max Johnson, "there is indeed a close parallel between what is asserted of Mary's Immaculate Conception in service of her ultimate role as Theotokos in the Incarnation and the ultimate role of . . . the community of the baptized, as the God-bearers of the incarnate Christ in the world as well. For baptism makes us all Theotokoi."[37] A member of the Charismatic Renewal describes this reality as follows:

---

32. Lubich, *Essential Writings,* 112.

33. Balthasar, *Glory,* 341.

34. The notion of archetypal experience is developed amply by Balthasar in *Glory,* 313: "The archetype, by its very nature, has a maternal form and under its 'protective mantle' it embraces the progeny that will imitate it."

35. In support of this position, see Second Vatican Council, *Lumen Gentium* 61–62.

36. Ouellet, "Beauty," 49.

37. Cf. Johnson, *Images,* 128–29.

> Jesus Christ continues to be born mystically of the Holy Spirit and of Mary . . . if we in the renewal want to proclaim Jesus to the world, we need the Holy Spirit and we need Mary, the Mother. Just as Mary was in the Upper Room at Pentecost, she is with us whenever we return to the Upper Room. If only we would welcome her as Mother as did the beloved disciple John, she will teach us: how to surrender to the Father's will, how to be faithful to Jesus unto the Cross, how to pray with a humble, pure and docile heart for more of the Holy Spirit, how to be one family. She is the spouse of the Holy Spirit and she knows better than anyone else how to yield to Him.[38]

Mary's intimate association with the Holy Spirit is an inspiration for a number of ecclesial movements. Msgr. Luigi Giussani, founder of Communion and Liberation, imprints upon his spiritual family the fact that the union between the Holy Spirit's work and Mary's *fiat* brings about the image of Christ in each baptized Christian.[39] Therefore he was fond of the invocation: *veni Sancte Spiritus, veni per Mariam*.[40] Mary's receptivity to the Holy Spirit is the ideal of the Legion of Mary and decisive for all of their evangelization efforts.

Many movements take their inspiration from Our Lady's *fiat*. Mary's receptive surrender at the Annunciation unites her with God and "allows" God to use her in order to become fruitful first *in* her and then *through* her. At the Annunciation, the Word became incarnate in the womb of Mary; on a much lower level Christ can and should truly grow spiritually in our hearts, as an actualization of baptism. For the Focolarini this means to grow in love for God and neighbor, to struggle, to die to self, and to mature into "another Mary."[41] *Fiat* means for her then and for us now: *where, when, how, and as long as He needs my witness!* Loyal perseverance to this commitment includes *standing beneath the cross,* an attitude fostered by the Silent Workers of the Cross movement.

The spirituality of some movements challenges its members to reenact or continue Mary's life on earth as *Via Maria, altera Maria, ens Marianum,* or as Memory of Mary. United with her in a covenant of love and sharing in Mary's mission, Schoenstatters strive to be committed to their daily ordinary duties, performing them in an extraordinary way in and for love thereby sanctifying the profane. For the member of Communion and

---

38. Mansfield, "Prayer," 115.

39. Giussani, *Holy Rosary,* Descent of the Holy Spirit on Mary and the Apostles.

40. Janaro, "Blessed Virgin Mary," 118–19.

41. Cf. Lubich, *Essential Writings,* 51.

Liberation, Mary is an "icon of God's self-diffusive goodness"[42] that they wish to emulate. The Legion of Mary endeavors to perform the weekly apostolate by imitating Mary's audacity; for with Mary's spirit of faith, nothing is impossible. The Focolarini strive to walk in her company, in order to better master "upheavals and inner tribulations," to "avoid spiritual pride . . . and find true humility."[43] Their lifestyle gives unequivocal expression to the Marian dimension of their charism of unity in everyday life. In the words of Chiara Lubich, "the environment in which we live and work . . . ultimately refers to harmony, order, beauty,"[44]—a very timely and concrete response to Pope Francis' *Laudato Si'*.

Many communities regard the Visitation narrative as a new way of evangelizing. Mary's experience of being inhabited by God awakens her longing of becoming a place of encounter with God for others. Like her, the first disciple and first messenger of Christ and His gospel, we are chosen in our time and age as *christóphoroi*—as those who bear and bring Christ to those who yearn for salvation. This image is especially dear to the family of Don Bosco, who engages in charitable work with the marginalized. The sons and daughters of St. John Bosco consider themselves to be a family "totally of Mary." Don Bosco himself always taught that it was "Mary who has done everything" and will continue to do so as long as we follow her as guide and teacher. Thus his followers strive to emulate Mary's self-forgetfulness and authentic commitment. At the Visitation, Mary found Elizabeth open to the mysteries of God. This is the experience of those movements, like Fatima's Blue Army and the Schoenstatt Rosary Campaign, who promote the traveling of an image of Mary. Numerous conversions can happen when we "not only speak of Christ, but in a certain sense 'show' him to them."[45]

Movements with a distinct Marian charism usually safeguard their being and working in, with, and through Mary in some form of consecration, dedication, alliance, or entrustment. The Militia of the Immaculata, for example, expresses the depth of their relationship to her through an act of entrustment and welcome. Their consecration to the Immaculata transforms them into evangelizers who wish to renew individuals and all of society by means of the mass media. Some movements like *Totus Tuus* or the Legion of Mary commit to or at least encourage their members to make the total consecration to Mary, according to St. Louis de Montfort. At the heart of

42. Giussani, *Holy Rosary*, Mary's Assumption into Heaven. "Our Lady indicates the ideal of Christian morality, the valuing of every moment, every instant."

43. Lubich, *Heaven on Earth*, 104.

44. Lubich, *Die Welt*, 26–27.

45. Rylko, "Christians, that is Christóphoroi," 179.

the Schoenstatt spirituality is a covenant of love with Mary, which enables the individual to grow through bonding with Mary into a Marian attitude. Mary's task as covenant partner is the education and formation of the new person and the new community, Christ's witness in the world.

Last but not least, a few movements are known through shrines, pilgrimages and/or Marian icons associated with them. Communion and Liberation promotes pilgrimages, especially to Loretto. Opus Dei's founder entrusted the Shrine of Torreciudad to his spiritual family with a special prayer to Our Lady "that she would work there miracles of conversion and peace and not physical miracles." The family of Don Bosco finds its spiritual home in the shrine of Valdocco. As mentioned above, more than 200 exact replicas of the Original Shrine of the Schoenstatt movement in Schoenstatt, Germany, have been built all over the world; moreover, as an expression of the domestic church, members of the Schoenstatt movement erect a home shrine, inviting Our Lady of Schoenstatt to make her dwelling in their homes, where she can be active as the educator of families.

The spirituality of Mary is the fundamental spirituality that contains, in a way, all spiritualities of the church in their pure state. As Mother of the Church, Mary safeguards that all communities in the church—religious and lay—preserve their unique witness to Christ. Moreover, she is the guarantee of a spirituality fully and authentically lived[46] since all are mirrored and renewed in her, making her the rule of conduct for all Christian witnessing.[47]

Bibliography

Abbott, Walter M., ed. *The Documents of Vatican II: All Sixteen Official Texts Promulgated by the Ecumenical Council, 1963–1965.* Baltimore: America, 1966.

Argüello, Kiko. "Neocatechumenal Way." In *The Ecclesial Movements in the Pastoral Concern of the Bishops*, 158–66. Vatican City: Pontifical Council for the Laity.

———. "Small Christian Communities for the New Evangelization." In *The Beauty of Being a Christian: Movements in the Church: Proceedings of the Second World Congress of the Ecclesial Movements and New Communities*, 99–105. Rome: Libreria Editrice Vaticana, 2007.

Astell, Ann W. "All Saints: The Universal Call to Holiness." Unpublished talk given at the University of Notre Dame, Jan. 19, 2008.

———. "Introduction." In *Lay Sanctity, Medieval and Modern: A Search for Models*, edited by Ann W. Astell, 1–26. Notre Dame: University of Notre Dame Press, 2000.

Astell, Ann W., and Danielle M. Peters. "Schoenstatt's Shrine for the Pilgrim People of God." *Claritas: Journal of Dialogue and Culture* 3/2 (2014) 68–84.

46. Cf. John Paul II, *Theotókos*, 35.

47. Cf. St. Ambrose, *De Virginibus* 2.2.15, in Migne and Vattasso, *Initia Patrum*, 222.

Balthasar, Hans Urs von. *The Glory of the Lord: A Theological Aesthetics.* Vol. 1, *Seeing the Form.* Translated by Erasmo Leiva-Merikakis. Edited by Joseph Fessio and John Riches. San Francisco: Ignatius, 1989.

Coda, Piero. "The Ecclesial Movements, Gifts of the Spirit: A Theological Reflection." In *Movements in the Church, Rome, 27–29 May 1998,* by World Congress of the Ecclesial Movements, 77–104. Vatican City: Pontificium Consilium pro Laicis, 1999.

De Sales, St. Francis. *Introduction to the Devout Life.* Translated by John K. Ryan. 1950. New York: Doubleday, 1972.

Francis. *Evangelii Gaudium.* November 24, 2014. w2.vatican.va/content/francesco/en/apost_exhortations/documents/papa-francesco_esortazione-ap_20131124_evangelii-gaudium.html.

———. *Laudato Si'.* May 24, 2015. w2.vatican.va/content/francesco/en/encyclicals/documents/papa-francesco_20150524_enciclica-laudato-si.html.

Giussani, Luigi. *The Holy Rosary.* www.clonline.org/articoli/eng/rosarygius.html.

Ihnatowicz, J. A. *Consecrated Life among the Laity.* PhD diss., Angelicum, Rome, 1984.

John Paul II. "Message to the World Congress of Ecclesial Movements, 1998." *Laity Today* (1999) 222.

———. *Theotókos: Woman, Mother, Disciple: A Catechesis on Mary, Mother of God.* Boston: Pauline, 2000.

Johnson, Maxwell E. *Images of Baptism.* Forum Essays 6. Chicago: Liturgy Training, 2001.

Hanna, Tony. *New Ecclesial Movements.* New York: Alba House, 2006.

Janaro, John. "The Blessed Virgin Mary in the Ecclesial Movement Communion and Liberation." *Marian Studies* 54 (2003) 117–28.

Lubich, Chiara. *Essential Writings: Spirituality, Dialogue, Culture.* Hyde Park, NY: New City, 2007.

———. *Die Welt wird eins: Franca Zambonini im Gespräch mit der Gründerin der Fokolar-Bewegung.* Munich: Neue Stadt, 1998.

———. "Focolare Movement." In *The Ecclesial Movements in the Pastoral Concern of the Bishops,* 148–54. Vatican City: Pontifical Council for the Laity, 1999.

———. *Heaven on Earth: Meditations and Reflections.* Translated by Jerry Hearne. New York: New City, 2000.

Mansfield, Patti Gallagher. "A Prayer Lavishly Answered." In *The Beauty of Being a Christian: Movements in the Church: Proceedings of the Second World Congress of the Ecclesial Movements and New Communities,* 111–15. Rome: Libreria Editrice Vaticana, 2007.

Migne, Jacques-Paul, and Marco Vattasso, eds. *Initia Patrum Aliorumque Scriptorum Ecclesiasticorum Latinorum ex Mignei Patrologia et ex Compluribus Aliis Libris.* Vol. 16. Studi E Testi Biblioteca Apostolica Vaticana. Rome: Typis Vaticanis, 1906.

Mitchell, Donald W. "A Life between Two Fires: Chiara Lubich and Lay Sanctity." In *Lay Sanctity, Medieval and Modern: A Search for Models,* edited by Ann W. Astell, 173–89. Notre Dame: University of Notre Dame Press, 2000.

Niehaus, Jonathan. *Brushstrokes of a Father.* Vol. 4. Bangalore: Brilliant, 2013.

Ouellet, Marc. "The Beauty of Being Christians." In *The Beauty of Being a Christian— Movements in the Church: Proceedings of the Second World Congress of the Ecclesial Movements and New Communities,* 41–57. Pontifical Consilium Pro Laicis. Rocca di Papa, May 31–June 2, 2006. Vatican City: Libreria Editrice Vaticana, 2006.

Paul VI. "Address of Pope Paul VI During the Last General Meeting of the Second Vatican Council." December 7, 1965. w2.vatican.va/content/paul-vi/en/speeches/1965/documents/hf_p-vi_spe_19651207_epilogo-concilio.html.

Pius XI, *Rerum Omnium Perturbationem*. January 26, 1923. w2.vatican.va/content/pius-xi/en/encyclicals/documents/hf_p-xi_enc_26011923_rerum-omnium-perturbationem.html.

Rylko, Stanislaw. "Christians, that is Christóphoroi at the Heart of the World." In *The Beauty of Being a Christian: Movements in the Church: Proceedings of the Second World Congress of the Ecclesial Movements and New Communities*, 179. Rome: Libreria Editrice Vaticana, 2007.

United States Conference of Catholic Bishops. *Catechism of the Catholic Church*. San Francisco: Ignatius, 1994.

Waaijman, Kees. "Toward a Phenomenological Definition of Spirituality." *Studies in Spirituality* 3 (1993) 1–57.

10

Hispanic Lay Movements in the Postconciliar Church

—Timothy Matovina

PUERTO RICAN CHICAGOAN ELISABETH Román "was raised in a strict Pentecostal household and indoctrinated from an early age about the evils of the Catholic Church." Faced with a personal crisis and lacking a spiritual home after a twenty-year hiatus from church attendance, she accepted a friend's invitation to a parish Mass imbued with the spirit of the Catholic Charismatic Renewal (CCR), an apostolic group centered on the gifts and the power of the Holy Spirit that seeks to renew Christian faith through community life, prayer, preaching, healing ministries, and evangelization. Román continued to worship at the Charismatic Mass each Sunday for three months. Impressed with the community's faith, her own sense of inner peace, and the fact that no one pressured her to become Catholic, she went through the process of being received into the Catholic Church, over the strong objections of her family members. Román avows that "the spirited [Catholic Charismatic] church I encountered, and the one I have learned to love and serve, seems to be what many Latinos are seeking." Román concludes that "for Hispanics, who must live between two cultures, charismatic Catholicism can offer the best of both worlds: participation in the sacraments and a personal, livelier form of worship, which is at the heart of our religious experience."[1]

1. Román, "Other Latin Mass."

Leaders of predominantly lay-led movements like the CCR note that their apostolic endeavors address situations that Latinos and Latinas like Elisabeth Román face in daily life. They underscore that Latinos and those who accompany them in grassroots Hispanic ministries face numerous difficulties. Most of these everyday trials and temptations are familiar to anyone who has even passing contact or knowledge of many working-class Hispanic communities: lack of opportunity, low educational attainment, drug and alcohol abuse, violence, teenage pregnancy, poverty, undocumented status, inadequate health care, and a general strain on family cohesion and personal wellbeing, among others.[2] Looking inward to the vitality of their own faith communities, Hispanic ministry proponents have frequently lamented that the upsurge of religious traditions like Pentecostalism and evangelicalism provides the most momentous challenge. Preserving the faith of immigrants is one element of this challenge. At least as urgent is the need to invigorate faith among Latinos—especially the younger generations—as they become more enmeshed in a pluralistic U.S. society with a range of religious options, including the choice for no religious affiliation.

The conviction that the most effective way to address such challenges is through smaller groupings of Catholics committed to common formation and apostolic activities is not new. Spanish subjects established *cofradías* (literally "brotherhoods" or "sisterhoods") throughout Latin America during the colonial period. While one appealing aspect of these pious societies was the communal support networks they provided, their primary purpose was to promote the requirements that members observe Catholic codes of conduct, receive the sacraments worthily, practice specific devotions, and, in many cases, organize an annual celebration for a particular saint or feast day. Pious associations remained the most prevalent form of Latino small faith community well into the twentieth century. For ethnic Mexican Catholics, the Guadalupana groups dedicated to Our Lady of Guadalupe are among the most popular and enduring of these societies. Latinos of other backgrounds supported their own associations, such as early 1960s Cuban exiles whose strong tradition of involvement in the lay organizations of their homeland centered their faith practice more on smaller communal settings than on the largely parish-based Catholicism they encountered in Miami and other U.S. locales. Parishes with significant numbers of Cuban congregants helped enable the transition to this predominantly congregational polity through parish-based sections of groups like Catholic Action,

---

2. For an analysis of the challenging social context for Hispanic ministry in one Chicago parish, see Dahm, *Parish Ministry*, chap. 2, "Mexican Families."

the National Council of Our Lady of Charity, and the Christian Family Movement.[3]

Apostolic movements eclipsed pious societies as the primary small faith groups during the second half of the twentieth century. Lay ecclesial movements with more protracted formation processes like Opus Dei, Focolare, Communion and Liberation, and the Neocatechumenal Way have exerted noteworthy influence over the course of the twentieth and twenty-first centuries in Europe; by one recent estimate nearly half the active Catholics in Spain relate to the church primarily through a movement rather than a parish.[4] While some Latinos are active in such movements in the United States, they have been more involved in apostolic movements with a greater tendency to have a parish base such as the CCR and a host of prayer groups, Bible studies, and other local initiatives. Members of these groups engage in common prayer, faith formation, and evangelization activities, often in smaller-sized communities that foster a stronger sense of commitment and belonging than many large parish congregations. For Hispanics, the new apostolic movements build on the strengths of their *cofradía* predecessors in their resonance with the devotional penchant of Latino Catholicism and their emphases on community and worthy reception of the sacraments. But they also reflect a more widespread and explicit stress among U.S. believers on a programmatic conversion to Christianity as an intentional way of life. In fostering intense religious experience, personal transformation, knowledge of one's faith, and fervor to evangelize others, apostolic movements are suited to the competitive religious environment of the United States and the pressures of modern urban life, including the unwieldy and oftentimes impersonal congregations in metropolitan areas.

Several apostolic movements have had noteworthy influence among Latinos from various national backgrounds. Founding national presidents Pat and Patty Crowley established the Christian Family Movement with other collaborators in 1949. It spread internationally and in 1969 Gustavo and Isabel Erviti became the first presidents for the new Spanish-language Movimiento Familiar Cristiano in the United States. Marriage Encounter (Encuentro Matrimonial) originated in Spain. Father Gabriel Calvo was the key leader and organized the first Encounter weekend in 1958. Calvo and Maryknoll priest Donald Hessler promoted the initial Encounter weekends in the United States in 1966. Subsequently the movement spread most rapidly among English-speaking Catholics, until the following decade

3. Torres, *The Paradox*; Pitti, "Sociedades Guadalupanas"; Poyo, *Cuban Catholics*, 93, 96.

4. Deck, "Where the Laity"; O'Connor, "Catholic Common Ground," 3–6.

when Roberto and Rosie Piña of San Antonio took the initiative to expand Marriage Encounter among the Spanish-speaking. RENEW is the
most widespread program in the United States centered on forming small
communities to enable people and parish congregations to foster spiritual
growth, integration of faith into daily life, and an evangelizing spirit. Established among Catholics in the Newark archdiocese in 1976, RENEW
has grown into an international network with its materials translated into
more than forty languages, including Spanish.[5] The two most widespread
apostolic movements among Hispanics, the Cursillo de Cristiandad (Short
Course in Christianity) and the CCR illuminate the potential of these movements to incite Catholics to live out their baptismal calling. An examination
of these two cases also reveals the pastoral challenges and opportunities the
movements present for ministry with contemporary Hispanic faith communities, including liturgical homiletics and animating the preaching mission of the baptized.

Cursillo de Cristiandad

The premier apostolic movement among Hispanics is the Cursillo. Eduardo
Bonnín and other Spanish laymen in Mallorca established the Cursillo in
the wake of World War II. In 1957 two of their countrymen assigned to a
Waco, Texas, military base collaborated with Father Gabriel Fernández to
lead the first Cursillo weekend retreat in the United States. Within five years
Cursillo weekends had spread to Puerto Ricans in New York, Cubans in
Miami, and among ethnic Mexicans in various locales. By 1978 some thirty
thousand Puerto Ricans in New York alone had participated in a Cursillo
weekend, exerting an influence so great that one observer noted, "In the
Puerto Rican community to be a *cursillista* and a Catholic was almost one
and the same." Seven years later a national survey of Latino Catholics found
that over one fourth perceived the Cursillo as "very important" or "somewhat important" to their faith, ranking the Cursillo highest among thirteen
choices on a survey question. It outranked other apostolic movements, the
National Hispanic Pastoral Encuentros, the U.S. bishops' pastoral letter on
Hispanic ministry, and even the Second Vatican Council. While the subsequent rise of other renewal movements moderated the centrality of Cursillo
among Latino Catholics, the 2014 National Study of Catholic Parishes with
Hispanic Ministry found that still thirty percent of 4,368 parishes engaged

---

5. Christian Family Movement Online, www.cfm.org; Rodríguez, "Hispanic Community," 220–21; RENEW International; Deck, *The Second Wave*, 73–75.

in Hispanic ministry had Cursillo activities, a prevalence that the study indicated only the CCR had surpassed among apostolic movements.[6]

According to New York Hispanic ministry leader Father Robert Stern, the Cursillo is "a highly and tightly organized, three-day, study-retreat weekend with a strong emphasis on community experience." It presents to participants "a theological understanding of the sacramental life, Christian maturity, and the responsibilities of the lay person in the church." As a movement initially conducted in Spanish but later also in English to attract Hispanic (and non-Hispanic) leaders and participants across generations, the Cursillos have deepened the experience of God, faith, and active church leadership commitment of many relatively passive Sunday worshipers. The Cursillos have also had a significant impact on Hispanics who felt isolated or disaffected in their faith and parish life. In Stern's experience, "after attending a Cursillo, the average participant is enthused, highly motivated, and disposed to active involvement in the apostolate in his or her local parish."[7]

More concretely, the bulk of time on the highly structured Cursillo weekend is dedicated to a series of presentations called *rollos* on the fundamentals of Catholic faith such as grace, sacraments, the vocation of the lay person, and what *cursillistas* deem the three pillars for grace-filled Christian living: piety, study, and action. Lay leaders who previously "made" a Cursillo weekend give most of these talks, intermixing content on the topic with personal testimony that often includes the way Cursillo has transformed them. These powerful testimonies from participants' peers and the convention of holding separate weekend retreats for men and for women heighten the emotional impact of the Cursillo, providing an environment that, for men especially, enables them to overcome aversion to self-disclosure and "bar[e] their souls to other men." The experience of friendship and intense, close-knit community over the three days both enhances and is enhanced by the bonds created in such conversations, resulting in an unabashedly affective style to the Cursillo that is consistent with Hispanics' devotional traditions. Songs, prayers, chapel visits, Mass, and Catholic devotions like Eucharistic adoration, the Way of the Cross, and the rosary, the latter sometimes prayed in the sacrificial posture of kneeling and outstretching one's arms in the form of a cross, give the weekend a deeply Catholic ambiance. Perhaps the most common participant testimony is that Cursillo enabled them to transcend faith as a mere custom or unconscious habit and enter into a deeper, more personal relationship with God in Christ. Many avow

6. Nabhan-Warren, *Cursillo Movement*; Rodríguez, "Hispanic Community," 215–19; Díaz-Stevens, *Oxcart Catholicism*, 109–10; Poyo, *Cuban Catholics*, 99–101; González and La Velle, *Hispanic Catholic* 133–34; Ospino, *Hispanic Ministry*, 17.

7. Stern, "Evolution," 312.

that the Cursillo experience brought them from being nominal Catholics to active participants in the church. A frequent highlight of the weekends is the reception of the sacrament of reconciliation, which participants describe as an experience of healing, encounter with a merciful God, and a new beginning of life with Christ.[8]

The final talk of the Cursillo, called "The Fourth Day," challenges participants to live the message and the personal relationship with God they have received beyond the confines of the close fellowship experienced on the weekend. Participants are particularly encouraged to be active in inviting their family, friends, and coworkers to future Cursillo weekends and to participate in follow-up group reunion meetings called *ultreyas* at their local parish or diocesan Cursillo center. The commitment and spiritual growth of many are further enhanced through the invitation to be on a team that presents a subsequent Cursillo, a responsibility that includes weeks of planning and for most the preparation of a *rollo* presentation through which they publicly witness to their faith. A number of *cursillistas* attest that, as powerful as their initial weekend was in awakening their faith, participation on a Cursillo team solidified their faith commitment even more deeply. Some participate on a number of teams and support Cursillo in their parish or diocese through other means such as *palanca*—prayers, sacrifices, and notes of encouragement offered for the spiritual benefit of those making a Cursillo. Past participants also attend the festive closing of subsequent Cursillo weekends, at which each new participant is invited to state what the retreat experience meant to them.

It is difficult to overestimate the significance of the Cursillo, which revitalized the faith of numerous grassroots Catholics and their parish communities. Indeed, one is hard pressed to find a Latino Catholic leader, especially those active during the initial fervor of the movement in the 1960s and 1970s, who has never had any involvement or contact with the Cursillo. In that sense it is not surprising that the Cursillo subsequently became less prominent in various locales; in a number of parishes a substantial majority of committed Latino Catholics had already been formed in the Cursillo experience and were now involved in other apostolic movements or activities. But even so Cursillo remains an important and vibrant apostolic movement among many Latinos today, both those who are making their first Cursillo and those who continue to participate in *ultreya* groups, some of which have met regularly for decades. Various bishops continue to appoint diocesan directors for Cursillo or even operate centers that advance Cursillo as a diocesan apostolate.

8. Hinojosa, "Mexican-American Faith," 117; Deck, *Second Wave*, 67–68.

Cursillo was not only the first and most significant apostolic movement to emerge out of Latino Catholicism, it was also the first to expand broadly to English-speaking Catholics and then to Protestants as well. *Cursillista* team members from previous Spanish-language weekends led the first English-language Cursillo in San Angelo, Texas in 1961. By the following year *cursillistas* had conducted weekends in numerous locales such as San Francisco, Kansas City, Chicago, Detroit, Cincinnati, Newark, Brooklyn, Baltimore, and Boston. Over the ensuing two decades nearly every diocese in the United States introduced the Cursillo movement, impacting literally millions of Catholics from a variety of backgrounds. Consciously or not, as Cursillo spread a number of retreat programs that closely emulate its core dynamics appeared: Teens Encounter Christ (TEC), Search and its Spanish counterpart *Búsqueda*, *Encuentros Juveniles*, Kairos, Christ Renews His Parish, and the Protestant Walk to Emmaus and youth-oriented Chrysalis retreats, among others. Teens Encounter Christ, for example, began in 1965 with a request from "a local adult faith community" in the diocese of Lansing, Michigan, that Father Matthew Fedewa assist them "in creating a similar faith encounter for their youth as they had experienced in Catholic movements like Cursillo." The Cursillo-inspired retreat movements have mirrored their predecessor in their wide impact, as is evident in the claim of Teens Encounter Christ leaders that since its establishment "hundreds of thousands of young people from multiple continents have encountered Christ through TEC." In both direct and indirect ways, the effects of Cursillo encompass the full range of these spiritual renewal movements. Religious studies scholar Kristy Nabhan-Warren rightly contends that the spiritual renewal movement Spanish-speaking *cursillistas* pioneered "has come to impact hundreds of thousands of U.S. Christian lives since the late 1950s—and millions globally."[9]

Catholic Charismatic Renewal

The most widespread apostolic movement among Latino Catholics today is the CCR. English-speaking U.S. Catholics founded the CCR in 1967. The initially tepid response of some Vatican officials warmed with the supportive backing of popes beginning with Paul VI, helping to spur the movement's growth to nearly 120 million participants worldwide by the early twenty-first century. More than sixty percent are Latin Americans, a number of whom brought the CCR spirit to the United States as immigrants and became leaders or founders of CCR groups in U.S. parishes. While a relatively

9. Teens Encounter Christ; Nabhan-Warren, *Cursillo Movement*, 253–54.

small group of Hispanics participated as the movement expanded among English-speaking U.S. Catholics during the early 1970s, subsequently rising immigration and the vibrancy of Spanish-language CCR groups fueled their increased involvement. Hispanic leaders established the Comité Nacional de Servicio Hispano (CNSH) in 1990 to promote the CCR and coordinate activities among the growing number of active Hispanic charismatics. The CNSH has three core commitments: to serve God in the Catholic Church and advance its mission of evangelization in the power of the Holy Spirit; to foment the experience of Pentecost as a grace of the Holy Spirit for the church; and to carry the fervor of the Charismatic Renewal to families, neighborhoods, parish communities, and all those who thirst for God. Structurally, the CNSH consists of a national coordinator, spiritual director, executive committee, and youth committee as well as representatives from eight regions spanning the United States and Canada. One of its major activities since its inception has been to conduct an annual leaders' meeting called the Encuentro Católico Carismático Latino de los Estados Unidos (Latino Catholic Charismatic Encounter of the United States), an initiative that provides opportunities for advanced training, networking, and greater cohesion among the national network of Latino CCR groups.[10]

The thousands of prayer groups that meet regularly in parishes or private homes are the most widespread manifestation of the CCR among Hispanics. Some clergy participate, but laity are the primary leaders in the vast majority of groups, which range in size from a handful to hundreds. The length of a meeting, order of service, and forms of prayer also vary and can encompass healing Masses, testimonies of God's action in people's lives, Marian devotion, prophetic utterances in which a participant speaks a word of admonition or encouragement in the name of God, teachings on CCR or other Catholic topics, Eucharistic adoration, periods of silent meditation, the ecstatic praise of speaking in tongues, spontaneous public prayer of praise and intercession, Bible reading, preaching, vibrant singing, and embodied worship such as hand clapping and raising one's arms in praise. A common experience of initiation is the baptism of the Holy Spirit or "second baptism," which for many Catholics who received the sacrament of baptism as infants entails a renewed adult commitment to live their faith in the power of the Holy Spirit. Prayer group leaders usually present the Life in the Spirit Seminar that prepares new CCR participants for this baptism. After what is often weeks or even months of preparation, the baptism is celebrated with group members laying hands on the initiates and praying

10. International Catholic Charismatic Renewal Services; Comité Nacional de Servicio Hispano.

with them that the Holy Spirit come upon them. Daily prayer, Bible study, parish involvement, witnessing to others, and inviting them to attend the prayer group are highly encouraged as some of the primary means to live as a Spirit-filled Catholic.

Extant surveys report a wide range of findings about the extent of Latino involvement in CCR groups. On the high end, the 2,000 Hispanic Churches in American Public Life (HCAPL) survey estimated that 5.4 million Latinos in the United States self-identify as Catholic Charismatics, substantially more than the 3.8 million that self-identify as Pentecostals. The 2014 National Study of Catholic Parishes with Hispanic Ministry found that the CCR is the most prevalent apostolic movement among Latinos, with one half of parishes engaged in Hispanic ministry having CCR groups or activities.[11] But even if every one of these CCR groups had 500 Latino members—a conservative estimate—cumulatively they would still comprise just over a million Latino Charismatics. The wide discrepancy between this estimate and the HCAPL survey is not easily explicated, though one important factor is the statistical gap between members regularly active in CCR parish groups and the much larger group of those who in some way identify with the Charismatic Renewal. A number of Latinos participate at least occasionally in home-based CCR activities or larger events apart from the parish-based prayer groups counted in the National Study of Catholic Parishes with Hispanic Ministry. In any case, a sizeable number of Latinos in faith communities across the country participate in the CCR.

The CCR has influenced a number of parishes and dioceses, enlivening the faith and evangelization efforts of numerous Latinas and Latinos. CCR leaders in the Galveston-Houston diocese (now archdiocese) established the Catholic Charismatic Center in 1972 with the support of Bishop John Morkovsky. The 1996 dedication of an ample new building for the center, originally housed in an old high school, marked the solid foundation and expansion of the ministry, which encompasses Spanish-language evangelization, youth, and leadership formation components. For over a decade Marina Carrion has been a paid staff member for the Diocese of San Bernardino, California, charged with overseeing the CCR and linking its members to parishes and diocesan formation programs. Her leadership has helped expand the number of Spanish-speaking prayer groups from 32 to 54, encompassing more than 60 percent of parishes and all regions within the diocese. She is most pleased to report that various vocations to the priesthood have come from the CCR and that Hispanics involved in the CCR have increased their participation in parish ministries and in diocesan

11. Espinosa, "Pentecostalization," 266; Ospino, *Hispanic Ministry*, 17.

formation programs. Monsignor Joseph Malagreca, the spiritual director of CNSH, has been involved with the CCR among Latinos in his home diocese of Brooklyn since 1975 and has seen an expansion from an initial four Hispanic prayer groups to 120. He estimates that one-third of Hispanic parishioners in his diocese are active CCR participants, who also comprise the majority of leaders in catechetical, evangelization, youth, liturgical, and other ministries. Nationally he cites as the most noteworthy features of the CCR its evangelistic fervor and especially its distinctive capacity to draw Hispanic men and young people more deeply into their Catholic faith.[12]

Pastoral Challenges and Opportunities

Bishop Agustín Román, the first Cuban exile named a bishop in the United States, aptly summarized the pastoral challenge and opportunity of movements like Cursillo and the CCR: "They are like a hurricane. They stir things up." Though apostolic movements such as these have received significant support from diocesan officials and pastors, some ministry leaders have criticized them. One charge is that they can drain parishes of their most active and talented lay leaders, who prefer to work in the more satisfying ministries of groups like the CCR and Cursillo rather than the everyday but necessary concerns of the parish. In the words of Latino pastoral leaders, apostolic movements can be a source of disunity when their members "adopt a quasi-sectarian attitude, focusing single-mindedly on their own activities and growth and neglecting the welfare of the parish."[13] Such critiques reflect the emphasis on the central role of the parish in U.S. Catholicism, which has led many pastoral leaders to value apostolic movements only to the extent they support the structures of parish life.

Pastors have also complained about various defects they perceive in apostolic movements and those who lead them. One is a divisive spiritual elitism among members of apostolic groups, often evidenced in the claim that their particular movement is the best or only authentic way of relating to God. An even more fundamental critique is that the movements merely succeed in inciting an emotional conversion, not a deeper and more lasting conversion that encompasses the intellectual, moral, faith, *and* affective dimensions of Christian life. Critics contend that this defect leads many apostolic movement participants to recurrently seek renewed emotional

---

12. Catholic Charismatic Center; Marina Carrion, interview by author, March 28, 2010; Msgr. Joseph Malagreca, interview by author, November 19, 2009.

13. Rodríguez, "Hispanic Community," 219; Bishops' Committee on Hispanic Affairs, *Hispanic Ministry*, on-site interview, section 3.

religious experiences through their communal prayer and other activities and, when those experiences are unavailable or no longer suffice, to fall away from their faith commitment.[14] Another critique comes from social activist Catholics, who have bemoaned what they perceive as a common apostolic movement focus on prayer and personal conversion that excludes or even openly resists faith-based social involvement. Competition between apostolic movements can further hinder their effectiveness. Infighting among apostolic movement group leaders is not uncommon and at times quite fierce. Leaders of parish or home groups resent the loss of members to larger apostolic organizations that attract followers in part through their mega-scale events and media savvy outreach.

CCR leader Andrés Arango, the CNSH national coordinator, avows that a root cause of difficulties in apostolic movements is a lack of adequate ministerial preparation among movement leaders. Many leaders participate exclusively in their movement formation programs, despite their directors' admonitions that these programs should complement rather than replace those of parishes and dioceses. Arango further opines that among groups rooted in the Charismatic Renewal "the biggest challenge we face is dealing with the issue of authority, especially leaders who want to be independent from any outside authority or influence," be it from diocesan or parish officials or from other CCR leaders like those of the CNSH.[15]

Yet pastoral leaders also attest to the many opportunities apostolic movements present. Arango points to the noteworthy successes of CCR groups in providing Hispanic immigrants a place to nurture their faith and develop their leadership within the U.S. Catholic Church, as well as forming bilingual leaders in the second and third generation who help revitalize the Catholic faith of both Latino and non-Latino youth alike. Father José Eugenio Hoyos directs the Hispanic apostolate for the diocese of Arlington, Virginia, where the Latino presence in the CCR has blossomed from some 150 in the late 1980s to an estimated 10,000 to 15,000 active participants in an array of home, parish, and diocesan-wide events. Hoyos deems Latino Charismatics the "engine of the Church" and attests that "a lot of [Latino] Pentecostals and other religions are coming back because of the Charismatic Renewal . . . They can express themselves very freely and feel a closer belonging to the Church than before." Many other Hispanic ministry leaders concur that the CCR provides a vital, Spirit-filled alternative to Pentecostal and other Protestant denominations. Allan Figueroa Deck, SJ, further asserts that the CCR "is arguably the single most important factor in

14. Deck, *Second Wave*, 68–69.

15. Arango, interview by author, July 8, 2008.

the new evangelization of Hispanics and in motivating new generations of them to serve in the church as lay ministers, deacons, priests and religious." The capacity of apostolic movements to form apostles is illustrated in one young Guatemalan who, after four years of seeking a place to belong after migrating to Chicago, finally found a spiritual home. His newfound young adult faith group stirred what he describes as a vocation: "I feel that God is calling me to not allow other *jóvenes* (young people) to go around lost and disoriented without finding a community that supports them and helps them to live their faith."[16]

Grassroots leaders and members of apostolic movements across the United States concur that their groups contribute extensively to the life of the church. Though many have felt misunderstood or unappreciated, even among their fellow Hispanic Catholics, they frequently express their allegiance to the traditions of the Catholic Church, its institutional leaders, and the overall wellbeing of their local parish. Leaders demonstrate their fidelity to church authority and doctrine in their citations of papal and other official teaching. Many state explicitly that they incorporate traditional devotions like Eucharistic adoration and the rosary into their communal prayer and group meetings to enhance the Catholic allegiance and identity of participants. They also incite participants to receive the sacraments fervently, especially the Eucharist and reconciliation, which have often been highlights of Cursillo weekends and the spiritual renewal fostered in other apostolic movements. The 2007 Pew Latino religion survey substantiated Latino Charismatics' emphasis on loyal participation in the life of the church, finding that they engage in parish ministries such as lector, choir, or parish council nearly twice as much as other Latino Catholics. Diocesan directors of Hispanic ministry confirm that "many Hispanics are energized and motivated to participate in the life of the parish by their activity in Charismatic Renewal and other prayer groups and in the different apostolic movements. They have a great thirst for knowledge of the Bible as well as for leadership formation."[17]

The influence of apostolic movements is not limited to greater church participation. They transform people and form them as evangelizers. Anyone who has worked in these movements is aware of the dramatic conversion testimonies people confess, ranging from recovery from alcohol or drug abuse to healing broken marriages, families, and lives. Their testimonies in prayer groups and in Cursillo and other retreat talks are one of the most

16. Arango, interview by author; Manetto, "Charismatic Spirit"; Deck, "Hispanic Ministry"; Díez de Sollano, "Perceptions," 31.

17. Pew Hispanic Center and Pew Forum, *Changing Faiths*, 39; Bishops' Committee on Hispanic Affairs, *Hispanic Ministry*, on-site interview section, part II.

effective forms of lay preaching in the U.S. Catholic Church. The preaching and general involvement of the baptized in apostolic movements build on Hispanics' familial and ethnic traditions and form them in a faith that is an intentional way of life. They also inspire them to give yet further witness to the mighty deeds of God and proclaim God's saving power to others. Since many members of the movements live and work in close proximity to their fellow grassroots Hispanics—friends, family, neighbors, and coworkers—collectively they have immense evangelizing potential.

Apostolic movements enrich the most abundant resource Hispanics provide for Catholicism in the United States: an energetic base of leaders committed to live the evangelizing call of their baptism. Unfortunately in various locales diocesan and parish leaders perceive apostolic movements as simplistic, misguided, or even a threat. Others simply ignore them. But thankfully a growing number recognize the dynamism of apostolic movements and their leaders' contributions to the missionary outreach of U.S. Catholicism. They seek to accompany, form, and guide the leadership base of the movements and integrate them more fully into the life and mission of the local church. More concretely, they encourage key leaders' participation in officially sanctioned programs so that the faith formation they receive will filter down to members of their apostolic movement. In other instances, they seek to shape the lay formation initiatives of the apostolic movements themselves through direct participation in them. Such pastoral efforts comprise one of the most strategic ways to foster baptismal witness in the world among today's Hispanic Catholics. More explicit attention to the baptismal call to preach the gospel can further enhance these formation initiatives and their participants' evangelizing work in prayer groups, spiritual renewal movements, and daily life.

The vitality of apostolic movements in Latino communities underscores the need to address them in a variety of pastoral ministries, including preaching. Even the brief analysis of pastoral challenges and opportunities offered above reveals that preachers can speak in concrete ways to themes like conversion, the relationship between prayer and action, ecclesial unity amidst a diversity of spiritual expressions, vocation, encountering Christ in the sacraments, and evangelization in everyday life. To take just one example, during the season of Lent a homilist could proclaim that conversion is a lifelong process and not merely a onetime, dramatic experience. The homilist could also avow that authentic conversion transforms every aspect of our lives and calls us to transform the communities and world around us. Emotional religious experiences can be gifts from God that inspire us, but they are not to be sought for their own sake. Moreover, they are all but worthless if they do not lead to the fruits of a changed heart and a changed life. Preachers who accompany Latinos in apostolic movements will have a greater capacity to incarnate messages such as these into sermons and into the lives of those who hear them. They will also open themselves to the enriching potential of the movements. Those who preach to the Eucharistic assembly can then more effectively proclaim the Word of God in a manner that animates our common baptismal call to preach the Good News in word and in deed.

Bibliography

Arango, Andrés. Interview by author, July 8, 2008.

Bishops' Committee on Hispanic Affairs. *Hispanic Ministry at the Turn of the New Millennium.* Washington, DC: United States Conference of Catholic Bishops, 1999.

Carrion, Marina. Interview by author, March 28, 2010.

Catholic Charismatic Center, Archdiocese of Galveston-Houston. catholiccharismatic center.org.

Christian Family Movement. www.cfm.org.

Comité Nacional de Servicio Hispano. www.rcchispana.com.

Dahm, Charles W. "Mexican Families in an American City." In *Parish Ministry in a Hispanic Community,* 24–60. Mahwah, NJ: Paulist, 2004.

Deck, Allan Figueroa. "Where the Laity Flourish." *America* 195 (August 14–21, 2006) 14–16.

————. *The Second Wave: Hispanic Ministry and the Evangelization of Cultures.* Mahwah, NJ: Paulist, 1989.

————. "Hispanic Ministry: New Realities and Choices." *Origins* 38 (2008) 405–11.

Díaz-Stevens, Ana María. *Oxcart Catholicism on Fifth Avenue: The Impact of the Puerto Rican Migration upon the Archdiocese of New York.* Notre Dame: University of Notre Dame Press, 1993.

Díez de Sollano, Dolores. "Perceptions of Popular Religiosity among Latino Jóvenes." In *Latino Catholic Youth and Young Adults in the United States: Their Faith and Their Culture,* edited by Carmen María Cervantes, 28–33. Stockton, CA: Instituto Fe y Vida, 2001.

Espinosa, Gastón. "The Pentecostalization of Latin American and U.S. Latino Christianity." *Pneuma: The Journal of the Society for Pentecostal Studies* 26 (2004) 262–92.

González, Roberto O., and Michael La Velle. *The Hispanic Catholic in the United States: A Socio-Cultural and Religious Profile.* New York: Northeast Catholic Pastoral Center for Hispanics, 1985.

Hinojosa, Gilberto M. "Mexican-American Faith Communities in Texas and the Southwest." In *Mexican Americans and the Catholic Church, 1900–1965,* edited by Jay P. Dolan and Gilberto M. Hinojosa, 9–125. Notre Dame: University of Notre Dame Press, 1994.

International Catholic Charismatic Renewal Services. www.iccrs.org/en.

Malagreca, Joseph. Interview by author, November 19, 2009.

Manetto, Nick. "Charismatic Spirit Spreads with Latino Catholics." *Our Sunday Visitor*, August 19, 2007.

Nabhan-Warren, Kristy. *The Cursillo Movement in America: Catholics, Protestants, and Fourth-Day Spirituality*. Chapel Hill: University of North Carolina Press, 2013.

O'Connor, Liz. "The Catholic Common Ground Initiative Explores Lay Ecclesial Movements." *Initiative Report* 12 (2008) 3–6.

Ospino, Hosffman. *Hispanic Ministry in Catholic Parishes: A Summary Report of Findings from the National Study of Catholic Parishes with Hispanic Ministry*. Chestnut Hill, MA: Boston College School of Theology and Ministry, 2014.

Pew Hispanic Project and the Pew Forum on Religion & Public Life. *Changing Faiths: Latinos and the Transformation of American Religion*. Washington, DC: Pew Hispanic Center and Pew Forum on Religion & Public Life, 2007.

Pitti, Gina Marie. "The Sociedades Guadalupanas in the San Francisco Archdiocese, 1942–1962." *U.S. Catholic Historian* 21 (2003) 83–98.

Poyo, Gerald E. *Cuban Catholics in the United States, 1960–1980: Exile and Integration*. Notre Dame: University of Notre Dame Press, 2007.

RENEW International. www.renewintl.org.

Rodríguez, Edmundo. "The Hispanic Community and Church Movements: Schools of Leadership." In *Hispanic Catholic Culture in the U.S.: Issues and Concerns*, edited by Jay P. Dolan and Allan Figueroa Deck, 206–239. Notre Dame, IN: University of Notre Dame Press, 1994.

Román, Elisabeth. "The Other Latin Mass." *U.S. Catholic* 73 (2008) 30–33.

Stern, Robert L. "Evolution of Hispanic Ministry in the New York Archdiocese." In *Hispanics in New York: Religious, Cultural and Social Experiences*, edited by Ruth T. Doyle et al., 2:283–357. New York: Archdiocese of New York Office of Pastoral Research, 1982.

Teens Encounter Christ. www.tecconference.org.

Torres, Theresa L. *The Paradox of Latina Religious Leadership in the Catholic Church: Las Guadalupanas of Kansas City*. New York: Palgrave Macmillan, 2013.

11

The Domestic Church and Witness

—Wendy M. Wright

At the risk of being perceived as irreverent, I have to begin this discussion of the witness of the domestic church[1] by reminding us that a mere fifty years ago, during the era in which the Second Vatican Council was convened, the primary "witness" to the world of a family's Catholicity was the number of children they produced. A family might also be recognized as Catholic by the fact that they engaged in devotional practices, avoided the churches of their Protestant neighbors, or did not divorce. Since the council, much has changed, including the context of family life and the church's thinking about Christian witness.

Vatican II, of course, did not happen in a vacuum and its pronouncements that would influence the Catholic domestic church and expand its sense of witness had been coalescing for some time. But the magisterial enunciation of two themes on which I wish to focus here, the universal call to holiness in *Lumen Gentium* and the mandate to turn in mission to the wider world expressed especially in *Gaudium et Spes* and *Ad Gentes*, have

---

1. I have come to see the domestic church as the smallest unit of church, a genuine community that attempts to realize Christian discipleship. And I have argued here that family takes many forms. I am aware that this is a different starting place than that taken in *Lumen Gentium* (II,11), in which the parish is generally conceived as the smallest unit of church and the domestic church is situated in the mystical body of Christ through the sacrament of marriage.

gradually shifted the ground upon which Catholic family life is planted and thus the way Catholic families might think of themselves and eventually witness to the wider human community.

These two highlighted conciliar themes—the universal call to holiness and mission to the wider world—seem to me to have profound consequences for contemporary Catholic families. They clearly situate the smallest unit of church where it actually has always been, but perhaps has not always seen itself: as having a vocation that is simultaneously individual and personal and at the same time social and political.[2] One disclaimer: While I hope that the following may be applicable to the majority of Catholic families, I am also aware that they are shaped by my own North American context.

The Universal Call to Holiness

Lumen Gentium clearly gives voice to the idea that all baptized are called to lead holy lives. Chapter 5 begins with the statement that the church derives its holiness from God who in infinite love united Himself to her as His mystical body, therefore "in the Church, everyone whether belonging to the hierarchy, or being cared for by it, is called to holiness."[3]

The increased participation of laity in all aspects of Catholic life in the years since the council as well as the rise in lay ministries indicate that this universal call, rooted in baptism, has been grasped by many of the faithful. However, it is not clear the extent to which the idea of holiness has seeped down to the level of the domestic church. My observation during twenty-odd years of teaching and ministry has been that it is a challenge for many families simply to reimagine their domestic life as a genuine spiritual path, a path whose point of immersion is distinctive from the path of priesthood or religious life but is nevertheless a profoundly incarnational path with its own particular dynamics, challenges, and joys.[4] The tendency, a carry-

2. In the April 30, 2015, issue of *Commonweal*, theologian Robin Darling Young, writing about climate change, made the point that Catholic tradition is ill-equipped to deal with a problem that is simultaneously social/political and individual/moral. In "Does the Earth Have Rights?" she questions how it is possible to balance individual moral responsibility described in the moral teachings of the church against a general human responsibility as developed in more than a century of Catholic social teaching. This seems to be a similar quandary faced in thinking about Catholic families: the individual moral dimension of life has been the primary focus of ecclesial ministry and attention.

3. Second Vatican Council, *Lumen Gentium*, 39–40.

4. On family life as spiritual path, see Wright, *Sacred Dwelling*; and Wright, *Seasons of a Family's Life*. A number of other recent books also treat this topic. Here's a recent selection: Benson, *Digging In*; Bourg, *Where Two or Three are Gathered*; Fischer,

over from centuries of assumptions about Christian "perfection," has been not only to assume that family life is a lesser way to follow Christ but that holiness is about imitating or replicating certain specific models held up for veneration as holy.[5] Classic models of holiness, the saints, have been for the most part celibates, persons who have "left the world," or those who have eschewed domestic life for another call. It is true that models and ideals have a powerful function as we grow in faith. Being inspired by a Mother Teresa of Calcutta or a Teresa of Avila, following in the footsteps of an Oscar Romero, or modeling one's life on the work of a Catherine McAuley can be profoundly formative and fruitful.

But two issues for families arise here. First, the church needs more saintly models that affirm the beauty and dignity of a domestic vocation. There are few days of liturgical observance reserved for persons whose family life has identified them as candidates for sainthood.[6] Obviously, this is a topic too large to address here, but it is one that needs attention.[7] Second, as essential as the witness of the saints is, even if we were to canonize those whose witness is primarily in the intimate world of the domestic church, the Spirit-led adventure of holiness is not something that can easily be copied, not to mention given specific perimeters. I don't believe that there is any true holiness that is generic. Instead, to paraphrase Francis de Sales, a favorite saint of mine, we are asked to "be who we are and be that well." Our baptismal challenge is to venture into the mystery of a life prompted by the Spirit of God and, aware of the gifts and liabilities we possess and in the specific context in which we find ourselves, and to say "yes" to the often unexpected and untried siren call of that Spirit. This was true for all of the saints that the church holds up for veneration. It is still true today. I have always liked theologian Karl Rahner's way of putting this. To paraphrase him:

Forgiving Your Family; Gaillardetz, *A Daring Promise*; Garland, *Sacred Stories of Ordinary Families*; Kelly et al., *Marriage in the Catholic Tradition*; Miller-McLemore, *In the Midst of Chaos*; Robinson, *The Busy Family's Guide to Spirituality*; Roy, *My Monastery Is a Minivan*; Rubio, *A Christian Theology of Marriage and Family*; Rubio, *Family Ethics*; Yust, *Real Kids, Real Faith*.

5. This tendency was countered as early as the seventeenth century when Francis de Sales's *Introduction to the Devout Life,* written for laity, made it very clear that a holy life was possible for all Catholics. De Sales's teaching is to a great extent the source for the teaching at the Second Vatican Council.

6. Obviously the process of canonization itself, which demands expensive and time-consuming sponsorship of dedicated communities, advocates, lengthy reviews of writings, testimonies and so forth, is a deterrent to opening an actual cause for persons whose witness is probably hidden and local. It is also true that many people name family members when asked about saints. Grandmothers are often at the head of the list. On the paucity of married saints, see Kenneth Woodward's by now classic *Making Saints*.

7. I have tried to raise this and similar issues in "Discovering God's Presence."

The saints are the pioneers in each era, bringing into being as yet unrevealed aspects of Christ's inexhaustible holiness.[8]

So there is no generic holiness. This is true for families as well as individuals. No two families are the same and no one pre-determined set of practices, decisions or arrangements "makes" a family holy. It is in the lived struggle, the creative and singular engagement with particularity and grounding in a universal faith that has a rich treasure of resources upon which to draw, that holiness is forged. If out of this struggle faith, hope and love flower, holiness can be identified. I mention this because it seems to me that, on the one hand, the church since the Second Vatican Council has attempted to address families as baptized Christians who are called to genuinely witness to the world. There are many programs available to aid families in crisis or to inform families of their responsibilities as members of the domestic church. There are diocesan offices for marriage and family life. Long-term marriages tend to be publically celebrated. Lay Catholics are encouraged to participate in most aspects of parish life.

On the other hand, the address to families or the teachings about family often seem to be so general and theoretical or so restricted to marriage preparation or sexual ethics that they may fail to inspire the longing for holiness in all aspects of life to which all Catholics are called. Spiritual formation of the laity needs to go beyond instruction in doctrine or catechesis. An example: the spirit of the council is clearly evident in *Familiaris Consortio* (on the family), Pope John Paul II's apostolic exhortation inspired by the 1980 synod on the family and promulgated on November 22, 1981.[9] The document begins by situating the domestic church in its present social and cultural situation. It then identifies the role that the family plays in the larger ecclesial body. The fundamental nature of family is identified as a communion of love particularly dedicated to the transmission and nurturing of life. The exhortation affirms the innate dignity of all members of the family, being specific to describe a family as consisting of two parents and their offspring while mentioning the importance of elders. It considers the family's prime ministry to be the spiritual nurture and education of children in the faith and in the fundamental values that allow human community to flourish. The exhortation likewise considers families as evangelizing communities rooted in the sacramental life of the church and offering service to the larger society and world. This is, clearly, for its moment, an expansive

---

8. Rahner, "Church of the Saints."

9. While the exhortation is decades old at this time, and subsequent statements on family such as Pope Francis' 2016 *Amoris Laetitia* may have modified its approach somewhat, pastoral practice focused on families is still deeply reflective of the vision offered by *Familiaris Consortio*.

vision and an important official placement of family life in its rightful position as one of the many sanctified paths to which baptism might lead. In general, it is a vision that still undergirds most church teaching and Catholic pastoral practice today.

However, *Familiaris Consortio* closes with a discussion of the pastoral care of families, again situating the domestic church primarily within the larger vision of the body of Christ and seeing it as fulfilling its assigned role and doing so by embodying the communion of love through a defined structure and practice. A final segment considers the pastoral care of "difficult" or "irregular" cases, families that one way or another fail to mirror or replicate the domestic church described in the foregoing discussion. Among these are mixed marriages, trial marriage, civil marriage, free unions, divorce, and remarriage.

I do not intend to discuss or raise objections to the moral, theological, or doctrinal issues pertinent here. But I must raise the question: Does a family witness to holiness primarily *because* it replicates a particular structure? Is a family holy *because* it consists of two parents and their children who fulfill all the criteria outlined in *Familiaris Consortio*? Are they holy *because* they show up together each Sunday at Mass? I would hope that a consistent immersion in the deep wisdom of the church's sacramental life *would* worm itself into the hearts of parents and children. That *is* the intent of attendance, is it not? But for attendance to move beyond obligation some fiery quickening of Spirit needs to occur. Put simply: Is holiness synonymous with behaving or appearing to behave in a prescribed way? Does a family's "irregularity" or "difference" inhibit the longing for or realization of the holy? Or is the attempt to foster and realize a communion of love in all sorts of circumstances actually what holiness in family is about?[10]

I would prefer to shift the focus a bit when thinking about the universal call to holiness and the domestic church by giving more attention to the spiritual capability of a variety of families actually found and to the arts of discernment. Holiness, I would contend, is as much about radical openness to the Spirit of God as it is about fulfilling obligations or expectations or the performance of duty. Please don't get me wrong here. I am not advocating that obligations should be shirked or that faithful practice is not essential in spiritual formation. I am simply saying that when we speak of family and holiness I think what is key is to nurture the arts of individual and communal discernment that enable radical availability to God's inrushing Spirit. This is a task not exclusive to the "model" Catholic family. Such discernment

---

10. Theologian Michael G. Lawler argued this some time ago in his *Marriage and Sacrament*.

involves individual and communal immersion in scripture and tradition, attentiveness to wise mentors and the prick of conscience as well as to actual experience, and the deepest of human desires. This is followed by the attempt to sift through all that is peripheral and then to listen again together, sifting and sorting competing impulses, demands and circumstances so that the plumb line that hones toward the ground of love can be felt. Parents need to learn and model these arts in order to be true teachers of their children.[11]

While I fully appreciate *Familiaris Consortio*'s description of the domestic church as a communion of love, I am a bit less convinced that the generalized vision it presents that is hung on the framework of what the "regular" or "not difficult" family should be like unlocks the full promise of the universal call to holiness. God's Spirit cannot pry us open, remake and transform us when we assume that it is only when we have no "problems" or only when we look like the idealized family, that God can and will meet us. Grace tends to find us, not in our sufficiency, as fine as that might be, as in the humility of our insufficiency, our brokenness, and in our particular unique situations. Perhaps what I am trying to say is that forgiveness, mutual compassion, and a shared effort to meet each other half way are some of the classic spiritual practices that allow families to aspire to the unique holiness to which each of them is called. The fruits of such earnest discernment cannot but be a witness to the wider world.

It may be that to really encourage the arts of discernment among Catholic families is a daunting idea to put into practice. But small faith sharing groups, renewal movements, days of reflection, parish missions, and programs in spiritual formation are some of the ways that might happen. Already, plenty of individual Catholics seek out associate programs offered by religious orders or attend prayer groups or seek spiritual direction. Further attention to genuine family formation beyond marriage preparation would be welcome.

Mission to the Wider World

The Vatican Council's later documents, *Gaudium et Spes* and *Ad Gentes*, as well as the ongoing tradition of Catholic social teaching, which seems to be wending its way into the consciousness of Catholic laity in the last several decades, prompt the domestic church to expand its sense of witness beyond the intimate confines of home and personal relationships. Members

11. Volume 4 of David M. Thomas and Mary Joyce Calnan, *The Catechism of the Catholic Church: Family Style*, subtitled "We Pray," does attempt to expand catechetical teaching into the language of family-friendly spiritual formation.

of families are not only parents, children, and in-laws but workers, citizens, consumers, and societal agents. Pope Francis certainly has encouraged the faithful to embrace a perspective that shifts attention away from preoccupation with internal ecclesial issues toward the poignant and pressing issues that trouble the wider human community: poverty, injustice, violence, and the unequal distribution of resources. He has drawn attention to the marginalized across the globe and brought into focus the teaching on the option for the poor that had its roots in the Latin American Episcopal Conferences that followed in the wake of the council.

Both John Paul II and Benedict XVI also oriented Catholics toward the contemporary world. For example, in his 1990 World Day of Peace address John Paul spoke of one of his favored themes, respect for life, and decried the lack of respect for life not only in the realm of individual morality but as evidenced in patterns of environmental pollution and global economic policies that result in the concentration of goods among the few and the creation of conditions of misery for much of the human community.

In light of this wider lens, families are invited anew to consider their lives, this time in the clear light of this broader global human family. The discernments called for here are myriad and require both individual and collective attention. Virtually every aspect of family life, especially in the global north, might well be examined with an eye thus widened. First, and this is what many Catholic families already do, in their roles as educators it is incumbent upon parents to teach their offspring to practice charity— perhaps they already donate toys to tots at Christmastime or visit a nursing home to spend time with the elderly or volunteer to work at Special Olympics games or distribute turkeys at Thanksgiving. These are all worthy charitable enterprises. And they are appropriate for helping children move beyond their own concerns.

But the more fundamental call than charity is justice. In today's global community, indeed in parts of most American cities, poverty, violence, and hunger are rampant. Human migrations caused by unjust policies, war, and economic necessity spill out across the world's borders and environmental degradation encroaches upon us all. This is what opening to the contemporary world means: to weigh the vision of a world inspired by divine love against the stark statistics of a very different global reality.

Parents may need first to inform themselves. They need not seek outside church agencies to be informed. Simply clicking on one of the links on the Catholic Relief Services webpage reveals a startling vision.[12] Then as

12. Nearly 842 million people worldwide are suffering from hunger. Ninety-eight percent of people suffering from hunger live in developing countries. Hunger kills more people every year than AIDS, malaria and tuberculosis combined. Hunger causes the

educators parents need to help their children as they grow older to learn of the reality of the world in which they are growing up and take responsibility for it. At this point in history such a perspective is not simply sentiment for those less fortunate but a clear-eyed assessment of an unstable world that is our questionable legacy to our children and grandchildren. The Catholic domestic church is not only a church of the hearth, a community of nurture and care. The Catholic family must be that, yes. But it must also be a witness to a truly Catholic vision of the dignity of the human person whom Catholic teaching defines as both sacred and social.

Because I have lived it, I am sympathetic to the complex challenges and discernments with which this two-pronged mandate to love confronts families. What does it mean to take care of the persons one has been entrusted to you? To nurture, feed, house, shelter, educate, and prepare your children for the future, to care for your elderly and infirm, to meet the demands of the work that sustains family life, and yet also attend to the cries of the world beyond charitable giving? What does it mean concretely for the domestic church to make an option for the poor? Again, I don't think there is one easy answer, nor one approach that can work for every family or for any given family all the time. And I am aware of the North American economic and societal context in which this must be negotiated, fueled as it is by an unforgiving ethos of individualism and the fierce competiveness of a market-driven economy. But the challenge is real. And the witness is real as well.

One contemporary theologian who has addressed this thoughtfully is Julia Hanlon Rubio, whose *Family Ethics: Practices for Christians* takes its cue from Catholic social teaching.[13] After surveying the resources of Catholic tradition and historical precedents for Catholic families as agents of social change, she suggests common sense practices that have broad social implications, including fidelity, eating justly, tithing, downward lifestyle mobility and prayer as resistance. In the interest of time, I will limit myself here to a consideration of tithing.

I recently taught Hanlon Rubio's book in a graduate course on family to Catholic ministerial students. I was not surprised that the adult participants were receptive to the notion of the family as a communion of love and the idea that marriage and family life could be genuine spiritual paths, although this was a new perspective for a number of them. What did surprise

---

deaths of about five million children each year. About seventeen million children are born underweight annually, the result of inadequate nutrition before and during pregnancy. Information from the Catholic Relief Services website.

13. Rubio, *Family Ethics*. The classic Catholic book on this topic by Kathleen and James McGinnis was updated as *Parenting for Peace and Justice: Ten Years Later*.

me was the extent to which these very good students, most preparing to do lay ministry, had difficulty imagining what it might mean to tithe or if not literally tithe ten percent, even to regularly allocate some portion of family income to others' needs. Parish collections were familiar to them and when most of them thought of service to others they assumed that their parish was attending to the needs of the poor.

They were conversant with the occasional missionary appeal, the Vincent de Paul poor box, or the Christmas food drive. None of them had been to a parish that had a twinning program with a parish in the developing world. Few had ventured out beyond the confines of a middle-class lifestyle. If they had traveled it was mainly to places of relaxation and pleasure. Few of them could imagine why a college-aged daughter or son would want to spend a post-graduate year in the inner city as a volunteer with the Jesuits or Capuchins or Salesians, insisting, in concert with the parents of many of such young people, that advancement toward a corporate job or a medical or law career was what really mattered for the future. Tithing of time and talent like this seemed to some of them to be a frivolous diversion from the expected post-grad itinerary toward *real* life.

The real surprise to me was the difficulty these exemplary Catholics had imagining how their individual families or the families to whom they minister might witness to the social and political dimension of life and, as the smallest unit of church, participate in the enterprise of social transformation. In fact, the options are endless. I am acutely aware that for many families simply making ends meet is a struggle and that in various phases of any family's life, resources, time, and availability are limited. A new baby, young children, job loss, death, elder care, family illness—all these must take priority at certain periods.

But any family can pick its choice of witness and not all witnesses require extravagant time commitments or resources. What it takes is the courage to imagine the Catholic family as a little bit countercultural, not only because of its sexual morality. Families are consumers and workers and citizens and what they buy and do not buy, what work they do, how they vote, what initiatives they support or do not support, how they relate to neighbors and those who are different from them, how and where they spend time, how they treat the land—all this is reflective of their faith. Here is a list of possible questions a Catholic family might ask itself. It is *far* from an exhaustive list. If we are not completely constrained in our work lives, does the work that we do and the way we do it accord with our faith values? What kind of housing do we need (not just want)? What kind of transportation do we have and how many vehicles can we justify? What about energy consumption, electricity, gas, fossil fuels? How much and what kind of clothing and possessions do we need or merely want? What about technology? Or home entertainment? How do our eating practices contribute to the global good and the environment? How do we witness against racial and gender and class stereotypes? How do we view domestic violence or human trafficking? How do we spend our leisure time? Do we monitor TV, cellphone and Internet use? Do we recycle? How do we teach compassion and other-centeredness to our children? What does the option for the poor and the marginalized look like for us? How does what we buy or consume or support affect others beyond our immediate relatives and friends?

These might seem to some families like questions that are only marginally connected to faith. In fact they are central questions entailing discernments that each family is encouraged by our tradition to engage. Certainly, not all families can address all issues at all times. But each can determine where their time and treasure might best be spent. And they might be encouraged from the pulpit to take their role as social agents seriously.

Preaching and Families

I will close with some suggestive reflections on preaching and the witness of the domestic church. I will draw on what might seem to be an unusual source. But my source seems an apt one in the conflicted cultural and ecclesial situation in which we find ourselves today. As suggested, I am a long-time student of Francis de Sales, the seventeenth century French-speaking Savoyard bishop and spiritual writer deemed by later generations a saint and doctor of the church. He is remembered for many things: his gentleness and humility (modeled on Matt 11:28–30) and his persuasive preaching. He also promoted what today we call the universal call to holiness. In fact his teaching was explicitly called upon at the council.[14] What is less known is that de Sales' pastoral style was forged consciously in the context of great conflict and violence. He was bishop of Geneva in exile from his diocese because Geneva was a Calvinist stronghold from which the Catholic faith was banned. Even more striking was the strife within his own Roman fold. France and its neighbors, including Savoy, were religiously divided. The militant (and I mean both militarily and ideologically militant) Catholic League, a zealous wing of the Roman church, opposed the Protestant minority and the accession to the French throne of Protestant-raised Henry of Navarre, who had converted to become king. The violence of the Catholic League extended to members of their own church who would take a more moderate stance toward the Protestant minority and toward Henry's claim.

14. See Suenens, "Saint François de Sales et Vatican II," 23–24.

As an adolescent Francis attended school in the Latin Quarter of Paris, a hotbed of militant Catholic zeal. A critical spiritual crisis—a terror of being eternally alienated from God—was precipitated when he learned of Calvinist theories of predestination and, perhaps more significantly, by the threats of heresy and damnation hurled by his militant co-religionists upon anyone who did not perceive God or the practice of the faith as they did. The story is more complex than can be recounted here but his resolution of the crisis had serious pastoral consequences.

De Sales's vision of a God whose heart is revealed in the gentle, humble Jesus and who enjoins all who hope to be disciples to love as they have been loved has implications for the way he preached. He preached heart to heart, proclaiming the beauty and generosity of a God who desired all to embrace the loving relationships to which they were called—relationships both divine and human. The astonishing thing, from a man living in such an unyieldingly oppositional confessional and intra-religious era, was that he never preached fear or shame or retribution or punishment. He did not denounce enemies, he sought to win friends. He did not preach what the faith was against but what it was for. He drew hearts with his gentle patience and his belief that each person has, deep within, the innate desire to return to the source of life. He did not scold but invite. He did not threaten but offered friendship.

His gracious and unrelenting campaign to counter the militant rigidity of his own confreres as well as those who stood outside the Catholic fold gained him some critics whose vision could not accommodate any mercy for those whose faith seemed less exacting or strictly defined than their own. But it also gained him the love and respect of generations. And it drew innumerable men and women—the majority of them laity—in his own time and since, into the fullness of faith. It shaped them as committed followers of Christ, as lovers of the divine lover who pursues us with persistent tenderness and care.

I have digressed here because all that I have suggested about family and witness in the present age can, I believe, best be approached with many of the same pastoral assumptions that the Savoyard saint held. We are in an era of promise, but also of conflict and division both within and outside the church community. The saint's positive tone, his belief that all persons have an innate goodness and desire to return love to the source of love, his pastoral respect for differences of perspective, his refusal to demonize, to instill fear, or incite division are all relevant in our own time. He sought to form lay persons in the spiritual life by teaching a prayer and discernment and preaching the practice of the virtues, especially the relational virtues of love and friendship. Then he trusted that grace would do its transforming work in those to whom he ministered.

Today in the wake of the ongoing reception of Vatican II, we can affirm with de Sales that all baptized Christians are called to witness to their baptisms through the holiness of their lives. We can also suggest that holiness is manifested chiefly in the quality of the relationships—the love, mercy, forgiveness, reconciliation, encouragement and so forth—that family members cultivate with one another. In terms of present day families realizing the community of love of which Pope John Paul II frequently spoke, more pastoral attention might well be paid to the internal dynamics of family spirituality rather than to particular external forms and behaviors of the ideal family. I have suggested elsewhere, for example, that forgiveness is one of the chief virtues that must be cultivated in the domestic church. I would name a number of other spiritual arts: the capacity to welcome and let go, the tending of an ear capable of deep attentive listening and a heart capable of stretching wide enough to embrace the unpredictable mystery of the others with whom one is called to grow over a lifetime. These are not negligible arts but challenging ones.[15] Families need to be encouraged when they grow and mature, when they fail and wound one another yet return to forgive and embrace one another, when they begin to live into a love that is wide enough to embrace diversity. We might also affirm that holiness is a lived experience of the challenging, healing Spirit moving among us not only in the idealized family but in the many forms of family life encountered today.

The new challenge for Catholic families today, especially as the baptismal call to all Christians to missionary discipleship catches fire, is to straddle the twin dimensions of a unique call that is simultaneously profoundly individual and personal and at the same time social and political. Families are, with the rest of the church, invited to the margins, called to evaluate the ways in which they might uniquely heed the signs of the times and respond to the call to mission in the wider world. To encourage this two-pronged call requires, if Francis de Sales has anything to teach us, an emphasis on transforming families' imaginations through persuasive love and gentleness, on *being* God's love rather than focusing on "getting it all right" or instilling fear and threatening exclusion. It involves deepened attention to the internal dynamics of family life as spiritual path and an expanded awareness of the social and political dimension of family and its missionary call to discipleship. In this way the domestic church might become a true, vibrant local witness to the mystery of God's surprising, unpredictable creative desire to transform the world.

15. These themes are outlined in my *Sacred Dwelling.*

Bibliography

Benson, Robert. *Digging In: Tending to Life in Your Own Backyard*. Colorado Springs: Waterbrook, 2007.

Bourg, Florence Caffrey. *Where Two or Three are Gathered: Christian Families as Domestic Churches*. Notre Dame: University of Notre Dame Press, 2004.

Catholic Relief Services. www.crs.org/get-involved/learn/hunger.

Darling Young, Robin. "Does the Earth Have Rights?" *Commonweal Magazine* (April 30, 2015). www.commonwealmagazine.org/does-earth-have-rights.

Francis. *Evangelii Gaudium*. November 24, 2014. w2.vatican.va/content/francesco/en/apost_exhortations/documents/papa-francesco_esortazione-ap_20131124_evangelii-gaudium.html.

Fischer, Kathleen. *Forgiving Your Family: a Journey to Healing*. Nashville: Upper Room, 2005.

Gaillardetz, Richard. *A Daring Promise: a Spirituality of Christian Marriage*. New York: Crossroad, 2002.

Garland, Diana R. *Sacred Stories of Ordinary Families: Living the Faith in Ordinary Life*. San Francisco: Jossey-Bass, 2003.

Hanlon Rubio, Julia. *A Christian Theology of Marriage and Family*. Mahwah, NJ: Paulist, 2003.

Hanlon Rubio, Julia. *Family Ethics: Practices for Christians*. Washington, DC: Georgetown University Press, 2010.

John Paul II. *Familiaris Consortio*. November 22, 1981. w2.vatican.va/content/john-paul-ii/en/apost_exhortations/documents/hf_jp-ii_exh_19811122_familiaris-consortio.html.

————. "Message of his Holiness Pope John Paul II for the Celebration of the World Day of Peace." January 1, 1990. w2.vatican.va/content/john-paul-ii/en/messages/peace/documents/hf_jp-ii_mes_19891208_xxiii-world-day-for-peace.html.

Kelly, Thomas, et al., eds. *Marriage in the Catholic Tradition: Scripture, Tradition and Experience*. New York: Crossroad, 2004.

Lawler, Michael G. *Marriage and Sacrament: a Theology of Christian Marriage*. Collegeville, MN: Liturgical, 1993.

McGinnis, James, and Kathleen, and McGinnis. *Parenting for Peace and Justice: Ten Years Later*. Maryknoll, NY: Orbis, 1990.

Miller-McLemore, Bonnie J. *In the Midst of Chaos: Caring for Children as Spiritual Practice*. San Francisco: Jossey-Bass, 2006.

Rahner, Karl. "The Church of the Saints." Translated by Karl H. Kruger and Boniface Kruger. In *Theological Investigations*, 3:97–99. New York: Helicon, 1967.

Robinson, David. *The Busy Family's Guide to Spirituality: Practical Lessons for Modern Living From the Monastic Tradition*. New York: Crossroad, 2009.

Roy, Denise. *My Monastery Is a Minivan: 35 Stories from Real Life*. Chicago: Loyola, 2001.

Second Vatican Council. *Lumen Gentium*. November 24, 1964. www.vatican.va/archive/hist_councils/ii_vatican_council/documents/vat-ii_const_19641121_lumen-gentium_en.html.

Suenens, Leon Joseph. "Saint François de Sales et Vatican II." In *Témoignages et Mélanges, Mémoires et Documents publié par l'Académie Salésienne*, 80:23–24. Ambilly-Annemasse: Franco-Suisse, 1968.

Thomas, David M., and Mary Joyce Calnan. *The Catechism of the Catholic Church: Family Style.* Vol. 4. Chicago: More, 1994.

Wright, Wendy M. *Sacred Dwelling: A Spirituality of Family Life.* Rev. ed. New London, CT: Twenty-Third, 2015.

Wright, Wendy M. *Seasons of a Family's Life: Cultivating the Contemplative Spirit at Home.* San Francisco: Jossey-Bass, 2003.

———. "Discovering God's Presence in His Holy Ones: the Feasts of Mary and the Saints." *Assembly: A Journal of Liturgical Theology* 37/2 (2011) 18–24.

Woodward, Kenneth. *Making Saints: How the Catholic Church Determines Who Becomes a Saint and Who Doesn't and Why.* New York: Touchstone, 1996.

Yust, Karen Marie. *Real Kids, Real Faith: Practices for Nurturing Children's Spiritual Lives.* San Francisco: Jossey-Bass, 2004.

12

Baptismal Witness in the World of Commerce[1]

—Oliver F. Williams, C.S.C.

BEFORE THE SECOND VATICAN Council the common understanding of the lay apostolate was participation in the apostolate of the clergy, for example, in such "inner-church" affairs as assisting in the diocesan or parish council, teaching catechetics, serving on financial committees, and serving as extraordinary ministers of the Eucharist. While these roles are not unimportant, Vatican II teaches that the role of the laity, based on baptism, is to evangelize the secular order.[2] The business person has a vocation as a lay apostle to bring the spirit of Christ into the professional world. As a baptized person, the business leader shares in the mission of the church to evangelize and, in fact, by the "Church," Vatican II means all the baptized, not just the clergy or hierarchy.[3]

---

1. Scripture quotations in this chapter are taken from the Holy Bible, New International Version®, NIV®. Copyright © 1973, 1978, 1984, 2011 by Biblica, Inc.™ Used by permission of Zondervan. All rights reserved worldwide. www.zondervan.com The "NIV" and "New International Version" are trademarks registered in the United States Patent and Trademark Office by Biblica, Inc.™

2. Second Vatican Council, *Lumen Gentium*, 31–37; *Gaudium et Spes*, 43; *Apostolicam Actuositatem*, 2–7.

3. Second Vatican Council, *Lumen Gentium*, 31.

It may be helpful to highlight some of the relevant texts from the three Vatican II documents celebrated in this volume. From the *Decree on the Apostolate of the Laity* (*Apostolicam Actuositatem*) comes the clear mandate:

> Christ's redemptive work, while of itself directed toward the salvation of men, involves also the renewal of the whole temporal order. Hence the mission of the Church is not only to bring to men the message and grace of Christ, but also to penetrate and perfect the temporal sphere with the spirit of the gospel. In fulfilling this mission of the Church, the laity, therefore, exercise their apostolate both in the Church and in the world, in both the spiritual and the temporal orders. These realms, although distinct, are so connected in the one plan of God that He Himself intends in Christ to appropriate the whole universe into a new creation, initially here on earth, fully on the last day. In both orders, the layman, being a believer and a citizen, should be constantly led by the same Christian conscience.[4]

The document goes on to say that the "apostolate of the lay person is that of the social milieu or temporal sphere"[5] and that "the laity are to make the church present in those places and in those circumstances where it is only through them that the church can be the salt of the earth."[6] In *Ad Gentes,* the church states: "All sons of the church should have a lively awareness of their responsibility to the world."[7] And in the pastoral constitution *Gaudium et Spes*, we are pointed to the purpose of business: "In the economic and social realms . . . the dignity and complete vocation of the human person and the welfare of society as a whole are to be respected and promoted. For man is the source, the center, and the purpose of all social life."[8]

The Purpose of Business: The Key Issue

In line with the quote above from *Gaudium et Spes* that the person "is the source, the center, and the purpose of all social life," the single-minded focus on making money in business has never been accepted in Catholic social teaching (CST). Religious social thought has long championed a wider role for the purpose of business than simply making profit. Catholic social thought expresses this well in the 1991 encyclical of Pope John Paul

4. Second Vatican Council, *Apostolicam Actuositatem*, 5.
5. Ibid., 7.
6. Ibid., 31.
7. Second Vatican Council, *Ad Gentes*, 36.
8. Second Vatican Council, *Gaudium et Spes*, 69.

II, *Centesimus Annus*. A central thesis of this document is that the purpose of business is not simply to make a profit, but rather, that business is a community of persons and that this community can foster development of society as well as people.[9]

What is thought to be the role of business in society today? I argue that we are in the midst of a major paradigm shift in our understanding of the purpose of business and that this new understanding holds much promise for business being a significant force for peace in our world. What we are seeing is the emergence of a view of the firm as a socially responsible political actor in the global economy and as an institution that can generate not only material wealth, but also wealth that nourishes the full range of human needs, what some call spiritual capital. The purpose of business, then, is to create sustainable value for stakeholders, including employees, suppliers, the community, the environment and, of course, the shareholders.[10] Mirroring the best of secular thought, a 2012 document from the Pontifical Council for Justice and Peace titled *Vocation of the Business Leader* (*VBL*) spells out what it means to create sustainable value for stakeholders by advancing the idea that the purpose of business is to create good goods, good work, and good wealth. Under these three rubrics, the document discusses how sustainable value might be created for the various stakeholders, including employees, suppliers, investors, the poor, the wider community, customers and the environment.[11]

Neoclassical economics asserted a strict division of labor between the private and public sectors. Governments are charged to provide public goods and deal with the challenges of social justice, while collecting taxes to pay for these services. If the people are not pleased with the way elected politicians establish priorities and mediate interests, they can vote them out of office. Business, on the other hand, has another task: to produce goods and services at a reasonable price while returning on investment. Business has made tremendous progress not only in the quantity of goods and services available but also in the quality of life. Technology that enables us to enjoy good music, medicines that increase life expectancy and decrease infant mortality, and machinery that humanizes work are only a few of the fruits of capitalism.

The strict division of labor between the private and public sectors is no longer a reality in our time. Under the rubric of corporate social

---

9. John Paul II, *Centesimus Annus*, 35.

10. For a discussion of the purpose of business, see Williams, *Corporate Social*, 30–50. Also Williams, *Sustainable Development*.

11. Pontifical Council for Justice and Peace, *Vocation*, 38–56.

responsibility (CSR), corporate citizenship or sustainability, companies are taking increasing responsibility for problems in the wider society. At least in practice, there is clearly a change in progress in the way the responsibilities of the private and public sectors are apportioned. Perhaps a major driver of this enlarged role of business in society is the changing expectations of consumers evidenced over recent decades. A 1999 poll by GlobeScan, the Prince of Wales Business Leaders Forum and The Conference Board revealed that two out of three respondents wanted companies to go beyond their traditional economic goals (provide jobs, create wealth, pay taxes and obey laws) and to help solve some of the problems in the wider society. Called the *Millennium Poll on Corporate Social Responsibility* and based on 25,000 interviews, the poll reported that one in five consumers claimed to reward or punish companies based on their perception of the companies' social performance.[12]

In contemporary business literature, the term "license to operate" is often used to convey the idea that meeting society's expectations is part of the implicit social contract between business and society. Failing to meet society's expectations can result in tough regulation, for example, the 2002 Sarbanes-Oxley law and the 2010 Dodd-Frank Wall Street Reform and Consumer Protection Act, resulting in a loss of discretionary power. This may explain why many companies have become proactive in meeting society's expectations; some, for example, by collaborating with NGOs in designing and implementing ethical norms for the global community. Companies either alone or partnering with NGOs have taken on numerous projects to assist the poor around the globe. Motives are always difficult to fathom, but clearly some business leaders want to reach out to the poor because they are concerned. In a November 2004 *Fortune* article about his company's projects throughout the world, Jeffrey Immelt, CEO of General Electric, commented: "The reason people come to work for GE is that they want to be about something that is bigger than themselves. People want to work hard, they want to get promoted, they want stock options. But they also want to work for a company that makes a difference, a company that's doing great things in the world."[13] Building community and doing great things in the world are goals that flow from the identity and culture of a business; for some business leaders they are intrinsic objectives and are not designed to make more money for the business.[14]

12. GlobeScan, *Millennium Poll*, 1999.

13. Gunther, "Money and Morals," 1.

14. Collins and Porras, *Built to Last*. See also Mackey and Sisodia, *Conscious Capitalism*.

What we are experiencing is that, under the influence of the wider society, there is a broadening of the values of many business people and, hence, a broadening of the values of capitalism. To be sure, this phenomenon is not present in all business, but a growing number of business people want to make a difference. They are asking about ultimate purpose, about what most deeply matters in life, and they want to chart a life plan that draws on the full range of resources of the human spirit. This new focus is what many describe as a focus on spiritual values. From this standpoint, sustainability reflects the connectedness of business with the wider society. Business must not only take responsibility for its own activities, but also for some of the problems in the wider society.

This wider vision of companies, the belief that doing well and doing good are not opposites, is championed by many management scholars and business leaders. Jerry Porras and Jim Collins in *Built to Last*,[15] as well as John Mackey of Whole Foods, discuss a number of these "visionary companies." A business leader, John Mackey, founder and CEO of Whole Foods, sees business as a high calling, a noble vocation, and its purpose is creating sustainable value for stakeholders. Value is not simply financial value, but value for employees, customers, the physical environment, communities, and so on. While Whole Foods employees feel good about their company and this has reportedly enhanced productivity and decreased turnover of employees, this concern for creating value for all stakeholders is part of the DNA of the company and is not single-mindedly driven by profit motivation. Companies that have an overarching view that their mission is to make the world a better place, which also creates more sustainable value for stakeholders, often have leaders who believe in the dignity of the human person based on human rights as, for example, stated in the UN's 1948 Declaration of Human Rights, or on the notion of a religious vocation.[16]

UN Global Compact

One relatively new initiative to promote and enhance peaceful societies based on the 1948 UN Declaration of Human Rights is the United Nations Global Compact. Founded in 2000 by the then-secretary-general of the UN, Kofi Annan, the Global Compact is intended to increase and diffuse the benefits of global economic development through voluntary corporate policies and programs. By promoting human rights and labor rights, enhancing care for the environment and encouraging anti-corruption measures,

15. Ibid.

16. Global Compact, United Nations.

the, principles of the Global Compact are designed to enable more peaceful societies. Initially composed of several dozen companies, the compact as of 2017 included over 9,000 businesses and 1,500 NGOs in 135 countries. The objective is to emphasize the moral purpose of business, with member companies setting a high moral tone throughout the world. Former UN Secretary-General Ban Ki-moon expressed the mission well: "Business practices rooted in universal values can bring social and economic gains."

The mission of the Global Compact is to foster the growth of humane values in global society. The underlying insight is that without the values embedded in the Compact—for example, trust, fairness, integrity, and respect for people—global capitalism would eventually lose legitimacy in the wider society.[17] There is much evidence from surveys on trust that people are increasingly losing trust in business. Public trust in business institutions and leadership is at a low level. For example, the 2012 Edelman Trust Barometer—an annual survey that measures public trust in business and institutions—found that globally, only 29 percent trust information about a business provided by the CEO. In the United States, only 38 percent trust business to do the right thing. As people come to trust business less and to judge that trusting the behavior of business is risky, there is more pressure for stronger organizational control systems, that is, rules, regulations and laws.

When people perceive that business is not only seeking its private good but also the common good, and that this is embodied in a mission statement and a widened purpose and activity, there is a slow retrieval of trust in business. This retrieval of trust is manifest in the response to some of the endeavors of signatory companies of the Global Compact. In the book, *Peace Through Commerce*, ten case stories of what companies are doing are presented in some detail.[18] For example, in rural sub-Saharan Africa, General Electric provided equipment, and, perhaps more importantly, management skills so that the indigenous people could be a part of the project, taking ownership and improving the clinics and hospitals. The GE program in Africa has been cited as a good example of how to aid a developing country. Employees of GE are proud to be part of this program.[19]

17. See Williams, "Responsible Corporate," 431–52.
18. Greenhut and Corcoran, "General Electric," 349–66.
19. Ibid.

Business Leadership as a Noble Vocation

This essay argues that a growing number of business leaders and firms are taking on projects in the wider society to alleviate poverty. This is done by many leaders, not because business caused these problems, but rather, because these executives are thinking and feeling human beings who realize that their organizations might have the managerial talent and resources to act where governments are unable or unwilling to do so. These leaders have a sense of being called upon to make a difference, to make the world a better place for them having been there.

This "calling" is often paired with the term "vocation." (The Latin vocare means to call).[20] This "servant leadership" perceives the interconnectedness among life and all its enterprises, especially business and the environment. While it is true that some of this activity is done simply to respond to society's expectations, there is a growing number of leaders who do it because they believe it is the right thing to do. When Pope Benedict XVI visited the United Nations in New York City on April 18, 2008, he wrote a powerful yet succinct message in the visitors' book: "Erit opus iustitiae pax" (Justice will bring about peace.) Taken from the Book of Isaiah (Is 32:17), this theme captures the flavor of much of CST.

Work can be understood in one of three ways: as a job, a career, or a vocation—or some combination of the three. When work is thought of as a job it is done for extrinsic motivation, for example students working for the summer flipping burgers may be only working for the money to pay tuition; they have a job. An accountant who has studied in college and mastered the skills to be an effective officer in a business has a career; she does work that is personally satisfying and has self-esteem based on successful achievements. This is intrinsic motivation. A person with a vocation has an overarching world view, some idea of what life is all about and how he fits in the grand scheme of things. He sees that talents and skills are to serve and develop others, in terms of the Christian message, to build up the Kingdom of God. In each of these three notions of work, leisure plays a differing role. In work as a job, leisure is amusement, activity that helps us forget the boring work we do. Perhaps it is playing on the Internet or drinking with friends. In work as a career, leisure is time out for a rest so that we can continue to be effective and productive. In work as a vocation, leisure is contemplation, time to receive what God has done for us; it entails such things as some solitude, weekly Mass and the habit of service.[21]

20. McGee and Delbecq have a good discussion of vocation in "Vocation," 94–110.

21. Pontifical Council for Justice and Peace, *Vocation*, 68.

Only with contemplation are we able to nourish and refresh our overarching world view as a co-creator in the Kingdom of God.[22] A problem for many Christians is that they regularly check their Christian values at the office door—they lead a divided life. *Gaudium et Spes* called this split "one of the more serious errors of our age."[23] "Dividing the demands of one's faith from one's work in business is a fundamental error which contributes to much of the damage done by business in our world today."[24] Business leaders who do not see themselves serving others and God in their working lives will fill the void of purpose with a less worthy substitute."[25]

The Vocation of a Business Leader: A Practical Handbook

As referred to in the previous pages, the notion of business as a vocation has been highlighted in a recent Vatican document. On March 30, 2012, Cardinal Peter Turkson, president of the Pontifical Council for Justice and Peace (now part of the Dicastery for Promoting Integral Human Development, headed by Turkson), issued a document titled *Vocation of the Business Leader: A Reflection.*[26] In practical, down-to-earth terms, these reflections outline CST and offer a set of questions designed to enlist business leaders in the difficult task of applying the principles.

The opening line of the executive summary of the document sets the tone of the reflections: "When businesses and market economies function properly and focus on serving the common good, they contribute greatly to the material and even the spiritual well-being of society."[27] Thus business not only produces goods and services but it also cultivates virtue; this is a remarkable affirmation of the role of business in society.

Following the approach of Cardinal Joseph Cardijn and the Young Christian Workers movement of almost a century ago, the document employs the three stages of seeing, judging, and acting.[28] A brief summary of these reflections may be helpful.

22. Ibid., 69.

23. Second Vatican Council, *Gaudium et Spes*, 43. This divided life is also a focus of *Vocation*, 10.

24. Pontifical Council for Justice and Peace, *Vocation*, 10.

25. Ibid.

26 25 The text is available at www.pcgp.it/dati/2012-05/04-999999/Vocation%20 ENG2.pdf.

27. Pontifical Council for Justice and Peace, *Vocation*, executive summary, 2.

28. This section summarizes some of the highpoints of paragraphs 15–80 in *Vocation*.

1. Seeing. While there is much that is good in our time, four new developments present major challenges. The developments are "signs of the times."[29]

    a. Globalization. Movement across borders has brought new efficiencies and vast new markets for business but it has also exacerbated inequalities and lessened the power of states to monitor and affect business for the common good.

    b. Communications technology. While technology has brought lower costs, much easier connectivity around the globe, and new products and services, the speed of communications has given new focus to short-term decision making and information overload.

    c. Financialization. Today the revenue and profits from the financial sector dominate the global economy. Emphasis on wealth maximization and short-term profits can easily overshadow concern for the common good.

    d. Broader cultural changes. We are living in a time when focus on individual rights often clouds concern for the common good. The erosion of family life, the stress of private goods at the expense of public goods, the neglect of duties that are entailed with rights, and the single-minded focus on wealth maximization are all factors that can lead to the neglect of shaping a healthy society.

2. Judging. For a Christian, the fundamental principles that inform all business decisions concern core principles of CST, such as respect for human dignity, the notion that business ought to be a community, and power as service for the common good. With these principles in mind, the business leader will try to produce goods and services that meet the needs of the world while at the same time considering the social and environmental issues involved, not only for the company but the supply and distribution networks, as well. Work will be structured taking into account the people involved and their flourishing. Justice will be sought in not only wages, but taxes, prices, as well as returns for shareholders. In all of this, business leaders are always alert to find new opportunities to serve the poor.

3. Acting. It is third dimension of acting as leaders who serve God that is the most troublesome for many in business. So often our definition of success and thus our judgment refers only to financial success. It is

---

29. *Gaudium et Spes* calls us to scrutinize "the signs of the times" and "to interpret them in the light of the Gospel," 4. *Vocation of the Business Leader* follows this call, 15.

very easy to compartmentalize, to check our ethical and religious principles at the office door. One may be a wonderful Christian at home and in the community but the workplace is off limits for Christian principles and action. This third dimension is a reminder that overcoming a divided life and bringing a vision into the world based on CST require an active spiritual life, prayer, and an acknowledgement of God's presence and gifts.

The document concludes with "A Discernment Checklist for the Business Leader." It is here that the genius of the document is most manifest. While there are hard questions here, there are no answers. The questions are informed by CST and the answers must come from those many intelligent business leaders who are pursuing a Christian way of life. It may be helpful to include the full text of the checklist here.[30]

A Discernment Checklist for the Business Leader

- Do I see work as a gift from God?
- Is my work as a "co-creator" truly a participation in God's original creative act?
- Do I promote a culture of life through my work?
- Have I been living a divided life, separating Gospel principles from my work?
- Am I receiving the sacraments regularly and with attention to how they support and inform my business practices?
- Am I reading the Scriptures and praying with the will to avoid the risk of a divided life?
- Am I sharing my spiritual path with other Christian business practitioners (my peers)?
- Am I seeking to nourish my business life by learning more about the church's social teaching?
- Do I believe that taking seriously the dignity of the person in my business decision-making will promote integral human development while making my company more efficient, more agile, and more profitable?

---

30. The checklist is taken directly from *Vocation*, appendix, 26–27.

Meeting the Needs of the World

- Do I see the responsibilities of my company as extending to all the participants who contribute to its life, not simply to the interests of the owners?

- Am I creating wealth, or am I engaging in rent-seeking behavior?

- Am I engaging in anti-competitive practices?

- Is my company making every reasonable effort to take responsibility for externalities and unintended consequences of its activities (such as environmental damage or other negative effects on suppliers, local communities and even competitors)?

- Do I recognize the importance of strong and lively "indirect employers" to ensure the right levels of labor protection and community dialogue?

- Am I sensitive to the fact that if corporate decisions are not deeply grounded in the dignity of the human person, they will be prone to instrumentalist and utilitarian constructs which fail to promote integral human development within business?

- Do I regularly assess the degree to which my company provides products or services which address genuine human needs and which foster responsible consumption?

Organizing Good and Productive Work

- Do I provide working conditions which allow my employees appropriate autonomy at each level? In other words, am I organizing human resources mindful of the subsidiarity principle in my company management system?

- Am I assuming the risk of lower level decisions to assure that his (*sic*) autonomy is genuine?

- Are jobs and responsibilities in my company designed to draw upon the full talents and skills of those doing the jobs?

- Have employees been selected and trained to be able to meet fully their responsibilities?

- Have these responsibilities and their scope been clearly defined?

- Am I making sure that the company provides safe working conditions, living wages, training, and the opportunity for employees to organize themselves?

- Have I embedded a set of comprehensively defined values and integrated that into my performance measurement process? Am I honest with my employees about their performance?

- In all countries where my company is engaged, is it honoring the dignity of those indirectly employed and contributing to the development of the communities hosting these operations? (Do I follow the same standard of morality in all geographic locations?)

- Do I place the dignity of all workers above profit margins?

Creating Sustainable Wealth and Distributing It Justly

- As a business leader, am I seeking ways to deliver fair returns to providers of capital, fair wages to employees, fair prices to customers and suppliers, and fair taxes to local communities?

- Does my company honor all its fiduciary obligations to providers of capital and to local communities with regular and truthful financial reporting?

- In anticipation of economic difficulties, is my company taking care that employees remain employable through appropriate training and variety in their work experiences?

- When economic difficulties demand layoffs, is my company giving adequate notifications, employee transition assistance, and severance pay?

- Does my company make every effort to reduce or eliminate waste in its operations, and in general to honor its responsibility for the natural environment?

The Ministry of Preaching and the *VBL*

In the Bible the term "vocation" or "calling" often has a broader meaning, that is, God's call for people to come to Christ and participate in the redemptive work in the world (Rom 1:6; Rom 8:28). In this reflection, vocation is used to mean God's guidance to advance creation in a particular kind of work (Gen 2:15, 19–20). Given the vast needs of the world and the unique gifts one might have received, a person is obliged to act. The Gospel for the Nineteenth Sunday in Ordinary Time, Year C, has the text that underlies Catholic social thinking on vocation: "From everyone who has been given much, much will be demanded; and from the one who has been entrusted with much, much will be asked (Luke 12:48). This text opens *VBL* and sets the tone for all of its reflections.[31]

Echoing Pope Benedict XVI in the encyclical letter *Caritas in Veritate*,[32] the notion of vocation or calling is built upon the "Logic of Gift." The call for business leaders to do great things in making the world a better place is based on the fact that these business leaders have been given great resources, not only high intelligence, but also a spirit of entrepreneurship and exceptional talents. *VBL* stresses that the meaning and purpose provided by CST gives the business leader the possibility for a happy and fulfilled life. Leaders come to see that God has a purpose for them in the work they do.

Moving beyond the notion of a life's work as a job or a career, a life's work as a vocation is informed by reflection on the scriptures, contemplation, and prayer. It is this kind of leisure which will likely enable a leader to "see" what should be done to advance the Kingdom of God. *VBL* states it well: "Sacramental worship is not an *escape* from the world of business—it gives us the space to see more deeply into the *reality* of the world and to contemplate God's work."[33]

Conclusion

Business leaders with a conscience will find a helpful moral compass with the guidance of CST, especially the document *Vocation of the Business Leader*. They will also find like-minded colleagues, men and women striving to lead sustainable businesses, in the membership of the United Nations Global Compact. Cardinal Turkson acknowledged this when he introduced the *Vocation of the Business Leader* in an address to the UNIAPAC World Congress in Lyon, France, on March 30, 2012: "Fortunately, we are witnessing a change in business, a new tendency among organizations, both public and private, to view profit as a *means for achieving human and social ends*— in other words, as an opportunity to serve the common good."[34] Today there are over a hundred local networks of UN Global Compact companies where

31. Pontifical Council for Justice and Peace, *Vocation*, 1.

32. Benedict XVI, *Caritas in Veritate*, 36.

33. Pontifical Council for Justice and Peace, *Vocation*, 69.

34. Turkson, "Vocation of the Business Leader."

leaders can share hopes and dreams, as well as learn from each other. I, for one, have great confidence that business can help us as we work towards a better world for all and empowering the lay apostolate with CST will play no small role in advancing the Kingdom of God.

Bibliography

Benedict XVI. *Caritas in Veritate*. June 29, 2009. w2.vatican.va/content/benedict-xvi/en/encyclicals/documents/hf_ben-xvi_enc_20090629_caritas-in-veritate.html.

Collins, James C., and Jerry I. Porras. *Built to Last: Successful Habits of Visionary Companies*. New York: HarperBusiness, 1994.

Corcoran, Robert, and Marshall Greenhut. "General Electric and Corporate Citizenship: Improving the Health of the Poor in Africa." In *Peace through Commerce*, edited by Oliver F. Williams, 349–66. Notre Dame: University of Notre Dame Press, 2008.

Delbecq, André L., and James J. McGee. "Vocation as a Critical Factor in a Spirituality for Executive Leadership in Business." In *Business, Religion, and Spirituality*, edited by Oliver F. Williams, 94–110. Notre Dame: University of Notre Dame Press, 2003.

GlobeScan. *The Millennium Poll on Corporate Social Responsibility*. 1999. www.globescan.com/news_archives/MPExecBrief.pdf.

Gunther, Marc. "Money and Morals at GE." *Fortune*, November 1, 2004, 1.

John Paul II. *Centesimus Annus*. May 1, 1991, w2.vatican.va/content/john-paul-ii/en/encyclicals/documents/hf_jp-ii_enc_01051991_centesimus-annus.html.

Mackey, John, and Raj Sisodia. *Conscious Capitalism*. Cambridge: Harvard Business Review Press, 2013.

Pontifical Council for Justice and Peace. *Vocation of the Business Leader: A Reflection*. www.pcgp.it/dati/2012-05/04-999999/Vocation%20ENG2.pdf.

Second Vatican Council. *Ad Gentes*. December 7, 1965. www.vatican.va/archive/hist_councils/ii_vatican_council/documents/vat-ii_decree_19651207_ad-gentes_en.html.

———. *Gaudium et Spes*. December 7, 1965. www.vatican.va/archive/hist_councils/ii_vatican_council/documents/vat-ii_const_19651207_gaudium-et-spes_en.html.

———. *Lumen Gentium*. November 24, 1964. www.vatican.va/archive/hist_councils/ii_vatican_council/documents/vat-ii_const_19641121_lumen-gentium_en.html.

———. *Apostolicam Actuositatem*. November 18, 1965. www.vatican.va/archive/hist_councils/ii_vatican_council/documents/vat-ii_decree_19651118_apostolicam-actuositatem_en.html.

Turkson, Peter. "Vocation of the Business Leader." Address to the UNIAPAC World Congress in Lyon, France. March 30, 2012. Text at *Union of Catholic Asian News*, spirituality.ucanews.com/2013/06/25/the-vocation-of-the-business-leader/.

United Nations. Global Compact. www.globalcompact.org/WHAT-IS-GC/OUR-WORK/SOCIAL/HUMAN-RIGHTS.

Williams, Oliver F. *Corporate Social Responsibility: The Role of Business in Sustainable Development*. Global Institutions Series 79. New York: Routledge, 2014.

———. "Responsible Corporate Citizenship and the Ideals of the United Nations Global Compact." In *Peace through Commerce*, edited by Oliver F. Williams, 431–52. Notre Dame: University of Notre Dame Press, 2008.

———, ed. *Sustainable Development*. Notre Dame: University of Notre Dame Press, 2014.

13

Lay Ecclesial Ministry as One Flowering of Baptismal Witness

—Zeni Fox

LAY ECCLESIAL MINISTRY IS a topic that I have thought about a great deal. In fact, I have been immersed in it, have not only researched it, but have taught many LEMs and had conversations with many, many more. It is the lay ecclesial ministers who have posed to me, by their lives in ministry, many of the questions that I am still pondering.

However, each time that I began to think about how to respond to the request to address "Lay Ecclesial Ministry as One Flowering of Baptismal Witness" it was a conversation with Fr. David Power, the great twentieth-century liturgist, that kept coming to mind. First, the back story. In August, 2001, ten theologians had been asked to spend eight days together in Collegeville, Minnesota, discussing papers we had prepared on lay and ordained ministry. We did not present the papers, rather we pondered together what we had written. We then sought points of convergence, of consensus, seeking to articulate a contemporary theology of both lay and ordained ministry.[1] One of the seven "points of convergence" was, "Baptism is an initiation into the life of Christ and the way of discipleship in the Church by which

---

1. Wood (professor at St. John's, then Marquette) had convened us and facilitated the conversation. She also edited the resulting volume, *Ordering the Baptismal Priesthood*.

all participate in the mission of the Church. It is the ground for all discussion of ministry . . . [T]he most fundamental ordering of the Church occurs in Baptism."[2] At some point in our discussion, David Power said that as a church community, we will truly recognize this when we celebrate baptism with the same solemnity as we celebrate Holy Orders. You can understand why this comment has stayed in my mind, and why I invite you to ponder this with me. My reflection here has four parts: a reflection on baptism, some stories about ritual, the emergence of lay ecclesial ministry, and some current developments in lay ecclesial ministry.

Looking Back to the Beginning

Let us first reflect briefly on the earliest writings of our church, first, the letters of Paul. An early articulation of the theological meaning of baptism is developed by Paul, especially in First Corinthians, Galatians and Romans. You know the text well:

> Do you not know that all of us who have been baptized into Christ Jesus were baptized into his death? Therefore we have been buried with him by baptism into death, so that, just as Christ was raised from the dead by the glory of the Father, so we too might walk in newness of life . . . The death [Jesus] died, he died to sin, once for all; but the life he lives, he lives to God. So you also must consider yourselves dead to sin and alive to God in Christ Jesus. (Rom 6:3–4, 10–11)[3]

In this passage we hear that baptism initiates us into union with Christ suffering and dying—something I will return to at a later point. And that it unites us with the Risen Christ, so that we may live a new life, including a life "for God"—which by implication describes sharing in the mission and ministry of Jesus.

In Acts, we note again and again that baptism was central to the life of the earliest Christian communities. Chapter 2 describes Peter's preaching on Pentecost, and concludes, "And he testified with many other arguments and exhorted them, saying, 'Save yourselves from this corrupt generation.' So

2. Ibid., 257.

3. Scripture quotations in this chapter are taken from the New Revised Standard Version Bible, copyright 1989, Division of Christian Education of the National Council of the Churches of Christ in the United States of America. Used by permission.

those who welcomed his message were baptized, and that day about three thousand persons were added" (Acts 2:40–41). In chapter 8 we read of Philip's preaching, and that when they believed Philip, who was proclaiming the good news about the kingdom of God and the name of Jesus Christ, "they were baptized, both men and women" (Acts 8:12). Paul himself was baptized by Ananias, during his time of retreat after his encounter with the Lord on the road to Damascus. A sense of urgency is in the words recording this: "He got up and was baptized" (Acts 9:18). Paul in turn baptized; in Corinth twelve men, already believers, were baptized in the name of the Lord Jesus. "When Paul had laid his hands on them, the Holy Spirit came upon them" (Acts 19:6). And when Peter visits the house of Cornelius, a Roman centurion, the inclusion in the community of the baptized expands beyond the Jews. "And as I began to speak, the Holy Spirit fell upon them just as it had upon us at the beginning . . . If then God gave them the same gift that he gave us when we believed in the Lord Jesus Christ, who was I that I could hinder God?" (Acts 11:15–17; cf. Acts 10:44–48). Acts attests to this practice of administering baptism to groups and individuals who believed in Jesus the Christ, based on the preaching of the apostles. This is almost like a refrain, sounded again and again, in this story of the early church.

A favorite early church writing of mine is *The Didache*, which some scholars date as early as AD 60 to 70. (I have always defined myself as a teacher, which is why this text for first-century teachers is so important to me.) It is very short, in my translation less than ten pages. It outlines the way of life Christians should follow and devotes two pages to beautifully describing the Eucharistic celebration. It also describes a ritual for baptism, saying in part, "Baptize as follows: after first explaining these points, *baptize in the name of the Father and of the Son and of the Holy Spirit,* in running water."[4]

All of these texts attest to the importance of baptism in the life of the early church, and, central to my thesis, the importance of the ritual celebration of baptism. The texts do not offer the same evidence of the ritual celebration of Holy Orders. The New Testament certainly does tell of Jesus calling disciples, and within that larger group, calling The Twelve. Further, it shows that the leadership of the Twelve was central in the early life of the community. The Pastorals, very late New Testament books, attest to a growing emphasis on the qualities that church leaders should have. *The Didache* also describes what qualities to seek in "bishops and deacons" but gives

---

4. Quasten, ed., *Didache*, 19.

much fuller descriptions of the teachers and prophets clearly active in the communities the authors knew.[5] The church's understanding of Holy Orders certainly developed over time. But in the early church, it was baptism (and Eucharist) which were most solemnly celebrated.

A small digression. The sense of the solemnity with which baptism was celebrated during the first millennium can be seen when viewing the truly grand baptisteries that were built, often adjacent to cathedrals—in Florence, Pisa, Rome, Parma, Ravenna, Padua, Aix-en-Provence, Kiev, to name just some. Often catechumens were catechized there, and of course baptism was celebrated by immersion. These beautiful structures remain to remind us of the solemn rituals they housed.

Twentieth-century Snapshots

My mother was born in 1915. Between her memory, shared in stories with me over the years, and my own, I would like to give some snapshots of the celebration of baptism during the middle of the twentieth century until today.

My mother attended my baptism, at a time when most mothers stayed at home; it was a simple ritual. She also went to the baptisms of my three younger siblings, but did not bring me. The font was not in the main church, and certainly not in a baptistery. Again, simple rituals, certainly valued by the Catholic faithful, but without the solemnity attested to by the great baptisteries.

As we move into the time after the Second Vatican Council, remember with me experiences of baptisms you have attended. In the generation of my nieces and nephews, each of them was baptized with many extended family members and friends gathered round. At one, two older siblings carried the small banner they had made for their sister; it hung in their living room for years. At another, each of the elders present was asked to trace the sign of the cross on the foreheads of the infants. (My bachelor uncle said it was the most beautiful baptism he had ever attended—I think because he was invited to participate in a meaningful way.) And now another generation, the baptisms of my grandnieces and nephews. At one, the priest invited all the children present to gather around the baptismal pool, to sit, to watch, to learn—putting their hands in the water to bless themselves, listening to

5. Quasten, ed., *Didache*, 22–24.

what was said, observing what was done, joining in the singing (catechizing, really). At my parish, at one Sunday Mass, the naked infant was lifted from the font and held high as we sang Alleluia; she was later carried in the recessional by the presider, as all rejoiced. These were solemn celebrations, at times with the font itself given new prominence, always with music and a gathered community.

Perhaps the fullest expression of this new consciousness is the celebration of baptism at the Easter Vigil at the conclusion of the RCIA (*Rite of Christian Initiation of Adults*) process. These rituals are actions of the entire gathered community; music and flowers accent the importance of the moment. There is deep intentionality, the catechumens, the sponsors, the RCIA team, the community itself, having shared in a slow journey, a journey of conversion, a journey of growth in understanding of baptism as a dying with Christ to one's old self, and a rising to new life. Here, full, conscious and active participation come to fruition and lead to greater participation in the life and mission of the church.

As we compare the celebrations of the first part of the twentieth century to those of the latter part, and of our own century, we can see the flowering of the teachings of Vatican II—the centrality of baptism in Christian life, full, conscious and active participation in the liturgy, the role of the entire community in our sacramental celebrations, and the role of music and art and symbolic gesture. This changed consciousness is present in the whole church—priests who plan participative celebrations, architects who design fonts so that they are once again central in our worship spaces, parents and family members who *show up* to celebrate.

During these years, I also participated in many celebrations related to ordination. In the 1950s, more than once my parish had a newly ordained's first Mass. Processions were always part of the life of my Polish community, and those for these Masses were rivaled only by Corpus Christi celebrations. (These included a procession to four altars placed around the entire block.) Every society participated, each with a distinctive banner, as ranks of altar boys, young girls in gowns, children in First Communion attire all slowly processed. Pillows on which the paten and chalice were enthroned were carried, there was a joyous pealing of the bells, as the procession proceeded a full block down the street from the school, and around the corner into the church, where the aisles were so full that periodically everything stalled.

And what of the conferring of Holy Orders? In recent years, I have attended more ordinations to the diaconate and to priesthood than I can count. And these are indeed solemn celebrations! A long procession of bishops, then priests. Joyous music. In the soaring space of the cathedral. The symbol-laden ceremonies themselves, so richly evocative—invocations,

promises, vestings, prostrations, calling on the saints of long ago and of today, receiving of symbols of office. At times they have taken my breath away.
These rituals, too, have been re-shaped by Vatican II—in fact, the permanent diaconate is re-born because of that council.

I wish I could ask David Power for his reflection on these post-council
rituals of baptism and Holy Orders. What would he say? And I wonder what
would happen if baptism were celebrated with much greater solemnity than
it is today? What greater changes in the consciousness of the faithful would
gradually take place as ritual and symbol did their work of shaping the religious imagination? Might this more effectively create missionary disciples
than words alone can do? Might the laity grasp more fully the way in which
we have died and risen with Christ, to live now in Him, to carry on His
work? These questions implicitly inform the next section of my reflections.

Emergence of Lay Ecclesial Ministry

Where did lay ecclesial ministers come from? I deeply believe that they arose
from the heart of the church, and that it was the Second Vatican Council
that initiated this gift. This conviction initially formed when I listened to my
students, young men and women who had embarked on a path preparing
for professional ministry. My dissertation, and then my work, *New Ecclesial Ministry: Lay Professionals Serving the Church*, were my first attempts
to explore the implications of this new development. To do so I traced the
multiple factors involved in calling lay men and women into professional
ministry—the work of the individuals themselves often first as volunteers
in ministry (actually, at the beginning, the word ministry was not yet even
used), invitations from pastors, the definition of roles by parish councils and
committees, formation programs offered by dioceses, colleges, universities
and seminaries. I also noted the involvement of groups such as the Canon
Law Society, professional organizations of ministers, liturgists and theologians—all of whom reflected on this sign of the times and sought to understand this development in light of our tradition. There was no single cause;
there was no directive from church authority, not in the local church, not in
the universal church. The church as a whole brought this forth, at the grass
roots. In 1980, in a document commemorating the fifteenth anniversary of
the proclamation of *The Decree on the Apostolate of the Laity*, the United
States bishops for the first time officially recognized "growing numbers of
lay women and men . . . preparing themselves professionally to work in the

church . . . ecclesial ministers . . . represent a new development. We welcome this as a gift to the Church."[6]

The number of lay ecclesial ministers grew rapidly. Msgr. Philip Murnion's studies of 1992 and 1997 indicated that "The number of lay parish ministers, i.e., religious and lay in pastoral roles . . . and paid for at least 20 hours a week, has increased by 35 percent, from 21,569 in 1992 to 29,146 . . . in 1997."[7] Today there are nearly 39,600 lay ecclesial ministers in the United States, nearly double the number there were in 1992.[8] It is important to note that these statistics do not have the precision of those relative to priests and permanent deacons, because there is a distinct moment when men become a priest, a deacon. There is no such clarity relative to lay ecclesial ministers, and even the definition has some variation from diocese to diocese.

In part, *New Ecclesial Ministry* reports the result of a survey of lay people employed in professional roles in parishes that I had conducted in 1985. One statistic is particularly relevant for our consideration here:

> The new ministers think that the authority they need to exercise their roles is delegated to them, and accepted by the parishioners. The ministers also state that they function as leaders in their settings. When asked to rank in order what gives them their authority for their work in the Church, they responded Baptism and Confirmation, with a strong preference for this response. Professional training and competence were ranked second, and a vocation from God third.[9]

Clearly, for the majority of these ministers, baptism and confirmation were central. However, in reviewing *Called and Gifted* and the document published fifteen years later, *Called and Gifted for the Third Millennium*[10] I noted that while call is given significant prominence, baptism is not. The most definitive work of the United States bishops on this reality, *Co-Workers in the Vineyard of the Lord*,[11] begins with a beautiful reflection on "The Call to All Believers," "The Call to the Lay Faithful," and "The Call to Lay Ecclesial Ministry." Discussing discernment of a call to lay ecclesial ministry, the bishops state: "Among the baptized, all of whom are called to serve the

---

6. United States Conference of Catholic Bishops, *Called and Gifted*, 4.

7. DeLambo and Murnion, *Parishes*, iii.

8. CARA Research Review, "Lay Ecclesial Ministers."

9. Fox, *New Ecclesial*, 62.

10. United States Conference of Catholic Bishops, *Called and Gifted*.

11. United States Conference of Catholic Bishops, *Co-Workers*, 7–11.

mission of the Church, some experience a further specific call to lay ecclesial ministry."[12] This is the only significant reference to baptism.

It seems to me that the concept of call, of vocation, has superseded the centrality of baptism. I think that part of the reason for this is that for both priests and vowed religious the discernment of their vocation has been so central in their lives, and therefore gradually it has been emphasized by and in reference to lay people. You might ask, what difference does it make? Vocation is a rich theological, spiritual concept, one honored in the life of the church. I see three reasons to favor baptism as the more central reality. First, it accords with the emphasis of the early church, in fact, for the church of the first millennia. Second, it is a more deeply ecclesial, a more radically communal experience and concept. And third, it reminds us that as Christians we enter into the suffering, indeed the death, of Jesus. I have already explored with you the centrality of baptism in the life of the early church. Let us think together about these additional reasons.

We live in an age and a culture where individualism is predominant. There is much that can be celebrated when we note the ways in which the individual is valued in our society—laws that protect, schools that foster personal growth (for example, critical thinking, and not rote learning), and an ongoing flowering of innovation. However, many forms of community life are significantly weakened, including that of our own parishes. Although as a church we emphasize that an individual's vocation must be both personally and communally discerned, it seems that the interior, personal, individual dimension of vocation is given more attention. This is even more true in the programs that educate and form lay persons, because, for the most part, there is no formal ecclesial process for affirming lay vocations. Unlike vocation, baptism, both ritually and in our theological understanding of it, is communal. It is an act of the ecclesial community, involving parents ("What do you want of the church?"), priests ("I baptize you . . . "), godparents and gathered family, and, at times, the assembly. Individualism can lead us to valuing "my ministry" and "my vision for the community," whereas baptism roots us within the People of God, whom we serve, and the particular community in which we minister.

In baptism, we are baptized into the death of Jesus; we enter the tomb with him. We enter into the suffering of Jesus. I believe that this belief has particular cogence today. Recently I attended the annual conference of the National Association for Lay Ministry, in Chicago. Most of our time was given to working in groups, considering the document *Co-Workers in the Vineyard*. Relative to each section of the document we pondered two

12. Ibid., 29.

questions: What is working and what is not working. The table conversations lent themselves to the telling of personal stories, too often stories of pain and anger. They echoed stories I have been hearing in recent years. You know, I am sure, some of the scenarios—a new pastor, and people lose their positions; a new bishop, and long-standing ministry formation programs are discontinued; a significant increase in the number of deacons in a particular local church and a parallel decline in the number of lay ecclesial ministers; cutbacks, sometimes radical cutbacks of diocesan staffs as a result of the financial impact of the clergy abuse crisis and the 2008 Great Recession. Lay ecclesial ministers who are living out their commitment to continue the ministry that Jesus began, who have a consciousness of their call to ministry, who see themselves as missionary disciples, suffer deep hurt when they can no longer minister as they had, or when they see fellow ministers in this situation. In light of this, remembering that baptism is a dying with Christ can give solace, strength and meaning to these events.

Positive Developments

In recent years, there have been many positive developments relative to lay ecclesial ministry. And yes, many that are not positive, but I will not address the latter today, rather a few that I think invite our further reflection.

A leader in the conversation about lay ecclesial ministry has been Saint John's School of Theology Seminary. They have sponsored two national symposia, in 2007 and 2011, drawing together hundreds of leaders of lay associations and organizations and diocesan offices, as well as academics and others with expertise on the topic. They also sponsored a second seminar of theologians.[13] The ultimate goal of each of these gatherings was that theologians and practitioners be in active conversation. A key conclusion was: "Lay ecclesial ministers serve in the name of the church." This is further explained: "The call to lay ecclesial ministry is rooted in the baptismal call to holiness and mission that is incumbent on every believer. Lay ecclesial ministers receive a further call to serve *formally and publicly on behalf of the church*."[14] It is because of this formal and public role—in the name of the church—that the question of the authorization of lay ecclesial ministers is so very important.

13. Key leaders of these efforts have been Jeff Kaster, Vic Klimoski, William Cahoy, Barbara Sutton, and Sr. Susan Wood.

14. Italics added in this text. A very helpful description of this practical theology method, with a focus on conversation, on listening, as well as the papers from the seminar, is given in Cahoy, *In the Name*, 213.

As a follow-up to the 2011 symposium, a study on the topic of authorization was commissioned by the Canon Law Society, and conducted by the Center for Applied Research in the Apostolate (CARA). It reports that while *Co-Workers* identified authorization as one of the four aspects of "pastoral applications," almost four in ten (38 percent) of respondents to the survey say that their archdiocese has no process for authorizing lay ecclesial ministry.[15] Lynda Robitaille, a Canadian canonist, sees the process of authorization as essential, if lay ecclesial ministry is to be an official ministry. She suggests that the structure that canon law could provide would be of great value in clarifying the rights, obligations, duties and roles of lay ecclesial ministers. The structure she proposes is that of office; a bishop could establish an office, or more than one, for his diocese. One value would be that the ministry would be emphasized, rather than the person in the ministry.[16] The Canon Law Society is planning to address the questions that the survey has raised.

In addition to the work done in the Collegeville seminars, Edward Hahnenberg's *Ministry: A Relational Approach* has provided additional insights into the theology of lay ecclesial ministry. He builds on the image of concentric circles of ministerial groups developed by Thomas O'Meara,[17] and develops his central point of ministerial relationships.

> Ministers are not primarily isolated individuals whose relationships of service are secondary or nonessential to their existence as ministers. Instead, one becomes a minister by entering into and being established in relationships of service. In a theology of ministry, relationship—qualified as a relationship of service—is the ultimate category.[18]

And ministers themselves have been actively involved in assisting the flowering of lay ministry not only individually, but by their cooperative action. One expression of this is the formation of The Alliance, a collaboration of the Federation of Diocesan Liturgical Commissions, the National Association for Lay Ministry, the National Association of Pastoral Musicians, the National Conference for Catechetical Leadership, and the National

15. "Authorization of Lay Ecclesial Ministers for Ministry."

16. Unpublished remarks from the presentation at the Collegeville National Symposium on Lay Ecclesial Ministry, May 20, 2015.

17. *Theology of Ministry*, see esp. 153. It is worth noting that two participants in the original Collegeville Seminar, Kenan Osborn (*Orders and Ministry*) and David Power (*Mission, Ministry, Order*) have each published significant books on ministry today, but neither treats the topic of lay ecclesial ministry as it has evolved in the United States and the document of the United States Bishops on this, *Co-Workers*.

18. Hahnenberg, *Ministry*, 93.

Federation for Catholic Youth Ministry. They have worked together developing the common competencies for lay ministry, and, in 2011, gained approval of their national certification standards and procedures from the United States Conference of Catholic Bishops' Commission on Certification and Accreditation.

Conclusion

The title for this chapter referenced a flowering of lay ecclesial ministry. My intention in this chapter was to say that this flowering has been nourished by the waters of baptism, and that a deeper consciousness of the centrality of baptism will support an even fuller growth. I have also wanted to indicate that in its initial emergence these flowers have been nurtured and tended by many in the church community. Lay ecclesial ministry is precisely ecclesial, communal, and, as our bishops have affirmed, "has emerged and taken shape in our country through the working of the Holy Spirit."[19]

This is a time to celebrate these developments; we have been part of calling forth this new reality, lay ecclesial ministry. And now moving forward into the next half century after Vatican II, the yet fuller recovery of the meaning of baptism is dependent on us as leaders. How we celebrate, how we preach—about Baptism, about ministry—will further impact the religious imagination of the church community. An enriched understanding and practice will strengthen our church communities in their inner life as the baptized, and will strengthen them for going forth to bring the Good News to the world.

Bibliography

Cahoy, William J., ed. *In the Name of the Church: Vocation and Authorization of Lay Ecclesial Ministry*. Collegeville, MN: Liturgical, 2012.

Canon Law Society of America. "Authorization of Lay Ecclesial Ministers for Ministry: A Report for the Canon Law Society of America." October, 2012. www.clsa.org/?page=LEMStudy.

Center for Applied Research in the Apostolate (CARA). "February 2015 Research Review: Lay Ecclesial Ministers in the U.S." cara.georgetown.edu/lemsummit.pdf.

DeLambo, David, and Philip Murnion. *Parishes and Parish Ministry: A Study of Parish Lay Ministry*. New York: National Pastoral Life Center, 1999.

Fox, Zeni. *New Ecclesial Ministry: Lay Professionals Serving the Church*. Kansas City: Sheed & Ward, 1997.

Hahnenberg, Edward. *Ministry: A Relational Approach*. New York: Crossroad, 2003.

19. USCCB, *Co-Workers*, 14.

O'Meara, Thomas. *Theology of Ministry.* New York: Paulist, 1983.

Osborn, Kenan. *Orders and Ministry.* Maryknoll, NY: Orbis, 2006.

Power, David. *Mission, Ministry, Order.* New York: Continuum, 2008.

Quasten, Johannes, ed. *The Didache* (compiled with four other ancient texts). Ancient Christian Writers. New York: Paulist, 1948.

United States Conference of Catholic Bishops. *Called and Gifted: The American Catholic Laity.* National Conference of Catholic Bishops. Washington, DC: United States Catholic Conference, 1980.

———. *Co-Workers in the Vineyard of the Lord.* www.usccb.org/upload/co-workers-vineyard-lay-ecclesial-ministry-2005.pdf.

Wood, Susan, ed. *Ordering the Baptismal Priesthood.* Collegeville, MN: Liturgical, 2003.

14

The Vocation of the Lay Theologian as Baptismal Witness

—Michael Downey

THE INVITATION TO ADDRESS the topic of the vocation of the lay theologian as baptismal witness has provided me occasion for some probing and pondering after more than three decades of doing theology in academic, ecclesial, and explicitly communal contexts: What is meant by "lay," what is "theology," and what, precisely, is a "lay theologian"? In what sense is theology a vocation? What sort of "witness" does a "lay" theologian give? And what might all this bear on the question of preaching, since "lay" persons, "lay" theologians specifically, do not exercise the ministry of preaching in the strict and formal sense?[1]

1. I acknowledge with gratitude my debt to Richard Gaillardetz for his insights in the course of several conversations on this topic, as well as in his writings on a more comprehensive view that moves beyond the impasses imposed by unhelpful clergy/lay distinctions. I also acknowledge gratefully the very helpful comments of Paul Wadell as this essay was being finalized.

A Contrastive View of the Laity

The very formulation of the topic is itself expressive of a premise that is problematic, or at least questionable, resting as it does on what Giovanni Magnani understands as a contrastive view of the laity.[2] In such a view the layperson is understood in terms of negation, that is, *non*-ordained, or *not* consecrated by religious vows. The layperson is thought to have a particular perspective that is brought to bear on the theological task by virtue of what is thought to be the "secular character"[3] of the lay state in contrast to that of the ordained or those in religious life. In addition, the layperson's perspective is, in the main, thought to be shaped by marital and familial commitments. It is often assumed therefore that the lay theologian has particular competence in topics ranging from the domestic church to the responsibilities of parenting. This is, in part, due to the fact that the majority of what might be thought of as a first wave of "lay" theologians in the conciliar and post-conciliar period, at least in North America, married after a period of active ordained ministry or after being released from religious vows. But some did not, have not and do not marry and have children.

Despite significant advances in the understanding of the laity in more positive terms rather than in terms of negation due in large part to the work of Marie-Dominique Chenu, Yves Congar, and Karl Rahner, the contrastive view of the layperson held sway in these thinkers, prevailing through the conciliar and early post-conciliar period. Such a view of the laity as non-ordained or non-religious, assuming their marital, familial and domestic moorings and thus their particular responsibility for the sanctification of the temporal order, or "the world," lies at the heart of the understanding of the laity expressed in John Paul II's post-synodal apostolic exhortation on the laity, *Christifideles Laici*.[4] In a different vein Edward Schillebeeckx maintained that such a view of the laity rests on "hierarchological" premises:

> This positive content [of a "theology of the laity"] is already provided by the Christian content of the word *christifidelis*. The characteristic feature of the laity began to be explained as their relation to the world, while the characteristic of the clergy was their relationship to the church. Here both sides failed to do justice to the ecclesial dimension of any *christifidelis* and his or her relationship to the world. The clergy become the apolitical men of the church; the laity are the less ecclesially committed,

2. Magnani "So-Called Theology?," 568–633.

3. Hagstrom, "Secular Character," 152–74.

4. John Paul II, *Christifideles Laici*, 393–521.

politically involved "men of the world." In this view, the ontological status of the "new humanity" reborn with the baptism
of the Spirit was not recognized in his or her own individual
worth, but only from the standpoint of the status of the clergy.[5]

Schillebeeckx hints of a tension between a contrastive theology of the laity
and another theology of the laity that focuses not on the secular character of
the lay state or the vocation of the layperson, theologian or other, but rather
on the primacy of baptism through which all share in the mission of Christ,
the mission of Word and Spirit in the world.

It appears that some of those gathered at the Second Vatican Council
envisioned a view of the laity more in keeping with Schillebeeckx's insights.
Above all, there was the choice to pull the matter on the church as the
People of God from its original location in a chapter on the laity and to
formulate a chapter on the People of God to be set before the chapter on the
hierarchy. This alternative view is also expressed in the council's frequent
use of the term *christifidelis* in reference to all the baptized, inclusive of the
ordained and those in religious vows. While the council documents might
be read as resting on the inherited lay/clergy distinction, it appears that the
council unleashed the possibility of a reexamination of this distinction by
using baptism and mission as the context for understanding the vocation of
the Christian, whatever his or her way or walk in life.

Even as he argues against a contrastive view of the laity, Magnani re-
tains the theological notion of "laity." However, he rejects the notion that the
laity constitute a distinct body of persons within the People of God. Such
terms as "lay," "laity," and "laicity" do not refer to specific persons within the
church, but rather to the church itself, for the mission of Christ, the mission
of the church, is none other than the *consecration or sanctification of the
world*. If such terms are used to designate that which is secular, that which
is "in the world," then it is the whole church which is lay because it is the
whole church which is inserted *in* the world to be and become a sacrament
in and to the world.

Magnani maintains that the council's wider ecclesiological vision suggests a more *intensive* approach to a theology of the laity. By this he means
that the life of the layperson is a more intensive realization of the situation
of all the *christifideles,* including those who are ordained or consecrated by
religious vows.[6] Laypersons exercise, as do all the baptized, the church's mission of "taking up the whole of *created reality,* the *world* and *history* in order

---

5. Schillebeeckx, *Church with a Human Face*, 157.
6. Magnani "So-Called Theology?," 611.

to bring them to fulfillment" (emphases mine) in Christ.[7] In a similar vein, Bruno Forte writes that it is the whole church that is marked by the world in its being and in its action. "The entire People of God must be characterized by a positive relationship with the secular dimension."[8] All of the baptized have a responsibility toward the temporal order, or "the world." This undercuts the notion of two separate spheres of existence—the holy and the profane, the sacred and the secular. It is rather that "there is the one sphere of existence with a complexity of definite relations that make up history."[9]

Points of Immersion

Why then speak of the "lay" theologian, and to do so in a way that implies that his or her task is different, and that his or her witness is different from other theologians'? This is what is implied in the topic assigned to me. And, this, as indicated above, is the problematic premise in the formulation of the topic.

Following Schillebeeckx and Forte, and especially Magnani, it is more helpful to set aside, or at least hold in abeyance, the adjectival and look at the substantive "theologian."

To speak of the vocation of the theologian is to recognize that theology is a whole way of life. What this means is that theology is not something that one does. It is most certainly not a job. Theology is rather the governing concern of a life. Indeed it is a whole tone of being, an entire way of life that requires setting aside, or relativizing, other options so that this way might be pursued as the way to make good on the one and only life one has to live. This is what it means to say that theology is a vocation, a whole way of life directed to probing theology's single most important question: Who is God? Whatever the topics or concerns taken up by the theologian, be it Monika Hellwig or dare I say Thomas Merton, these spring from her or his sense of call to search out an answer to the question beneath and behind all the questions, that is, to theology's prime question. This may seem more monastic than academic, which is itself an indication of the "slippery-ness" of all these terms.

In considering the theologians who were influential in my own theological formation—Avery Dulles and David Power to name just two—and in looking with gratitude to a theological conversation partner such as the late Catherine LaCugna or Mary Milligan, or to colleagues and friends in

7. Magnani "So-Called Theology?," 613, and elsewhere.

8. Forte, *Church: Icon*, 54–55.

9. Ibid., 58–59.

theology such as Thomas Rausch, Richard Gaillardetz, or Linh Hoang, I do not think that it is all that helpful to think in terms of their "state in life" as ordained, religious, lay, married or single, as the principal reason for the kinds of the theological questions they have raised, the sort of theology at which they have worked, or the theological corpus some have left us. Is a "lay" theology really all that different from that done by a cleric or religious? If so, is it because of the supposed difference—ontological or other—between the cleric and the religious or the lay person? I suggest not. The differences rest, rather, in the different "social locations," from which one searches out, or lives into, the answer to the theological question(s) engaged.

Whether looking at Justin or Origen, Irenaeus or Athanasius, it must be recognized that their theological writing was done with pastoral intent in the face of new questions, in light of shifting modes of perceiving and being. Athanasius's preeminent concern with the Incarnation, that God had spoken and is speaking in human flesh, gave rise to a sustained argument against any effort to denigrate human flesh. In their different "todays," Aquinas and Bonaventure, Karl Rahner and Hans Urs von Balthasar, Schillebeeckx and Congar, or Anne Carr and Peter Cho Phan have been motivated by the pressing questions of their day.[10] Their concern is quite concrete: God's presence in *these* circumstances—in *this* time—and in *this* place—anything but an abstraction. Their focus, one and all, is with the mystery of Christ's identification with the human reality. The life's work of each one can be understood as a Spirit-assisted search to find the idiom and form in which the Christian mystery is rendered accessible.

The revelation of Christ, the mission of Word and Spirit, is in and to the world. If we don't know much about the world in which we live, or care much about it, if we do not understand ourselves to be first and finally members of a people in *our own time and place*, then we won't know much about revelation.[11]

In line with Magnani's notion of intensification, it may be more useful to think of the witness the theologian gives by setting aside the slippery term "world," resting as it often does on the church/world, sacred/secular distinction, and speak of different *points of immersion* in the *humanum*.[12]

10. For example, see Vorgrimler, *Understanding Karl Rahner*; Schindler, *Hans Urs von Balthasar*; Kennedy, *Schillebeeckx*; Nichols, *Yves Congar*; Puyo, *Jean Puyo interroge*.

11. See Second Vatican Council, *Gaudium et Spes*, par. 1.

12. Here I follow Schillebeeckx, who uses the Latin neuter adjective *humanum* to suggest that what it is to be human cannot be defined by a noun. The term conveys the sense of a project, involving the whole self, individuals and community, persons and peoples. The *humanum* entails constant transformation through God's initiative and our response.

While it is true that some of those mentioned above have spoken and written from within the circles of the academy, what should not be overlooked is that the primary immersion in the *humanum* of some takes the form of life in communities whose commitment has been and remains to those at the edges of both society and church. Margaret Farley's immersion in a sisterhood born in Catherine McAuley's efforts in Dublin's Lower Baggot Street to care for those who are "poor, sick and ignorant," has given shape to a moral theology alert to the concrete circumstances in which people strain, indeed struggle, to make and keep commitments in the face of sometimes insurmountable obstacles. Elizabeth Johnson's immersion in a community of women who, from roots in Le Puy, have sought to express a profound love of God and neighbor without distinction so that all may be one, has led to the construction of a theology alert to a range of voices vastly different, with an ear tuned to those neglected and often unheeded. David Power's theology is shaped through and through by a governing concern for the mission of a community of men immersed in the life of the poor who are to be evangelized and who in their turn evangelize, as well as by an abiding respect for the differences discerned in the working of the Word and Spirit in diverse languages, cultures, and peoples. While all three have done theological work via pen and podium, each has done so as part of a community of immersion that seeks to respond to the needs of those at the edges rather than the center of both church and society. All three, while pursuing academic careers, have found their principal point of immersion by "following" their sisters and brothers to the edges, to what Pope Francis has repeatedly referred to as the "existential peripheries."[13] The theology of each can only be fully appreciated in view of these various points of immersion in the *humanum* that has shaped their theology not principally as an academic exercise, but as a form of witness to the world. This finds echo in Pope Francis' remarks on December 6, 2013, when he addressed the International Theological Commission:

> Theologians, then, are "pioneers . . . in the Church's dialogue with cultures. But being pioneers is important also because sometimes we think they [theologians] stay back, stay in the barracks . . . No, they are on the frontier!"

In the same address in Rome he also linked the work of theologians with a listening to the sense of the faithful, insisting that they must be "attentive to

---

13. Jorge Mario Bergoglio used this term in his four-minute presentation to the cardinals who would elect him pope shortly thereafter. In his writings and speech, the importance of the church going to/living at the "existential peripheries" has been a recurrent theme.

what the Spirit says to the Churches through the authentic manifestations of the *sensus fidelium*."

Autobiographical Interlude

Here allow me a few remarks about the point of immersion from which I have sought to live out the vocation of the theologian. Early on I was drawn to live "up close" with the wounded and the weak, particularly those with developmental disabilities. A course of discernment and study led me through a rather thorny path of trying to combine this attraction with another equally persistent pull, call it "intellectual," that ended, or began, in becoming the first "lay" person to receive a PhD in theology from The Catholic University of America, in 1982. My dissertation topic, combining these two seemingly incompatible "vocations," emerged as I was living between two worlds—the academic community of The Catholic University of America in Washington, DC, and a l'Arche community in Trosly-Breuil, France. In the face of considerable resistance from significant voices in the department of theology at the time, and with the unstinting support of my director, mentor, guide, and friend, the late David Power, the topic I chose, with which I aimed to build a systematic theology rooted in the philosophy of Jean Vanier as well as the praxis of living up close with the wounded and the weak in the l'Arche communities, was approved by the faculty and successfully defended. Looking back on more than thirty years of work in academic, ecclesial, and communal settings, it is the point of immersion in l'Arche and in similar contexts at the edges that has been the principal factor in the shaping of my own vocation in search of an answer to theology's prime question, and whatever witness I may have given while straddling three "worlds" in service of the *humanum*.

A Point of Immersion: Jean Vanier and L'Arche

The story of Jean Vanier and the communities of l'Arche cannot be recounted in full here. A few salient points will suffice.

After resigning from a brief but distinguished career in the Royal Navy and later the Royal Canadian Navy, Vanier joined l'Eau Vive, a small community of students, predominantly lay, situated in a poor neighborhood near Paris, while doing philosophical studies. In 1962 he successfully completed his doctoral dissertation in philosophy at the Institut Catholique de Paris, entitled *Le Bonheur: principe et fin de la morale aristotélicienne*,[14] focusing on the Aristotelian triad of justice, friendship, and contemplation, which together make for the good and happy life. But Vanier notes something lacking in Aristotle—the centrality of love, which is later disclosed in the Pasch of Jesus Christ.

Shortly after beginning his career as professor of moral philosophy at Saint Michael's College in Toronto, Vanier moved to Trosly-Breuil, France. There he bought a small, dilapidated house, which he called l'Arche, the Ark, Noah's Ark—which he saw as a symbol of refuge, diversity, and hope. The name also bespeaks an arch that bridges different points: nations and races, languages and cultures, strong and weak, believer and unbeliever. On August 4, 1964, Vanier welcomed two mentally handicapped men, Raphael and Philippe, into his home.

From the seed sown in Trosly-Breuil in August 1964, l'Arche has grown to include roughly 135 communities worldwide, ranging in size from family-like homes to small villages, all founded on the belief in the uniqueness and sacredness of each person, whether disabled or not. Motivated by the affirmation of the primacy of the beatitudes in Christian and human living, the gifts of each person are to be nurtured and called forth with predilection for the poorest, weakest, and most wounded in community, society, church. The handicapped (core members) and the non-handicapped (assistants) strive to live together in the spirit of the beatitudes. The "normal" are not there to "help" the disabled. Rather, Vanier learns from the disabled that the wounded and the weak are often the *teachers* of the clever and the strong. And what they teach is that the person does not just have a heart, but *is* the heart, understood as the fundamental capacity of the human person to be in relation. In the disabled—the disfigured—he sees the contours of a reconfigured understanding of human being. For Vanier, looking to the disfigured, we learn something about what it means to be human—through this point of immersion in the *humanum*.

Theological Orientations

Nearly forty years since the criticisms raised by some of the theological faculty of Catholic University as to whether one could build a theology from the philosophy of Jean Vanier and the praxis of l'Arche, it is a singular delight to spell out the theological orientations that emerge from this point of immersion in the *humanum* situated at the existential peripheries, those "frontiers" to which we are urged to go, and indeed to live and work, by Pope

14. Vanier, *Bonheur*.

Francis. This is done so as to be of some help to others in various theological disciplines whose approach may be quite different. Further, these orientations might provide some *jalons de la route* for good preaching, precisely because this is an eminently practical theology meant for proclamation. Here we have a theology that has come to life in a community of the broken, a proclamation in word and deed from and to those who are inheritors of the promise of the beatitudes.

First, speech about God is rooted in the praxis of life in community. While Vanier was formed in classical currents of philosophy and theology still evident in his writings to the discerning eye, it is living up close to the wounded and the weak that gives rise to what is said and written about God, and indeed what is preached, in l'Arche. Whatever is known or said of God is itself based in love, since it is rooted in the heart as the capacity for relationship, and looks to the weak and the vulnerable who reveal the mystery of God often hidden from the clever and the robust. Prayer, indeed contemplation, is of the mystery of God revealed in the weak, as well as of the weakness of Jesus in his infancy, and at his agony and passion, death and descent. Though Vanier and the communities do not speak in these terms, this approach to knowledge and speech about God is deeply resonant with John Paul II's message to theologians in *Fides et Ratio*. There he spells out what he sees as the "current tasks for theology."[15] He writes: "The very heart of theological inquiry will thus be the contemplation of the mystery of the Triune God."[16] Further, "From this vantage point, the prime commitment of theology is seen to be the understanding of God's *kenosis*, a grand and mysterious truth for the human mind, which finds it inconceivable that suffering and death can express a love which gives itself and seeks nothing in return."[17] In the praxis of l'Arche, there is an ongoing consent to the *kenosis* of God in Jesus Christ through which contemplation of the Triune God is made possible in an encounter with the broken bodies and the fractured minds, the very emptiness, of the wounded and the weak.

Second, the Gospel is the norm for the life of this community. Whatever the rules governing the life of a community, these are in service of being and becoming a people of the beatitudes. While not able to preach the gospel in the strict and formal sense, in his writings and speeches, Vanier's focus is consistently on the Gospel, with a preference for the Gospel of John, which he sees as the gospel of relationship.[18] In his most recent public ad-

15. John Paul II, *Fides et Ratio*, par. 92–99.

16. Ibid., 93.

17. Ibid.

18. See Vanier, *Gospel of John*.

dress on the occasion of receiving the Templeton Prize, in London on May 18, 2015, his focus was on Luke 14:12–14, "proclaimed" in halting speech and thickened tongue by one of the core members of l'Arche in the Church of St. Martin-in-the-Fields, Trafalgar Square. Amidst the elite of London, dignitaries from around the world, and core members of l'Arche, Vanier reminded us that it is when we welcome the blind, the lame, the hungry to our table, that we will be blessed. What good is it to invite your family and friends when you know you will be repaid?

Third, the charisms at play in each and every member of the community—core members and "assistants," lay, clergy, religious—are to be respected and invigorated for the life of the local community and for the *humanum*, with predilection for those who are most vulnerable and wounded, the last, lost, littlest, and least. This is expressed when Vanier asks if we can reasonably have a dream of a world where people, whatever their race, religion, culture, abilities, or disabilities, whatever their education or economic situation, whatever their age or gender, can find a place and reveal their gifts.

Fourth, those at the "edges" of the community hold pride of place. For those whose vocation is to search out an answer to the "question" *Who is God?*, our speech is incoherent and indeed implausible, our view of God obscured and obscure, if we are inattentive to the lives of those who sometimes cannot even find words to speak, let alone speak of God. From them we learn that theological language is always to some degree the language of unsaying.

Fifth, immersion in l'Arche is a life of "contrast" experience as understood by Edward Schillebeeckx, rather than as explained by Magnani above. For Schillebeeckx, suffering bears hefty theological weight. It makes it possible for us to imagine that for which we are hoping. The fullness of life for which we long, flourishing in the *humanum,* dare we say salvation, is manifest in juxtaposition to human suffering. Here Schillebeeckx introduces the notion of negative contrast experience.[19] This he describes in terms of injustice, oppression or suffering that gives rise to nay-saying in the form of protest and a yea-saying that impels us in activities to bring about change. Schillebeeckx maintains that in such contrast experiences we recognize an *intuitive* awareness of duty. We simply *know* that we must strive to make things different. This "intuitive knowledge" is deeply resonant with Vanier's understanding of knowing in/by the heart. God is present even and especially in suffering, in failure, even in death. The clever and robust experience weakness and vulnerability when scientific and rational measures are no match in the struggle with the suffering of the body, the mind and the spirit.

19. See Schillebeeckx, "Church, Magisterium," 143–66, esp. 155–56.

It is often in experiences of powerlessness or raw suffering that we are able to lean into the God who is to be found there, in the deepest movement of contemplation at the edge of mystical union.

Sixth, this lends to a reconfiguration of the "good life," the goal of the *humanum*, based on what is known through living up close to those who are "disfigured," those who disclose to the clever and robust hints of an answer to the question *Who is God?*

From Disfigurement: Reconfiguring a Curriculum for the *Humanum*

Recall that Vanier's study of Aristotle focused on justice, friendship, and contemplation, the triad on which rests happiness, the good life. He gives evidence of his perception, even at the time of writing his dissertation, that Aristotle's rather singular focus on reason and intellect stands in need of a corrective.[20] Such a focus leaves out of its scope the great majority of people who could never attain human fulfillment and perfection because of a lack of intellectual ability, education, or leisure.[21] Further, the priority given to the powers of intellect, especially in contemplation, leaves little room for the affective, relational dimension—what he calls the heart as a way of "naming" the human capacity to be in relation—antecedent to intellect and will.

His vision, even at the time of his study of Aristotle, was developing around the notion of the heart as the foundation of the human person.[22] In l'Arche, Vanier continually encountered people who, by Aristotelian standards, could never arrive at a point of true human flourishing. Not exhibiting the ability for greatness in Aristotelian terms, they were nonetheless capable of living simple and joyful lives with deep compassion, joy, and an ability to forgive, reconcile, and celebrate.[23] With very little intellectual ability, or ability to produce things by the work of their hands, the people of l'Arche taught Vanier that there is something deeper, richer, more profound and fundamental to the human person than the intellect,[24] efficiency, and productivity.[25]

20. Vanier, *Bonheur*, 418–21.

21. Ibid., 419.

22. Ibid., 418–21.

23. Vanier, *Eruption*, 45–46.

24. Ibid., 47.

25. Ibid., 45.

Vanier then perceived that the little child, the very old[26] and persons in situations of distress and vulnerability often manifest extraordinary human qualities that lend to a deepening of communion.[27] Vanier expresses this by saying that a person *is* the heart, the qualities of which must be developed by all.[28] Because all persons have the capacities of the heart, *this provides the common basis and groundwork for true advancement and progress among peoples*, that is, for a new approach to the *humanum*, a renewed social order. Compassion, joy, reconciliation, forgiveness, and celebration, which stem from what is deepest in the person, are finally the dimensions that internally vivify us all, making possible the unity desired by all.[29] What is needed, according to Vanier, is a revolution of the *heart*, of love, of care, of forgiveness, of compassion, of joy and celebration.[30]

For Vanier, a new social order does not lie in programs and policies, but in *all, together, reflecting and seeking truth and meaning*. This brings us back to the Aristotelian triad, shaped by immersion in l'Arche. *Justice* is an activity of seeking to build a world in which *all* may grow, the activity that seeks to create an "alternative space"[31] in which all may grow and flourish in the pursuit of the *humanum*. *Friendship* becomes possible between and among people living *together* who are vastly unequal. And is not contemplation *seeking truth and meaning*, beholding the truth with another, indeed with all others? *Contemplation* is now understood as the non-pragmatic regard for God, creation, and persons—especially for the wounded and weak who are "useless" and seemingly have nothing to achieve in a society of the useful and productive. Thus this new social order rests on a reframed understanding of justice, friendship, and contemplation.

In this renewed social order there is a reconfiguration of justice, now understood as the pursuit of the good for the many in obedience to the mandates of the heart transformed by love. The exercise of justice is aimed at the establishment of an order in which the knowledge of the heart has an important place, and the weak, wounded, and vulnerable have priority.

Friendship comes about by response to the knowledge of love as we ourselves are prompted by the attractions of love and of the heart in another,

---

26. Vanier, *Community and Growth*, 79.

27. Vanier, *Eruption*, 42, 48.

28. Vanier, *Be Not Afraid*, 12.

29. Ibid., 12ff.

30. Vanier, *Eruption*, 102.

31. Pope Francis urges the creation of alternative spaces of self-giving and respect for difference in his *Letter to All Consecrated People*, II.2.

making friendship possible between any two persons, even those who are vastly unequal in terms of human capacity.

The goal of knowledge given in contemplation is itself based in love, since it is rooted in the heart, and looks to the weak and the vulnerable in the search for God.

Insights from Immersion at the Edge

What does all this say, then, about the vocation of the theologian as baptismal witness?

First, in our own time and place there are points of immersion, "existential peripheries," or "frontiers" that are integral to the life of the theologian whose vocation is in service to the *humanum*. Theology and proclamation only come to life when one is immersed to some measure in the life of people and peoples, not at the center, but at the edges of both society and church.

Second, immersion in life at the existential peripheries, going to the frontiers, is not only the vocation of the "lay" theologian in witness to the world, but is ineluctably a part of any theological vocation whatever one's "state" in life.

Third, from immersion in life at the peripheries, the theologian more clearly recognizes that the necessary intellectual rigors of our discipline can lead to writing and speech from and to "north of the neck," that is, a highly rationalist, cognitive, indeed scientific, exercise. Too often we are inclined to relegate and marginalize "intuitive knowledge"—the affective, the heart, as well as contemplation—to what is thought of as the fluffy, soft discipline of spirituality. Theology limps as a result.

Fourth, a reconfigured understanding of the theological vocation emerges as the pursuit of the good life rooted in the Aristotelian triad of friendship, justice, and contemplation:

Friendship. No matter how solitary our vocation may seem at times due to the lonesome task of research, study, and writing, theology takes place within the context of a community or, better, as a conversation between and among friends. Theology is an act of welcoming and befriending the other so that we might see the world and God differently, more clearly, more adequately. Theology is a vocation that calls us to befriend God, others, and the world, requiring both humility and hospitality in search of an answer to theology's prime question.

Justice. As an exercise of justice, in writing, speech, and teaching, the theologian seeks to create "alternative spaces" in which there is room enough for those at the edge of the classroom or other places, those who have little or nothing to say, those who are illiterate in the well-worn but often tired responses to what we judge to be pressing questions. Finding or making room for persons in unlikely places is required, not simply desirable, in search of a fuller expression of the *humanum* and a more adequate understanding of God.

Contemplation. No longer understood in strictly Aristotelian terms as the mind's pure gaze on eternal, unchanging truth, contemplation is rooted in the heart understood as the capacity to be in relation with another, others, every living creature, creation, and God. John Paul II reminds: the prime task of theology today is understanding the mystery of God's *kenosis*; in doing so we will be led to the contemplation of the Triune Life.[32] The mystery of the divine *kenosis* is perhaps nowhere more manifest than in those persons and peoples at the peripheries. From the vantage point of *kenosis*, God comes without pretension, in contrast to the hubris of reason unaided, putting a bold question mark before reason's effort to figure it all out. The divine mystery does not rest in God's inscrutability, but that God should appear in such a fashion. *Kenosis* is the scene on which God appears, refusing to identify with human achievement, resisting our inordinate need to perform and succeed. These defy the logic of gift, the emptying out of the divine self, indeed our very selves, in order to appear on the scene of human weakness and vulnerability, to identify with human beings in the concrete circumstances of their lives.

This is the mystery to which theologians give witness in the world with the one and only life we have to live.

Bibliography

Forte, Bruno. *The Church: Icon of the Trinity*. Boston: Pauline, 1991.

Francis. Address of Pope Francis to Members of the International Theological Commission. December 6, 2013. w2.vatican.va/content/francesco/en/speeches/2013/december/documents/papa-francesco_20131206_commissione-teologica.html.

———. *Letter to All Consecrated People*. November 21, 2014.

Hagstrom, Aurelie A. "The Secular Character of the Vocation and Mission of the Laity." In *Ordering the Baptismal Priesthood: Theologies of Lay and Ordained Ministries*, edited by Susan K. Wood, 152–74. Collegeville, MN: Liturgical, 2003.

John Paul II. *Christifideles Laici. AAS* 81. 1989.

John Paul II. *Fides et Ratio*. 1998.

Kennedy, Philip. *Schillebeeckx*. Outstanding Christian Thinkers. Collegeville, MN: Liturgical,1993.

32. John Paul II, *Fides et Ratio*, 93.

Magnani, Giovanni. "Does the So-Called Theology of the Laity Possess a Theological Status?" In *Vatican II: Assessment and Perspectives: Twenty-five Years After (1962–1987)*, edited by Rene Latourelle, 1:562–633 New York: Paulist, 1988.

Nichols, Aidan. *Yves Congar.* Outstanding Christian Thinkers. Wilton, CT: Morehouse-Barlow, 1989.

Puyo, Jean. *Jean Puyo interroge le Père Congar.* Paris: Centurion, 1990.

Schillebeeckx, Edward. "Church, Magisterium, and Politics." Translated by N. D. Smith. In *God the Future of Man*, 141–66, New York: Sheed and Ward, 1968.

———. *The Church with a Human Face.* New York: Crossroad, 1985.

Schindler, David L., ed. *Hans Urs von Balthasar: His Life and Work.* San Francisco: Ignatius, 1991.

Second Vatican Council. *Gaudium et Spes.* 1965.

Vanier, Jean. *Be Not Afraid.* New York: Paulist, 1975.

———. *Community and Growth.* New York: Paulist, 1979.

———. *Eruption to Hope.* Toronto: Griffin House, 1971.

———. *Gospel of John, Gospel of Relationship.* Cincinnati: Franciscan Media, 2014.

———. *Le bonheur: principe et fin de la morale aristotélicienne.* Paris: Desclée de Brouwer, 1965.

Vorgrimler, Herbert. *Understanding Karl Rahner: An Introduction to His Life and Thought.* Translated by John Bowden. New York: Crossroad, 1986.

15

Naomi and Ruth in the House of Bread[1]

—Anna Carter Florence

LAST FALL I WAS asked to lead a retreat for a group of pastors. There were about twenty of them, most of them from rural settings, serving churches of fifty to a hundred members; they were tired, and they were ready for something different: rejuvenating, yes, but also, maybe even a little wild and reckless, something they could do without their congregations looking over their shoulders. I suggested we read scripture, because when I think, "wild and reckless," I think, *Scripture, awesome! Let's get into it!*—which says a lot about me, or maybe about preachers. You want to have some fun on a Thursday night? Get some preachers and a pot of coffee, maybe even some adult beverages, and let 'em loose with the biblical text. You will see verbs you never thought were there in the Holy Writ. And the funny thing is, they *were* there; they were there in the Bible all along. They were just waiting for you to cut loose and notice them, which you don't always do when you're alone on a Saturday night, trying to write your sermon.

So these pastors and I, we decided to cut loose with the book of Ruth. We had twenty-four hours, and it seemed plausible that we could get through four chapters in some lively way, plus there was the whole threshing floor scene in chapter 3 that promised to be really fun. Off we went to the

1. Scripture quotations in this chapter are taken from the New Revised Standard Version Bible, copyright 1989, Division of Christian Education of the National Council of the Churches of Christ in the United States of America. Used by permission.

retreat center, Bibles poised, hair down, ready to indulge, because nothing says *scriptural escapist fantasy* like the book of Ruth and twenty pastors of the Lutheran persuasion. And guess what? It wasn't a wild and crazy overnight at all. It was an utterly practical experience. Ruth, we were shocked to learn, is a manual for preachers. *Ruth!*—which has no preachers in it at all! *Ruth!*—which *looks* like a cult classic, throbbing with romance and ancient intrigue, but is *actually* a postmodern homiletical treatise in disguise, and who knew?! Who knew that a story about two stranded women could have so much to say about our life in the pulpit?

It seemed obvious that I had found my text for the conference, so here we are. What I'd like to do is walk through some of the text with you, and ask you to imagine that you are listening as a very tired preacher. Will that be too much of a stretch? A very tired preacher somewhere between the land of Moab and the house of bread, which is, of course, Bethlehem. And on the way there are these two women, Ruth and Naomi, who invite you into some of their verbs. I have become obsessed with verbs, in the last few years; I've been reading texts verbs first, preaching them verbs first, because I've found that focusing on the verbs is a good way to get into the deep end of the pool fast when you read scripture, and I'm writing a book on it, so when you get me, these days, you get verbs. Which is a good thing, I might add: verbs lead us to the script in the scripture; *our* script. And when you find that, you find your life, life in the house of bread.

I would tell you I have three points—three verbs this text offers preachers, one for each of the first three chapters—but then I would be giving it away, ruining the inductive moment, which of course I wouldn't. Let's just say that if you are an orderly sort of person for whom the rule of three is a comfort, well, you can look for it. But now the text, first from chapter 1.

> In the days when the judges ruled, there was a famine in the land, and a certain man of Bethlehem in Judah went to live in the country of Moab, he and his wife and two sons. The name of the man was Elimelech and the name of his wife Naomi, and the names of his two sons were Mahlon and Chilion; they were Ephrathites from Bethlehem in Judah. They went into the country of Moab and remained there. But Elimelech, the husband of Naomi, died, and she was left with her two sons. These took Moabite wives; the name of the one was Orpah and the name of the other Ruth. When they had lived there about ten years,

both Mahlon and Chilion also died, so that the woman was left without her two sons and her husband.

Then she started to return with her daughters-in-law from the country of Moab, for she had heard in the country of Moab that the Lord had considered his people and given them food. So she set out from the place where she had been living with her two daughters-in-law, and they went on their way to go back to the land of Judah. But Naomi said to her two daughters-in-law, "Go back, each of you, to your mother's house. May the Lord deal kindly with you, as you have dealt with the dead and with me. The Lord grant that you find security, each of you in the house of your husband." Then she kissed them and they wept aloud. They said to her, "No, we will return with you to your people." But Naomi said, "Turn back, my daughters, why will you go with me? Do I still have sons in my womb that they may become your husbands? Turn back, my daughters, go your way, for I am too old to have a husband. Even if I thought there were hope for me, even if I should have a husband tonight and bear sons, would you then wait until they were grown? Would you then refrain from marrying? No, my daughters, it has been far more bitter for me than for you, because the hand of the Lord has turned against me." Then they wept aloud again. Orpah kissed her mother-in-law, but Ruth clung to her. So she said, "See, your sister-in-law has gone back to her people and to her gods; return after your sister-in-law." But Ruth said, "Do not press me to leave you or turn back from following you! Where you go, I will go; Where you lodge, I will lodge; your people shall be my people, and your God my God. Where you die, I will die—there will I be buried. May the Lord do thus and so to me and more as well, if even death parts me from you!" When Naomi saw that Ruth was determined to go with her, she said no more to her. (Ruth 1:1-18)

Our text begins with a famine. It seems there is always a famine somewhere; the people of God are always traveling between a place of fullness and a place of empty. On one side is home, or what you thought was home, until the fields dried up and the sermons, too, and how can you be home when you have no bread? On the other side are foreign territories, where you must always be a stranger, but where the people seem to eat regularly and well; call it the land of Moab. When there is famine at home, you must go to Moab; everybody knows that. And maybe in the land of Moab you won't have to worry about membership numbers and stewardship campaigns and youth sports tournaments that go out of their way to happen on Sundays.

Maybe in the land of Moab preachers can remember why they got into this ministry thing in the first place. But let us be clear: you have to leave home to get there. *The land of Moab.*

Let us be clear about another thing: the famine that starts all this movement is in Bethlehem, or, quite literally, in the house of bread. There is no bread in the house of bread. And if that sounds impossible, maybe it's because you haven't talked to a very tired preacher lately. Maybe you haven't sat in on a meeting of the church council this year. Maybe you haven't stopped by the airport bookstore and thumbed through the "inspirational literature" kiosk. Maybe you haven't heard the breathtaking silence from so many churches in the wake of Ferguson and New York and Baltimore and Charleston. Is there bread in the house of bread? That's a fair question these days. And a lot of us are hungry and looking toward the land of Moab.

The land of Moab is where Elimelech and Naomi went when famine came to Bethlehem. They crossed the border, found a place, got the green card, learned the language, sent their kids to Moabite schools, and in a few years, they were out of the woods: immigrant success stories. No more famine. Their boys grew up bilingual and when it came time to choose a bride, no one insisted that they go back to the old country, choose a girl of the same denomination; this was a forward-thinking family. Move ahead, boys. Marry those nice Moabite girls you took to your high school prom; we'll teach the grandkids to speak Hebrew, and maybe they'll even be proud that their ancestors came from Bethlehem and that they left Judah to make a home for their families in the land of Moab.

Except home is a very fluid concept, isn't it? Part people, part landscape, part roof-over-your-head-and-food-on-your-table. If you're a preacher, add bodies in the pews and a sermon on the laptop, every Saturday night. One of those factors disappears, and your security is at risk; "home" is at risk. There you are, staring another famine in the face. It happened to Naomi. Elimelech died, her sons died, and there was nothing left for her in the land of Moab but foreign daughters-in-law, who much as you love them, aren't going to replace what you had.

If you're a very tired preacher, wandering somewhere between the land of Moab and the house of bread, here's the first verb sequence Naomi tosses your way: *turn back*. Not "turn around," as in repent, regroup, begin again. We can all use a chance to turn around and reboot from time to time, and if we need prompting, John the Baptizer is always ready with that. But "turn back"? That's something else entirely. When you turn back, you give up. Turn back, my daughters-in-law, because where I'm going, you don't want to be. Turn back, because where I'm headed, there is no future for anyone. Turn back, because this road is over; it's a dead end, with no home in sight.

Turn back. That's famine talk. It's a verb that comes from a place of anxiety, rather than a place of trust: it's a verb of amnesia. Or worse, it's a verb of nostalgia. And it is all over the church. Whenever the anxiety goes up, the refrain starts to hammer and whine: Turn back, preacher. Turn back, church. The times, they are bewildering; the famine, it is fierce; so let's turn back to something we recognize, something we don't have to decipher digitally or untangle pastorally or translate into emergent-speak. Surely, if we put our minds to it, we can just turn back the clock and the church to a simpler time when no one had to define marriage or question authority or worry about things like police brutality in our communities: how did we get to this place? And how do we get out of it? Naomi is so bereft that she has one verb to offer, in the first chapter of this text. You want security? Turn back, because I got nothing else for you here.

One of the daughters-in-law decides this verb makes a lot of sense, under the circumstances: Orpah cuts her losses, says her goodbyes, and turns back, while she still can. The other daughter-in-law is Ruth, and she doesn't. Ruth has another verb in mind: *cling.* It's an unfortunate translation given contemporary English, because the first thing I think about is the stage one clingers in the youth group, those adolescents who are so happy to be dating someone that they breathe new meaning into the word "smother." In Hebrew, "cling" doesn't mean clutch and suffocate. It means remain steadfast, as one who abides. It means keep close and hold tight. It means grasp, embrace, hang on—and not to your own security, by the way. To another human being. To the person whose life and hope are most at risk. To the least of these. Orpah turned back, but Ruth joined herself to Naomi and clung to her.

I want to suggest that if you're a very tired preacher, wandering somewhere between the land of Moab and the house of bread, every time you open the biblical text, someone is going to offer you the verb "turn back," and there will be a lot of incentive to take it. Parishioners who are tired of the way things are and longing for the way things were. Councils who don't particularly like it when you agitate the masses. Listeners who want you to preach sermon series about the thirteen thrifty practices of positive-thinking people, in which the prayer of Jabez figures prominently. You get a lot of chances to turn back when you're a preacher. And maybe most of those are coming from someone like Naomi, who must have been a fearless spitfire back in the day, but is now sad and tired and worn down with loss, devoid of the imaginative resilience she once possessed in spades. Now she is so empty she can hardly stomach the idea of reading scripture. She'd rather you turn back and skip it altogether, quote platitudes that we at least know aren't true rather than a living word of resurrection. Turn back, preacher. Don't raise my hopes when I know there's nothing coming. There is no bread in the house of bread. And you know what? It can be easier to believe her than not. Be like Orpah: turn back.

But I guess there's a reason why we call it the book of Ruth. The book of Orpah would have only been a few verses long; turning back tends to cut things short. Ruth chooses a different verb. And I want to suggest that if you're a very tired preacher, wandering somewhere between the land of Moab and the house of bread, you can choose it, too. Cling. Abide. Keep close and hold fast. Not to security. Not to the church's business of survival, which, as South African cleric and theologian Allan Boesak once said, is really none of our business; that is up to God and God alone.[2] No, cling and abide and hold fast to the Word. Practice resurrection. Speak it to Naomi, who so desperately needs to hear it: *Release to the captives. Recovery of sight to the blind. Freedom for the oppressed, and joy for the broken-hearted.*

I wonder what our lives would be like, as preachers, if we made a promise to ourselves, this week, that no matter what happens when we open this text, we will not turn back from following that path. We will not choose the verb of Orpah. We will choose the verb of Ruth: cling. Abide, remain steadfast, hold on, hang in, don't you let that text go; don't you even think about it! Ruth's verb is like a marriage vow: join yourself to this Word and the two of you shall become one. Which is why I tell my students that when you become a preacher, you take on another life partner: it's the text. Like it or not, the two of you are an item. And like any relationship, yes, it taxes your patience and tests your courage and absolutely ruins your need for order and certitude, but that's okay: live in the tension. It's so postmodern.

But there's more. When we choose Ruth's verb, we're not just clinging to and abiding with the text. We're saying something about the whole hermeneutical process, how we read the Bible with other human beings. You want to know what it looks like to interpret scripture with the community of faith? It's this: we read together, and we stay together, no matter what, because texts do things to people, and we know that. So where you go in this scripture, I'll go. Where you lodge in it, I'll lodge, and if it dumps you down

2. See Allan Boesak sermon, "The Reuben Option," in *A Chorus of Witnesses*, edited by Thomas G. Long and Cornelius Plantinga Jr. (Grand Rapids: Eerdmans, 1994), p. 137.

for the night and there's no room in the inn, I'll pitch us a tent. I'll be right beside you, no matter where it takes you or what it shows you or what it puts you through to read it, both good and bad. So don't you tell me to leave you or turn back from following you! I am picking Ruth's verb, not Orpah's, and Ruth's verb is feisty.

Second verb, in chapter 2. I'm not going to provide the whole thing, but read the passage below, just to get a sense.

> Now Naomi had a kinsman on her husband's side, a prominent rich man, of the family of Elimelech, whose name was Boaz. And Ruth the Moabite said to Naomi, "Let me go to the field and glean among the ears of grain, behind someone in whose sight I may find favor." Naomi said to her, "Go, my daughter." So Ruth went. She came and gleaned in the field behind the reapers. As it happened, she came to the part of the field belonging to Boaz, who was of the family of Elimelech.
>
> Just then Boaz came from Bethlehem. He said to the reapers, "The Lord be with you." They answered, "The Lord bless you." Then Boaz said to his servant who was in charge of the reapers, "To whom does this young woman belong?" The servant who was in charge of the reapers answered, "She is the Moabite who came back with Naomi from the country of Moab. She said, 'Please, let me glean and gather among the sheaves behind the reapers.' So she came, and she has been on her feet from early this morning until now, without resting even for a moment." Then Boaz said to Ruth, "Now listen, my daughter, do not go to glean in another field or leave this one, but keep close to my young women. Keep your eyes on the field that is being reaped, and follow behind them. I have ordered the young men not to bother you. If you get thirsty, go to the vessels and drink from what the young men have drawn." Then Ruth fell prostrate, with her face to the ground, and said to him, "Why have I found favor in your sight, that you should take notice of me, when I am a foreigner?" But Boaz answered her, "All that you have done for your mother-in-law since the death of your husband has been fully told me, and how you left your father and mother and your native land and came to a people that you did not know before. May the Lord reward you for your deeds, and may you have a full reward from the Lord, the God of Israel, under whose wings you have come for refuge!" Then she said, "May I continue to

find favor in your sight, my lord, for you have comforted me and spoken kindly to your servant, even though I am not one of your servants." At mealtime Boaz said to her, "Come here, and eat some of this bread, and dip your morsel in the sour wine." So she sat beside the reapers, and he heaped up for her some parched grain. She ate until she was satisfied, and she had some left over. When she got up to glean, Boaz instructed his young men, "Let her glean even among the standing sheaves, and do not reproach her. You must also pull out some handfuls for her from the bundles, and leave them for her to glean, and do not rebuke her."

So she gleaned in the field until evening. Then she beat out what she had gleaned, and it was about an ephah of barley. She picked it up and came into the town, and her mother-in-law saw how much she had gleaned. (Ruth 2:1–18a)

What's the verb that stands out from that chapter? *Glean*—which may not be a verb you rely on for everyday discourse unless you are agriculturally minded, but which occurs twelve times in this chapter alone. That's enough for an MVP trophy, in my book: *Glean*, the most valuable verb of Ruth, chapter 2. It means what the text describes: to gather slowly and laboriously. To pick up what the professionals missed. To collect by hand, and from the ground. *Glean*. It's the same verb given to the children of Israel, when they gather manna in the wilderness. Daily bread, bit by bit, which you can't hoard, and you can't save.

Of course, in this text, gleaning is poor people's work. You don't glean unless you have no fields of your own, and have to rely on the kindness of others. The Torah makes very clear allowances for this: the poor are to be permitted to glean behind the reapers in any field, so that they may at least gather a portion of their daily bread. But you never know, with gleaning. You might pick up enough to sustain you, and you might not. You might follow behind some deliberately sloppy reapers, or you might not. It all depends on the field and who owns it. Ruth got lucky: Boaz took a liking to her. But not every owner is as generous.

Gleaning also falls into the category of slow production: there is nothing mechanized about it. You may have the latest combine machinery, the most current technology for efficient reaping, but there is always going to be a percentage of the harvest that falls to the ground and needs to be collected by hand. So you glean. Thousands of years of farming improvements have not been able to correct that. Gleaning is an irrepressible verb. You upgrade, update, download "reaping 2.0," and it still bounces back, telling you it's time to get out there and stoop between the rows.

Preachers know the verb *glean*. We know it very well. We kind of hoped we wouldn't, that the homiletical harvest would be fast and industrial. We kind of hoped that writing a sermon would be like working a combine, that you'd sign onto the text, hand over your loyalty verbs—*cling* and *abide* and *remain steadfast*—and someone would point you to the corner of the field with your name on it for the week: go to it. We kind of hoped that the text would just fall down and yield, if you asked politely. Preferably in neat rows, by 5:00 p.m. on Friday. Alas. It turns out that your loyalty to the Word of God in no way guarantees that it will produce quickly and efficiently. And, there is no combine. There's just you, on your hands and knees, trudging up and down the rows, picking up the leftover bits of wisdom the text sees fit to throw your way. Slow, laborious work. And so random. You never know what you will find, and if it will be enough to feed Naomi, let alone a congregation.

If you're a very tired preacher, wandering somewhere between the land of Moab and the house of bread, preaching feels like gleaning—or maybe it would be more accurate to say that reading the text for preaching feels like gleaning. And maybe that is as it should be. The moment interpretation turns into some sleek, reliable machine of production, that is the moment it has been taken over by empire. Pharaoh and Herod have no time for gleaning; gleaning doesn't fill the storehouses. They would like us to spend our time on brick making and building monuments to their splendor. They would like our interpretive processes to be as predictable and uniform as everybody downloading the same sermons from the same imperial source, week after week. That, you can control. But gleaning? There's no profit in it. There's no containment. It's just tiny bits of scattered seed and grain that the imperial machines missed, and who knows what will grow from those seeds if they're planted?

Gleaning. It's your right, as a preacher to go between the rows of any field and any text, to see what's there. To take your time and go slowly. To make the nourishment of Naomi and not the feeding of the empire your goal. If *cling* is the first interpretive move a preacher makes, *glean* is the second; once again, Ruth has the verbs. She knows that the Lord provides manna in the wilderness, and it is ours to glean and gather.

The third and final verb I want to offer you is a little more complicated, and you will need to exercise the same interpretive freedom that allows us to insert Ruth chapter 1 into so many wedding ceremonies: "Where you go, I will go," are the words of a woman to her mother-in-law, but whatever. We could get in big trouble if we took that literally, and we could get in big trouble if we did the same with chapter 3.

～ ～ ～

There is one more verb that needs our attention: *uncover*. It speaks to the *why* of all this interpretive homiletical work. Why do we cling to the text and remain steadfast to one another while we read it? Why do we do the slow work of gleaning? Because there is something that needs to be uncovered, and I don't just mean Boaz. The passage below is from chapter 3.

> Naomi her mother-in-law said to Ruth, "My daughter, I need to seek some security for you, so that it may be well with you. Now here is our kinsman Boaz, with whose young women you have been working. See, he is winnowing barley tonight at the thresh-ing floor. Now wash and anoint yourself, and put on your best clothes and go down to the threshing floor; but do not make yourself known to the man until he has finished eating and drinking. When he lies down, observe the place where he lies; then, go and uncover his feet and lie down; and he will tell you what to do." Ruth said to Naomi, "All that you tell me I will do."
>
> So Ruth went down to the threshing floor and did just as her mother-in-law had instructed her. When Boaz had eaten and drunk, and he was in a contented mood, he went to lie down at the end of the heap of grain. Then Ruth came stealth-ily and uncovered his feet, and lay down. At midnight the man was startled, and turned over, and there, lying at his feet, was a woman! He said, "Who are you?" And she answered, "I am Ruth, your servant; spread your cloak over your servant, for you are next-of-kin." He said, "May you be blessed by the Lord, my daughter; this last instance of your loyalty is better than the first; you have not gone after young men, whether poor or rich. And now, my daughter, do not be afraid, I will do for you all that you ask, for all the assembly of my people know that you are a worthy woman." (Ruth 3:1–11)

Let us bracket, for the moment, the questions about seduction and impro-priety and how two women alone in the ancient world sometimes have to work it in order to live. We do not need lessons in Hebrew sexual innuendo. The point I want to make is that in order for Ruth and Naomi to be restored to the community, something has to be uncovered. And uncovering is a dangerous verb. It takes us way deeper than most of us want to go or to see.

If we're uncovered, we have to look at our own nakedness. All we are, like it or not. All we've done. All we've tried to cover up with fig leaves so God wouldn't notice that we haven't exactly followed every rule in the gar-den; there was one tree whose fruit we just had to taste; sorry. *Uncovered*. It's exposed and vulnerable and usually not your default posture of choice. And let's be clear. It isn't only individuals who can be uncovered. Communities can, too. Churches. The people of God in all our human collectivity.

Ruth and Naomi's community was in need of a little uncovering. Boaz on the threshing floor was just the designated rep, standing in for the rest of the townsfolk; really, they were all under the microscope, in need of a little truth-telling. Look at us. Look at how some of us have all we could want and others of us are growing up in abject poverty. Look at how we treat foreigners who come across our borders. Look at how we resist claiming the connection between us and Naomi, so much so, that she and Ruth have to enact this elaborate ritual to get us to call them family. Is this really how we want to live? Is this God's vision for us and human flourishing?

Uncovering is a call to truth-telling and justice. It's a call to action. And it starts when a very tired preacher lifts up the corner of the community and shows us what's underneath: that we're really family, and it's time to claim one another. That we have a shared history and a lot of it in this country is painful and difficult to tell. That Pharaoh still has a grip on us, and will, until we uncover and work through our own addictions to privilege. Uncovering. It's the courage to be truly authentic in front of God and everybody. And in this time of Ferguson and New York and Baltimore and Charleston, it has never been more critical for us.

The Book of Ruth. It's a script for a very tired preacher, wandering somewhere between the land of Moab and the house of bread. And if you can resist the urge to turn back, if you can hold onto Ruth's verbs, you'll make it to chapter 4, which of course is the chapter of redeeming. Redeeming is God's verb. It means to restore to fullness, which is what I pray for you. Amen.

Bibliography

Boesak, Allan. "The Reuben Option." In *A Chorus of Witnesses*, edited by Thomas G. Long and Cornelius Plantinga Jr., 131–38. Grand Rapids: Eerdmans, 1994.

16

Preaching to the Baptized in a Secular Age

The Role of Classic Homiletics as Cultivator of the Biblical Imagination

—Timothy O'Malley

ALTHOUGH TRADITIONAL SECULAR THEORY has proved inadequate for understanding American religiosity, there is an acknowledgment that religious life in the United States has been colonized by an internal form of secularization.[1] This internal secularization has led to an attenuation of the theological imagination, one in which the particularity of the religious narrative is reduced to a vague sense that God exists and requires human beings to be decent citizens of a thin moral order.[2] In this context, preaching has a particular vocation to make available to the late modern person God's salvific plan that unfolds through an encounter with the Scriptures in the milieu of divine worship.[3]

This essay suggests that in the setting of a secular age, Catholic homilists need to look for models of preaching in the classic sermons that make up the Christian tradition. The essay will proceed in three parts. In the first,

1. See Smith, "Moralistic Therapeutic," 55–74.
2. O'Malley, 45–50.
3. Grasso, *Proclaiming*, 47–48.

I define what constitutes a secular age, at the same time noting ways that homiletics is challenged by the presumptions of secularity. In the second, I turn to three icons of classic homiletic methodology who conceived of the preaching act as a participation in the biblical narrative. These preachers include Augustine of Hippo, Romanos the Melodist, and John Henry Newman. In the third, I gather together the results of this inquiry, arguing that preaching to the baptized in a secular age will necessitate a move away from exclusive attention to historical-critical exegesis in scriptural interpretation, as well as deeper attention to the poetics of human speech.

Preaching in a Secular Age

Awareness of the effects of modernity upon the religious imagination is by no means new. In his assessment of the prospects for his own Romantic construct of religion in modernity, Friedrich Schleiermacher notes that in Germany, the apotheosis of the scientific method "knows nothing of this living acquisition, of this illuminating truth, of the true spirit of discovery in childlike intuition . . . where things are only to be seen and handled as they have already presented themselves."[4] Modern theology has constantly responded to the shift in human consciousness away from a sanctified cosmos to a utilitarian universe in which there is nothing more to matter than meets the eye.

Charles Taylor's account of secularity takes up this analysis of religiosity in the modern world. Secularity, for Taylor, is not ultimately about either the separation of religion from the political order or the disappearance of religion from human consciousness. Such an understanding of secularity has been put to rest by sociologists attentive to the vigorous presence of religiosity in the modern world.[5] Rather, for Taylor, the practice of Christianity has moved "from a society where belief in God is unchallenged and indeed, unproblematic, to one in which it is understood to be one option among others, and frequently not the easiest to embrace."[6] For Taylor, this is not simply a matter of finding oneself doubting the existence of God. Rather, the assumptions that Christianity depend upon are challenged by alternative worldviews that contest these assumptions. Further, the Christian conception of reality is not merely an equal challenger to secular ontology

---

4. Schleiermacher, *On Religion*, 127.

5. See Casanova, *Public Religions*; and Davie, *Europe*.

6. Taylor, *Secular Age*, 3.

but conceived as a boutique philosophy that has no authentic standing in the public sphere.[7] As Taylor writes:

> There is a secular reason which everyone can use and reach conclusions by—conclusions, that is, with which everyone can agree. Then there are special languages, which introduce extra assumptions, which might even contradict those of ordinary secular reason. These are much more epistemologically fragile; in fact you won't be convinced by them unless you already hold them. So religious reason either comes to the same conclusions as secular reason, but then it is superfluous; or it comes to contrary conclusions, and then it is dangerous and disruptive. This is why it needs to be sidelined.[8]

Thus, the baptized Christian operating within the public sphere must deal with this clash of worldviews on a regular basis. A secular age is less a matter of sociological necessity and instead is an experience of disorientation that the religious person has existing in a cosmos in which her worldview is only one (insufficient) option among many. In this context, a person in a secular age will either find oneself isolating spheres of life, relegating religion to a certain private activity beneficial for human flourishing; or, this person will depart from the religious tradition, entering the growing ranks of the "nones."

In fact, among Americans, the former option, at least thus far, seems to have been the more prominent one. As Christian Smith's own research has discerned, the dominant American religious mentality discernable among adolescents but passed on from parents is Moralistic Therapeutic Deism, a credo in which God exists, people must be generally good, and if they are, they will find themselves bound for heaven. Such a religious perspective, in fact, enables the existence of multiple worldviews that do not conflict. As he writes:

> Like American civil religion, Moralistic Therapeutic Deism appropriates, abstracts, and revises doctrinal elements from mostly Christianity and Judaism for its own purpose. But it does so in a downward, apolitical direction. Its social function is not to unify and give purpose to the nation at the level of civil affairs. Rather, it functions to foster subjective well-being in its believers and to lubricate interpersonal relationships in the local public sphere.[9]

7. See Milbank, *Theology*.

8. Taylor, "What Does Secularism Mean?," 320.

9. Smith with Denton, *Soul Searching*, 169.

In the religious sphere, Americans practice religion "to help people succeed in life, to make them feel good, and to help them get along with others—who otherwise are different—in school, at work, on the team, and in other routine areas of life."[10] In such an outlook, the particular claims of religious traditions dissipate. One does not attend to particularity but instead looks for general truths accessible to every person.

In the context of preaching, there is a significant problem with this internal secularization in American religion. The particulars of the scriptural narrative are passed over often by both the preacher and the baptized who are participating in the preaching act. The one who encounters the scriptural text performs an internal act of eisegesis in which the text must be conformed to the thin credo of Moralistic Therapeutic Deism. Among my students, for example, a reading of the Parable of the Good Samaritan immediately means that human beings should be generally good to one another, taking up small acts of kindness for all those whom one encounters. While this is a fine moral philosophy, it passes over the radical hospitality of the Samaritan and the violent context of the parable in which Jesus extends the possibility of salvation to those perceived as outside the covenant. The listener of the parable is invited to become neighborly to those most in need of compassion, extending oneself beyond ethics to christological self-gift.[11] To rectify the thin reading of the parable brought about by MTD, it is necessary to discover anew practices of scriptural reading that pay attention to details rather than interpret the text as a cipher of an already determined meaning.

For this reason, it is necessary to form both the preacher and the baptized alike in encountering the particulars of the text once again. Yet, for the most part, modern forms of reading do not encourage this kind of contemplative encounter with text. In his essay, "Retreat from the Word," George Steiner describes the change in humanity's relationship to language precipitated by higher-level mathematical discourse. Words are no longer meant to attune the human person to reality but instead are understood as formula themselves: conveyers of symbolic meaning from the speaker to the recipient. He writes:

> The language of Shakespeare and Milton belong to a stage of history in which words were in natural control of experienced life. The writer of today tends to use far fewer and simpler words, both because mass culture has watered down the concept of

---

10. Ibid.

11. Johnson, *Gospel of Luke*, 173.

literacy and because the sum of realities of which words can give
a necessary and sufficient account has sharply diminished.[12]

Steiner is not simply a literary aesthete, decrying a world in which human
discourse has become less sophisticated. Instead, he is noting that there is
little attention to the particularities of *every* word, the rhetorical and literary function of human speech, in light of the epistemic predominance of
scientific discourse in society. Words do not conform the human being to
participate in reality but instead they are conveyers of already assembled
truths to the human person.

In such a society, the faithful approach the Scriptures oriented toward
the text as a conveyer of propositional truths, often inattentive to the particular imagery of the scriptural word. In this reduced literary context, the
Scriptures express moral truths about existence in parabolic form or are
intended to elicit a certain experience in the listener.[13] Nonetheless, the listener of the Scriptures is not attentive to the literary dimensions of the text,
the metaphors that shape Christian existence. As Janice M. Soskice writes:

> The smitten rock, the riven side, the foundation of life, death
> by water in the flood and life by water in baptism and the res-
> urrected Christ—these images appear again and again in litur-
> gies, in homiletics, on baptismal founts, in church mosaics and
> friezes, on stained glass, and in countless paintings. They form
> an inescapable background to Christian thought, with each new
> reflection bringing to mind those that went before it. But this is
> not static—the image of living water can be renewed and embel-
> lished by each individual who reflects upon it.[14]

The task of the theologian, and thus the preacher, is to attend to the specific
images of the text, showing not only how these images have been interpreted historically but also how these central Christian motifs still remain
powerful for the shaping of a life here and now.

Therefore, formation in homiletics for preaching to the baptized in
a secular age cannot simply rely on introducing the homilist to practices
of communication. Instead, what is needed is a renewed attention to the
pedagogy of scriptural reading. Classic homilies, for the most part, were attuned to a variety of practices of reading that brought the listener or reader
of the homily to an encounter with the scriptural word and thus Christ's

12. Steiner, "Retreat," 25.

13. For an essay on the homilist's own temptation to move beyond imagery, see
Martin, *Breaking*, 103–18.

14. Soskice, *Metaphor*, 157.

very presence dwelling among the assembly. To study these practices is to develop homiletic strategies that will renew the imagination of the baptized in a secular milieu.

Icons of Scriptural Reading in the History of Preaching

In speaking to those involved in Catholic preaching, it is often surprising to discover the few occasions in which seminarians or deacon candidates immerse themselves in the homiletic methodologies employed by classic preachers in the Christian tradition. Although one must be careful to avoid a naïve antiquarianism in the preaching act with historical retrieval of homiletic practice, reading classic homilies might serve as a pedagogical aid in the renewal of practices of scriptural reading attached to the work of preaching itself. In this second part of the essay, I will attend to short sections of three "classic" homilies delivered (or written) by Augustine of Hippo, Romanos the Melodist, and John Henry Newman. Each of the homilies encounter the scriptural text less as a way of conveying already perceived moral truths to the believer and instead perceive scriptural reading as performed within the homily as a manifestation and thus encounter with divine love.

Augustine of Hippo

Among patristic preachers, Augustine is unique in his rather direct attention to homiletic pedagogy. In his *De catechizandis rudibus*, he combines his hermeneutics of love employed in his reading of the Scriptures to the pedagogical formation that the preacher should receive. To Deogratias, a deacon asking for assistance in delivering a sermon at the moment of first evangelization, he notes that the preacher must remember:

> [B]efore all else, Christ came so that people might learn how much God loves them, and might learn this so that they would catch fire with love for him who first loved them, and so that they would also love their neighbor as he commanded and showed by his example—he who made himself their neighbor by loving them when they were not close to him but were wandering far from him.[15]

This Christo-centric hermeneutics of love, one attentive to every particular detail of the text,[16] is made incarnate in the person of the preacher himself.

15. Augustine, *Instructing Beginners* 1.4.8.

16. Books II and III of *De doctrina christiana* form the preacher to attend to the

In addressing Deogratias's own boredom at repeatedly elucidating the most basic elements of the narrative, Augustine exhorts the deacon to remember that "if our understanding finds its delight within, in the brightest of secret places, let it also delight in the following insight into the ways of love: the more love goes down in a spirit of service into the ranks of the lowliest people, the more surely it rediscovers the quiet that is within."[17] In this way, the preacher offers a commentary upon the thread of love running through the scriptural narrative so that the assembly might discover in the preaching itself an encounter with this love. And this encounter with the salutary speech of the Scriptures mediated through the preaching act effects a healing of the assembly so that they might learn to love God and neighbor aright. As John Cavadini writes, "God's eloquence gives everything else a voice, invests the world of temporal things with significance, but only by keeping our attention fixed on God's eloquence can anything else speak."[18]

Augustine's preaching is an immersion into the signs of God's eloquence incarnate in the Scriptures, allowing listeners or readers to discover the humility of divine love and thus become themselves this sacrificial eloquent offering. Although significant attention to Augustine's homiletic corpus might draw this out more clearly, in the present context close attention to a single passage will be sufficient. In his *Enarrationes in Psalmos*, homilies on the psalms delivered to an assembly and then later edited, Augustine exegetes the meaning of praise in Psalm 150. Augustine's homilies carefully attend to every phrase in the psalms, unfolding how the particular scriptural word is an icon of divine speech, drawing the listener into a reformed way of life. In Psalm 150, Augustine's assembly has heard a hymn of praise in which the voice, the trumpet, and the lyre all participate in doxology. For Augustine, this is no accident, for "Our psalm has not left out any kind of sound, for it has indicated the voice by speaking of choral song, the breath or air in its mention of the trumpet, and percussion in the lyre."[19] Augustine suggests the diversity of musical praise of the psalm is an analogy "intended to suggest the mind, the spirit, and the body."[20] For this reason, praise offered to God is never merely a matter of the voice but implicates the entire person. The singer of the psalm is called to become an authentic doxologist.

---

particularities of the signs of the Scriptures so that these signs may be used for the enjoyment of the faithful in their encounter with God.

17. Augustine, *Instructing Beginners* 1.10.15.

18. Cavadini, "Sweetness," 169.

19. Augustine, *Expositions*, 150.8.

20. Ibid.

And at the very conclusion of his sermon, Augustine exhorts his assembly to become a society of divine praise. He preaches:

> When, at the beginning of the psalm, he invited us to *praise the Lord in his saints,* to whom was he speaking, if not to the saints themselves? And in whom were they to praise God, if not in themselves? The psalm is as good as saying, "You are his saints, for you are his strength, but only because he deploys his strength in you. You are his powerful ones, you are the vast extent of his greatness, because of the great deeds he has wrought in you. You are the trumpet, the psaltery, the lyre, the drum, the choir, the strings, the organ, and the cymbals that sound so splendid because they are attuned to each other." You are all these instruments, and when you listen to the psalm do not think of anything in this orchestra as worthless or transitory or lacking in dignity.[21]

Augustine has provided a close reading of the psalm in which all creation praises God precisely because it is created out of God's very goodness. The assembly takes up their identity as divine instruments of praise, ones that are importantly attuned to each other. The assembly itself is addressed through the psalm, which Augustine underlines through taking up the role of the psalmist himself, as if David himself is speaking to the assembly. This psalm (and in fact the entire psalter), as Augustine's homily discovers, is about the harmony of the saints who are attuned to one another in love. Augustine is teaching a way of listening closely to the Scriptures so that the baptized may discover in the text an image of what it means to belong to the church. The next time that the reader or listener encounters Psalm 150 (or any use of instrumentation in the Scriptures), they have developed the technologies of reading to long for the church's final destiny in a chorus of praise. Singing in church itself is no longer a mere religious practice but has become an icon of the church's final destiny. And, everyone within that assembly functions as an instrument of praise—an ecclesial ethics of sacramental love.

Augustine's method of preaching thus invites close attention to the particulars of the text. Yet, even more, through specific rhetorical techniques, he invites the assembly to see themselves as instruments of praise performing within the orchestra of the saints. There is an enrichment of the biblical imagination, one that results in a transformation of human life conceived doxologically.

21. Ibid.

Romanos the Melodist

While prose defines much patristic preaching, the sermons of Romanos the Melodist offer a fascinating counterpoint. Romanos, a sixth-century Greek poet, composed a number of homiletic *kontakia* that would have been chanted after the Gospel. These hymnic and acrostic sermons, taking place in a liturgical context, formed the Christian in seeing oneself as a participant in salvation history. As Derek Krueger writes:

> The rites and offices of the church offered the forum where Byzantine Christians learned to apply a penitential Bible to themselves. The liturgy produced not only the body and blood of Christ, but also a Christian congregation—itself a body of Christ—situated in liturgical time, revisiting the life of Christ in the course of the liturgical calendar. Throughout the festal cycle, hymns and sermons inculcated certain dispositions to teach Christians who they were within the history of salvation.[22]

The biblical narrative, rather than being relegated to the past, becomes a present performance within the liturgy as the listener of the chanted sermon enters into the dramatic roles presented by the poet.

Romanos's sermon "On the Resurrection" embodies his homiletic pedagogy. He begins by focusing the attention of the listener on the narrative that is to unfold in the Gospel of the day: "Though you descended into the tomb, O Immortal/yet you destroyed the power of hell,/and you arose as victor, O Christ God,/calling the myrrh-bearing women, 'Rejoice!'/and giving peace to your apostles, O you/*who grant resurrection to the fallen.*"[23] The hymnic homily begins not addressed to the assembly but to the resurrected Christ. Already, the listener is invited into a relationship with God through the homily, which is not mundane prose but already prayer.

As the homily continues, Romanos offers a poetic re-telling of the Resurrection, one in which the assembly gathered in the church participates:

> To the Sun who was before the sun and yet had set in a tomb/ myrrh-bearing maidens hastened towards dawn,/seeking him as the day, and they cried to one another:/Friends, come, let us anoint with spices/the life-bearing yet buried body,/the flesh which raises fallen Adam and now lies in the grave./Come, let us hurry, like the magi/let us adore and let us offer/sweet spices as gifts to the One who is now wrapped,/not in swaddling clothes,

---

22. Krueger, *Liturgical Subjects*, 218.
23. Romanos, "On the Resurrection," 167.

but in a shroud./Let us weep and let us cry, "Be roused, Master, *who grant resurrection to the fallen.*"[24]

The narrator in the first three stanzas has knowledge, through the Scriptures, that Christ's death is not the end of the narrative. A kind of paradox is presented that the very eternal Sun of life has like the created sun been "set" in a tomb. Gathering to celebrate the resurrection of Christ at dawn, Romanos is inviting the assembly to imagine itself in the Resurrection narrative, hastening to the tomb. And indeed, the assembly takes on the role of myrrh-bearing women. They come forth to anoint the Christ who will be the source of all life. Here, Romanos seems to be implying that the women who showed up to the tomb to anoint the dead body of the Lord already operated out of faith in the Resurrection. In fact, they could perceive a link between their own anointing of Christ and the gift of the magi at Christ's birth, when he was already wrapped in swaddling clothes. The assembly come to offer this gift of love to Christ with the women, crying out for the resurrection of the Lord, aware that Christ's resurrection is the meaning of all of history.

This same dialogical quality unfolds throughout the entire chanted sermon in which the narrator, the characters of the Gospels, and the assembly become part of salvation history. The text of the Scriptures does not function as a past event but as a present reality in the lives of the faithful. After twenty-three stanzas of poetic, scriptural narration, and dialogue, the poem concludes with a single voice crying out to Christ in prayer:

> May my dead soul, O Savior, rise again with you./Do not let grief destroy it, and may it not come to forget/those songs that sanctify it./Yes, O Merciful, I implore you, do not abandon me/ who am stained with offenses,/For in iniquities and in sins my mother bore me./My Father, holy and compassionate,/may your name be ever hallowed/be my mouth and be my lips,/be my voice and be my song,/Give me grace as I proclaim your hymns, for you can do so, *who grant resurrection to the fallen.*

The death that has been overcome is now the sinner's. Importantly, Romanos does not conclude his sermon with the narrator exhorting the assembly to avoid sin. Instead, through the homily the assembly once again become prayerful penitents before the risen Lord. The hymns of Easter, sung throughout the liturgy thus far, are not simply to be enjoyed unto themselves. Instead, the very singing of the hymns is to become a participation in

---

24. Ibid.

the resurrection of Christ. Christ's resurrection unfolds now in the history of the church.

Thus, Romanos the Melodist, all the while employing textual exegesis of the Scriptures, transforms the homiletic act into a participation in sacred history. There is no separation between the assembly and the biblical narrative, precisely because the story of salvation made manifest in the Scriptures unfolds now in the liturgical act. The particular details of the text are interpreted not simply through the modality of explanation but through a poetics of participation whereby the assembly takes up the voice of the characters in the Gospel. And through assuming these roles, the assembly at the level of the individual self is gradually formed so members see their own lives as immersed in saving history.

John Henry Newman

John Henry Newman's Anglican homiletics must be located within the broader context of English religious practice in the nineteenth century. In Newman's "plain" preaching,[25] there are two approaches to religious practice, both of which Newman finds insufficient. The first, evident in Newman's "Religion of the Day," sees religion as part of social conduct not radically affecting human action in the world. This "enlightened" religion believes that as "reason is cultivated, the taste formed, the affections and sentiments refined, a general decency and grace will of course spread over the face of human society, quite independently of the influence of Revelation."[26] Scriptural phrases that are deemed too severe are dismissed by such rational Christians. Instead, this religion of the day is "adapted to please men of skeptical minds . . . who have never been careful to obey their conscience, who cultivate the intellect without disciplining the heart, and who allow themselves to speculate freely about what religion *ought to be,* without going to Scripture to discover what it really is."[27] Rational preaching in this context was less interested in discerning what is revealed in the Scriptures and more focused on discussing current events in the church and world. Tractarians, including Newman, "sought to minimize discussions of potentially divisive issues because any controversy that provoked could detract from the raison

---

25. For an account of "plain" versus "university" preaching, see Ellison, "The Tractarians' Sermons," 36–44.

26. Newman, "Religion of the Day," in *Parochial and Plain*, 199.

27. Ibid., 202.

d'être of the sermon: the preacher's appeals for his people to live more fully Christian lives."[28]

At the opposite end of the spectrum, Newman was equally concerned with the rise of English evangelicalism and the implicit theory of conversion operative in such preaching. Horton Davies describes the style of these evangelization preachers: "Their own use of preaching was threefold: to awaken men from apathy or formality and thus to convert them with the aid of the Holy Spirit; to build men up in the faith—edification; and to teach men how to manifest the fruits of the Spirit-sanctification."[29] For Newman, the desire to bring those who received the preaching act to conversion and a deeper holiness was integral to the preaching act. Nonetheless, Newman was concerned that such evangelical preaching was intended primarily to elicit affections, detracting the listener of the sermon from the normal way of holiness: the sacraments and ordinances of the church. Therefore, in his sermon "Religious Emotion," he is careful to caution the assembly to remember:

> One secret act of self-denial, one sacrifice of inclination to duty, is worth all the mere good thoughts, warm feelings, passionate prayers, in which idle people indulge themselves. It will give us more comfort on our deathbed to reflect on one deed of self-denying mercy, purity, or humility, than to recollect the shedding of many tears, and the recurrence of frequent transports, and much spiritual exultation.[30]

In this way, Newman's homiletic theory was an immersion of the listener into the saving grammar of the Scriptures, together with a description of those central practices that might enable the Christian to seek after holiness of life.

Newman's sermon for the feast of Christmas, "The Mystery of Godliness," embodies this two-fold concern for immersion into the sacramental narrative of the Scriptures together with fostering concrete religious practice among the assembly. At the beginning of the sermon, Newman focuses the assembly on what takes place during the season of Christmas:

> Our Saviour's birth in the flesh is the earnest, and, as it were, beginning of our birth in the Spirit. It is a figure, promise, or pledge of our new birth, and it effects what it promises. As He was born, so are we born also; and since He was born, therefore

28. Ellison, "The Tractarians' Sermons," 19.

29. Davies, *Worship*, 3:228.

30. Newman, "Religious Emotion," in *Parochial and Plain*, 122.

we too are born. As He is the Son of God by nature, so are we
sons of God by grace; and it is He who has made us such.[31]

This initial focal point is a commentary upon Heb 2:2, "Both He that sanc-
tifieth and they who are sanctified are all of one: for which cause He is not
ashamed to call them brethren."[32]

Yet, while Hebrews may be the proximate source of the sermon, "The
Mystery of Godliness" knits the listener or reader of the sermon into the
narrative of the Scriptures such that it is nearly impossible to distinguish
between Newman's own speech and the scriptural word:

> This is the wonderful economy of grace, or mystery of godliness,
> which should be before our minds at all times, but especially at
> this season, when the Most Holy took upon Him our flesh of "a
> pure Virgin," "by the operation of the Holy Ghost, without spot
> of sin, to make us clean from all sin." God "dwelleth in the Light
> which no man can approach upon;" He "is Light, and in Him is
> no darkness at all." "His garment," as described in the Prophet's
> Vision, is "white as snow, and the hair of His head like the pure
> wool; His throne the fiery flame, and His wheels burning fire."[33]

Newman is reading across the Scriptures in the presence of the assembly.
The scriptural narrative is the source of all sacred history. And the very
words of the Scriptures matter so much to Newman that he first lets them
speak before he contributes his own word about the Word: "He it was who
created the worlds; He it was who interposed of old time in the affairs of the
world, and showed Himself a living and observant God . . . Yet this great
God condescended to come down on earth from His heavenly throne, and
to be born into His own world."[34] His speech is only possible because he has
first allowed God to speak a narrative of salvation through the mediation of
the scriptural word.

Newman concludes the sermon with an exhortation to practice what it
means to live in a post-Christmas world:

> Let us at this season approach Him with awe and love, in whom
> resides all perfection, and from whom we are allowed to gain it.
> Let us come to the Sanctifier to be sanctified. Let us come to Him
> to learn our duty, and to receive grace to do it. At other seasons
> of the year we are reminded of watching, toiling, struggling, and

31. Ibid., 1014.
32. Ibid.
33. Ibid.
34. Ibid., 1015.

suffering; but at this season we are reminded simply of God's gifts toward us sinners.[35]

During this season of gift-giving, to which Newman is making reference, the Christian is to practice abiding within the space of gift. The season of Christmas is "a time for innocence, and purity, and gentleness, and mildness, and contentment, and peace."[36] To practice Christmas is to take up these virtues, to live them out more fully so that "each Christmas . . . find[s] us more and more like Him, who as at this time became a little child for our sake, more simple-minded, more humble, more holy, more affectionate, more resigned, more happy, more full of God."[37] Here Newman is inviting the listener of the sermon to imitate the virtues of the God-child, born in a stable, so that they might become more divine.

Thus, Newman's homiletic pedagogy involves an immersion into the scriptural narrative, necessary even before the preacher can adequately exhort the assembly to do anything. The scriptural quotations are not proof-texts, but seeds intended to water the scriptural imagination of the assembly. Newman makes the scriptural text into a reality being performed in the present, a text that manifests God's tender compassion for the human condition. And, by concluding the homily with implications of this immersion, he prescribes concrete practices whereby the assembly be renewed in holiness in light of this encounter with the Scriptures.

The Renewal of Preaching in a Secular Age

The three homilists studied in this essay, although occupying distinctive places in the history of Christianity, offer to the contemporary homilist a series of strategies that might be employed in preaching to the baptized in a secular age. First, they each employ methods of scriptural interpretation that are not simply historical-critical in approach. Instead, they immerse the reader into the Scripture using a variety of reading strategies. Second, through the use of poetic speech, the three homilists proclaim the narrative of the Scriptures in the subjunctive mode, inviting the assembly to perceive the scriptural proclamation as unfolding even within the present.

35. Ibid., 1020.
36. Ibid., 1021.
37. Ibid.

Reading Strategies

Historical-critical exegesis, of course, is not to be discounted in the work of homiletics even within a secular age. *Dei Verbum* notes that "the words of God, expressed in human language, are in every way like human speech, just as the Word of the eternal Father, when he took on himself the weak flesh of human beings, became like them."[38] In this sense, the scriptural word has a history, and to discover this biblical history is to discern the ways that God has acted in human history itself.

Yet, the problem with historical-critical exegesis is less with its results than the mentality that may develop if the reader employs it as the univocal strategy.[39] As John J. O'Keefe and R.R. Reno write:

> For Irenaeus and for the patristic tradition in general, the Bible was not a perfect historical record. Scripture was, for them, the oriented, luminous center of a highly varied and complex reality, shaped by divine providence. It was true not by virtue of successfully or accurately representing any one event or part of this divinely ordained reality. Rather, the truth rested in the scripture's power to illuminate and disclose the order and pattern of all things.[40]

The focus of reading is not primarily on determining the historical references made in the text but "to learn from and to come to know the Teacher, a knowledge that uncovers the deepest meaning of the texts themselves."[41]

In other words, the reading strategy of historical-critical exegesis attends to the intentions of the historical author of the text. Without other reading strategies, it is likely that the homilist will forget that the primary purpose of preaching is to illuminate what God is authoring through the biblical narrative. The privileging of historical-critical exegesis in scriptural formation has led to homilists unable to encounter the text as still authoring the church into existence. Rather than serve as a source of arcane historical knowledge or moral teachings, the Scriptures are God's continual authorship of humanity.

In Augustine, Romanos the Melodist, and John Henry Newman, readers find themselves immersed again in an exegesis that takes seriously the Scriptures as divine history, which is still unfolding in the present. The

---

38. Second Vatican Council, *Dei Verbum*, 13.

39. For a closer study of the rise of historical-critical exegesis in biblical commentary and homiletics, see Frei, *Eclipse*.

40. O'Keefe and Reno, *Sanctified*, 11.

41. Levering, *Participatory*, 63.

instruments used in Old Testament psalmody are now applied to the very life of the church herself. Characters within the resurrection narrative are not simply used for arguments within early Christianity about who saw Christ first but are intended to form the subjectivity of the present reader to encounter the resurrected Lord. Christmas is not only about the event in Bethlehem but the birth of God in the life of the believer. The reading of classic homilies might elevate alternative reading strategies, renewing scriptural exegesis in the process; and thus inviting the baptized into forms of reading that see the Scriptures not as archaic narratives but as a salvific story unfolding even now. Such a reading strategy is a tactic that can aid the church in preaching in a secular age.

The Poetics of Preaching in the Subjunctive Mood

Most homilies delivered in parishes function as monologues in which the priest or deacon speaks to the assembly about his particular insights drawn from the Scriptures. The listener of the homily encounters often, in this discourse, not the immediacy of the scriptural narrative but the preacher's words about a text. Ironically, in this context, the homily actually distances the listener from the Scriptures instead of knitting them into the narrative of salvation.

Yet, there are forms of speech better suited to sacramental proclamation than the kind of direct address employed in homilies in the present. As Paul Ricoeur writes, "Revelation . . . designates the emergence of another concept of truth as adequation . . . a conception of truth as manifestation, in the sense of letting be what shows itself. What shows itself is each time the proposing of a world, a world where I can project my ownmost possibilities."[42] Preaching may find it beneficial to re-tell the narrative already proclaimed in the Scriptures, yet in such a way that in the re-telling the listener is invited to participate anew in the narrative. Homilies can employ poetic language, inviting the listener to participate with wonder in the paradox of the Incarnation where the God became flesh. The homily can move from proclamation to prayer, addressing itself no longer to the assembly but to God, thus moving the baptized to see that the narrative of salvation is still unfolding in the present. Poetics operate in the "subjunctive mode," constructing "a third space . . . where we create, experience, and share alternative realities and orders."[43]

42. Ricouer, "Naming God," 223.
43. Puett et al., *Ritual*, 72.

This kind of "subjunctive" poetics, presenting the drama of salvation, is noticeably absent in present homiletic discourse where it is presumed that the preacher's immediacy is what is required. There is not a creativity in discourse in which the baptized are invited to refigure the world in light of the narrative of salvation unfolding in Christ. Yet Augustine performs this poetics often, inviting the assembly to imagine itself as an instrument within the Scriptures. Romanos allows the doxological subject to take on the characters of the Scriptures by introducing poetic drama into homilies, and in the process re-forming the self for the activity of worship. Newman quotes Scriptures as his own speech, and thus, the text once again becomes a narrative of salvation in the present. He lets the listener contemplate meaning before he interprets it for them. In each case, the speech of homilies gives play for the imagination, which is necessary for inviting the baptized toward reconceiving the cosmos as sanctified.

Such work in forming preachers in pre-critical exegesis together with a poetics of human speech are required if the Scriptures are again to function for the baptized as a sacramental encounter with God's salvific speech. Homiletic training that depends solely on either communications theory or peer assessment has not steeped the homilist into the luminous worldview of the Scriptures present in classic homilies that must be communicated in the present, secular age. In the liturgy, the Scriptures again function no longer as a book in the library, but as the sacramental encounter with God's saving words. And to the baptized, who grow accustomed to hearing homilies inspired by classic homilies, their own private reading of the Scriptures, and thus their very imaginations, will be renewed. As Jean-Louis Chrétien writes:

> The white in the margins of the Bible, that emptiness which surrounds that writing, that unsaid which borders and fringes the said, is the place not built but always buildable, where you may edify, listener, if you wish, the Bethlehem of your reading and response, the future, in you and for you, of the sacred story. It matters little that you do it in haste and that a single word should be reborn in you, a single verse, for then you will soon go to bed in another today than the one in which you awoke this morning. For each time God speaks and is heard, the sacred story is today, and today is the sacred story.[44]

Preaching as an act of telling again the always present sacred story is perhaps the most important task for combating internal secularization.

44. Chrétien, "Reading the Bible Today," 5.

Formation for such preaching would benefit by learning from those who have preached this sacred story in the history of the church.

Bibliography

Augustine of Hippo. *Expositions of the Psalms*. Vol. 6. Translated by Maria Boulding. New York: New City, 2004.

———. *Instructing Beginners in Faith*. Translated by Raymond Canning. New York: New City, 2006.

Casanova, José. *Public Religions in the Modern World*. Chicago: University of Chicago Press, 1994.

Cavadini, John. "The Sweetness of the Word: Salvation and Rhetoric in Augustine's *De doctrina christiana*." In *De Doctrina Christiana: A Classic of Western Culture*, edited by Duane W. H. Arnold and Pamela Bright, 164–81. Notre Dame: University of Notre Dame Press, 1995.

Chrétien, Jean-Louis. "Reading the Bible Today." In *Under the Gaze of the Bible*. Translated by John Marson Dunaway. New York: Fordham University Press, 2015.

Davie, Grace. *Europe—The Exceptional Case: Parameters of Faith in the Modern World*. Sarum Theological Lectures. Maryknoll, NY: Orbis, 2002.

Davies, Horton. *Worship and Theology in England: From Watts and Wesley to Martineau, 1690–1900*. Vol. 3. Grand Rapids: Eerdmans, 1996.

Ellison, Robert H. "The Tractarians' Sermons and Other Speeches." In *A New History of the Sermon: The Nineteenth Century*, edited by Robert H. Ellison, 15–57. Boston: Brill, 2010.

Flannery, Austin, ed. *Vatican Council II: The Basic Sixteen Documents*. Northport, NY: Costello, 1996.

Frei, Hans W. *The Eclipse of Biblical Narrative: A Study in the Eighteenth and Nineteenth Century Hermeneutics*. New Haven: Yale University Press, 1974.

Grasso, Domenico. *Proclaiming God's Message: A Study in the Theology of Preaching*. Notre Dame: University of Notre Dame Press, 1965.

Johnson, Luke Timothy. *The Gospel of Luke*. Sacra Pagina 3. Collegeville, MN: Liturgical, 1991.

Krueger, Derek. *Liturgical Subjects: Christian Ritual, Biblical Narrative, and the Formation of the Self in Byzantium*. Philadelphia: University of Pennsylvania Press, 2014.

Levering, Matthew. *Participatory Biblical Exegesis: A Theology of Biblical Interpretation*. Notre Dame: University of Notre Dame Press, 2008.

Martin, David. *The Breaking of the Image: A Sociology of Christian Theory & Practice*. Vancouver: Regent College, 2006.

Milbank, John. *Theology & Social Theory: Beyond Secular Reason*. 2nd ed. Malden, MA: Blackwell, 2006.

O'Keefe, John J., and R. R. Reno. *Sanctified Vision: An Introduction to Early Christian Interpretation of the Bible*. Baltimore: Johns Hopkins University Press, 2005.

O'Malley, Timothy P. *Liturgy and the New Evangelization*. Collegeville, MN: Liturgical Press, 2014.

Puett, Michael J., et al. *Ritual and Its Consequences: An Essay on the Limits of Sincerity*. New York: Oxford University Press, 2008.

Newman, John Henry. *Parochial and Plain Sermons*. San Francisco: Ignatius, 1997.

Ricouer, Paul. "Naming God." In *Figuring the Sacred: Religion, Narrative, and Imagination*, edited by Mark I. Wallace and translated by David Pellauer, 217–35. Minneapolis: Fortress, 1995.

Romanos the Melodist. "On the Resurrection." Translated by Ephrem Lash. In *On the Life of Christ: Kontakia*, 165–79. Sacred Literature. San Francisco: HarperCollins, 1995.

Schleiermacher, Friedrich. *On Religion: Speeches to Its Cultured Despisers*. Translated by John Oman. New York: Harper & Bros., 1958.

Smith, Christian. "Is Moralistic Therapeutic Deism the New Religion of American Youth? Implications for the Challenge of Religious Socialization and Reproduction." In *Passing on the Faith: Transforming Traditions for the Next Generation of Jews, Christians, and Muslims*, edited by James Heft, 55–74. New York: Fordham University Press, 2006.

Smith, Christian, with Melinda Lundquist Denton. *Soul Searching: The Religious and Spiritual Lives of American Teenagers*. New York: Oxford University Press, 2005.

Soskice, Janet Martin. *Metaphor and Religious Language*. Oxford: Clarendon, 1985.

Steiner, George. "The Retreat from the Word." In *Language and Silence: Essays on Language, Literature, and the Inhuman*, 12–36. New York: Atheneum, 1967.

Taylor, Charles. *A Secular Age*. Cambridge, MA: Belknap, 2007.

———. "What Does Secularism Mean?" In *Dilemmas and Connections: Selected Essays*, 303–25. Cambridge, MA: Belknap, 2011.

17

A Priesthood Worthy of *Gaudium et Spes* and *Apostolicam Actuositatem*

—Rev. Donald Cozzens

THIS CHAPTER HAS THE provocative title "A Priesthood Worthy of *Gaudium et Spes* and *Apostolicum Actuositatem*." Here's the plan. First I'd like to address the state of the priesthood today which, sadly, will reveal a wounded and fractured priesthood. We'll spend some time here because the state of the priesthood provides the lens I will use to take the measure of "a priesthood worthy of *Gaudium et Spes* and *Apostolicum Actuositatem*."

Secondly, we'll grapple with my contention that many priests today are indeed worthy of the Vatican constitution and decree in question and why some priests might appear to be unworthy of them. This section of the chapter will examine the tension inherent for priests when we try to minister in our modern world and minister alongside our lay colleagues.

Finally, we'll put the "cancer" of clericalism under a surgeon's examining light and consider how we might excise this ecclesial tumor.

The State of the Priesthood

A few years ago I gave a talk to priests at St. Patrick's College in Maynooth, Ireland. It is Ireland's only remaining seminary. The talk was titled "The Last

Priests in Ireland." If I were to give a similar presentation to U.S. priests, I'd title it "The Last Priests in America."

If you've ever visited the seminary at Maynooth, you will remember being impressed with its size. It's huge; established in 1795 to accommodate 700 seminarians, in 2013 it had an enrollment of approximately 70 seminarians preparing to meet the pastoral needs of Irish Catholics.

I've come to see that the state of the priesthood in the U.S. is pretty much the state of the priesthood in Ireland, Europe, and Central and South America.

Here in the U.S., our seminaries are, for the most part, less than half full. And researchers report that for every hundred priests who retire, resign, or die in a given year, fewer than thirty are ordained. It's clear our numbers are down, our median age is up, our morale is low, and yet we remain mostly happy men who are humbled and grateful to preach God's word and serve God's people. Let's probe this apparent paradox.

We American priests are wounded men. A small but significant number of us have sexually abused children and teens, leaving the rest of us confused, embarrassed, and sad. The impact of the sexual abuse scandals on the morale of priests is difficult, of course, to measure. But it has shaken us to our core and raised questions we have long chosen not to face. We priests, who are charged to comfort the afflicted, have in our ranks men who have inflicted terrible suffering on countless victims.

Still, most active Catholics continue to signal us that we remain their friends and that they still trust us. That show of understanding has humbled many of us. Wounded? Yes. Sad? Yes—and at the same time, happy. But we shouldn't be surprised. For the gospel reminds us that Jesus made it quite clear that we can find peace, even joy, in the midst of suffering.

But there are other wounds. Some are self-inflicted. We find it easy at times to hide behind canon law instead of making pastoral decisions that might get us in trouble with the chancery office. Under the veil of prudence, we find it easy to avoid the prophetic, challenging homily likely to upset some of our parishioners. We play it safe. We wait for our next day off, our next vacation, and we count the years to our retirement.

Father Kilian McDonnell, the Benedictine theologian and poet, wrote these lines, which hit me square in the forehead. Of monks and priests, he writes:

> No grand betrayals
> We lacked the impudent will
> We died of small treasons.

Small treasons! Yes, that's what many of us are guilty of. Sex and drink remain real challenges, but so many silent cuts wound us too. We priests can gossip with the best and some of us stand in good company with cynics and those who make snarky judgments of others' manners and behaviors. After a while, our small treasons become invisible to us. And we don't realize just how badly our wounds of betrayal are wounding others.

If we priests are a wounded lot, we are also a divided lot. And the split in our ranks is deep and painful. Now we know the priesthood, like the church itself, has always, at least to some extent, been divided. And the divide is natural enough. It's partly the result of different temperaments—some clergy are simply more cautious than others while others are more adventurous. Some priests are simply conservative by nature. Others of us are more progressive by temperament. So, temperament is a factor, but the divide we priests are coping with goes well beyond temperament or personal leanings toward stability versus change. Let me put it this way, the chasm separating priests today is profoundly existential—it touches the core of our souls by upsetting our sense of identity and our understanding of what it means to be an ordained minister in our church.

Interestingly, the priesthood's present split was deepened, if not caused, by Vatican II's Decree on the Ministry and Life of Priests—*Presbyterorum Ordinis* (the order of priests). The decree points to two theologies or models of priesthood that may be complementary in theory, but often not in the daily life and ministry of the priest. The cultic model, endorsed at the Council of Trent, holds that priests receive a "sacred power" for "offering sacrifice and forgiving sins" (PO 2). Here, the priest is presented as a sacred figure, a mediator between God and humanity. He was called to a special and more perfect state of holiness. Such status, such dignity required, even demanded, that he be a man "set apart."

Special training, special discipline, the sacrifice of the human and sexual fulfillment of marriage and family—all this created an aura of an elite caste of religious heroes. I'm reminded of the recruitment ad, "The few, the proud, the Marines!" The priesthood had become the "Marines" of the Christian foot soldiers marching into battle against the forces of darkness and evil. Priests knew who they were and they knew their mission—the salvation of souls and the building up of the Kingdom of God in history.

But the very same Vatican II decree on the priesthood went on to say that the priest was a man set in the center of a Eucharistic, compassionate community of believers. He was not an elite officer of the church living in princely splendor but a human being living in the midst of a community and charged with preaching the Word of God and servant-leadership. Like the people he served, the priest was a disciple.

A woman parishioner entered the sacristy after Mass to take strong exception to a part of the priest's homily. The conversation grew uncomfortably heated. Exasperated, the woman said loudly, "After all, we're all disciples." The priest shot back, "I'm *not* a disciple!" Implied, of course, was the message that he was a priest—and she wasn't. He was the teacher; she was the disciple.

In the servant-leader model, the priest's identity is grounded in his baptism as well has his ordination. He's not so much a man "set apart," as a disciple set in the center of the community charged with the spiritual and pastoral care for his fellow disciples. Here the priest is a trail guide to a pilgrim people. Moreover, as a disciple himself, he needs the friendship, support, and encouragement—that is, ministry—of his community.

This division within the ranks of the priesthood shouldn't be exaggerated because the dividing line between the two models is porous and flexible. Both priests of the cultic model and priests of the servant-leader model often work well together within the same parish community. At the end of the day, they understand they share in a common ordained ministry. In fact, we regularly see characteristics of the cultic and servant-leader models in the same priest. But still, the division holds and is the source of real distress in the lives of many priests. In the midst of this distress priests find energy and hope in "serious conversations leading to blessed communion," in the words of Walter Brueggemann.

Worthy of *Gaudium et Spes, Apostolicam Actuositatem*

"The joys and hopes, the griefs and the anxieties of the men of this age, especially those who are poor or in any way afflicted, these are the joys and hopes, the griefs and anxieties of the followers of Christ." (GS 1)

Perhaps this single sentence holds the most memorable words of the Second Vatican Council. How do we priests hear them? How do we read the "signs of the times" if we remain focused on our parish ministry? Priests hear the council fathers telling them to pay attention to the modern world. Many clergy trained in pre-Vatican II seminaries—and in many post-Vatican II seminaries—were told not to take the modern world too seriously. The world that mattered was the heavenly world, the Kingdom of God.

Gaudium et Spes (*Pastoral Constitution on the Church in the Modern World*) challenged priests to recalculate their mission. We were told to reclaim the prophetic dimension of the priesthood, to awaken a "prophetic imagination." Our preaching, Dominican theologian Mary Catherine Hilkert reminded us, was to "name Grace," to name God's healing mercy in a violent and ruthless age. Many of us were more comfortable naming sin.

Thomas O'Meara, longtime professor of theology at the University of Notre Dame, titled one of his books *Loose in the World*. He wrote that the Holy Spirit was truly loose in the world, that God's grace and mercy permeated the world and was not restricted to the official channels of grace. Pope Francis gets this.

Gaudium et Spes instructed priests to see the fundamental goodness and dignity of the human person and to embrace the relational, communal heart of our faith. The "here and now" was as sacred as the "end time" and the "after time."

This pastoral constitution left the thinking priest both enthused and confused. It dawned on us priests that we were more liberators than enforcers. He not only had to preach the gospel of Jesus Christ, he was to bear witness to it. He was no longer to teach and govern and administer from the comfort of his rectory, he was to enter into authentic human relationships where he was an adult among adults.

For those men more grounded in the cultic model of the priesthood, this broader focus of ministry in the world was and is unsettling. They seemed to have little interest in ecumenical and inter-faith activities. And they remember that theologians Karl Rahner and Joseph Ratzinger both believed *Gaudium et Spes* was too optimistic about the human condition and the cultures of the world.

On the other hand, priests more grounded in the servant-leader model discovered a fresh rush of energy enlivening their ministry. For these men, parish boundaries seemed to dissolve. Now the world was their parish. Now the inner city and the sprawling suburbs presented pastoral challenges that required creative ministries. Racism, sexism, political corruption, and injustice of whatever stripe needed to be confronted. And most servant-leader priests were eager to meet these challenges.

∼ ∼ ∼

Let's consider now a priesthood worthy of the Decree on the Apostolate of the Laity (*Apostolicam Actuositatem*). But first a brief step back to the time of Pope Pius X, who insisted that the church is an unequal society made up of pastors and flock. In his words: "So distinct are these categories [of pastor and flock] that with the pastoral body only rests the necessary right and authority for promoting the end of the society [the church] and directing all its members toward that end." Pius continues, "[T]he only duty of the multitude is allow themselves to be led, and, like a docile flock, to follow the pastors" (*Vehementer Nos*).

When Msgr. George Talbot, an English priest of the Victorian era was asked about the role of the laity, he responded: "To hunt, to shoot, to entertain. These matters they understand, but to meddle with ecclesiastical matters they have no right at all."

Well, the laity has come a long way since the days of Pius X and Msgr. Talbot.

Priests can tip their hats to theologians Marie-Dominique Chenu and Yves Congar who shaped the renewed theology of the laity that remains one of the cornerstones of Vatican II.

But Vatican II stands with World War II in liberating Catholic laity from the passive role that held them in check for centuries. World War II's G.I. Bill opened the doors of America's colleges to working-class Catholics. And at the university, a multitude of American Catholics learned how to think and how to question. They were no longer ready to simply "pray, pay, and obey." Or as I prefer to put it, "to believe, behave, and be saved."

Apostolicam Actuositatem makes it clear that the Christian vocation is also a vocation to the apostolate and that the laity exercise a genuine apostolate, a genuine ministry. The decree defines the apostolate as "[A]ll activity directed to the goal for which the Church was founded: to spread the Kingdom of Christ for the glory of God enabling all to share in redemption and enter into relation with Christ."

Lay men and women bring the gospel and holiness to their sphere of influence where they are embedded in the various levels of society. And they should remember that they have a right to exercise their charisms for the building up of the church.

Some priests are reassured when they read in the decree that the "laity are fully subject to the hierarchy in the teaching of Christian doctrine, certain aspects of liturgy, and in the care of souls." Most Catholics are comfortable with this affirmation of the role of the teaching church, but they are likely to wince at the phrase, "laity are fully *subject* to the hierarchy." The *sensus fidelium* has become a part of the laity's vocabulary.

Most priests, I think, have a healthy respect for the laity and their role in the mission of the church. But I also think that many of the laity aren't so sure about that.

And clericalism is one of the reasons many of the laity are put off by us priests. Wherever clericalism exits, the reforms and vision of the Vatican II are repressed. So, let's consider briefly the phenomenon of clericalism.

Clericalism

Finally, there appears an issue that our divided church can agree on. Catholics of all stripes, conservatives and progressives and in-betweens, are declaring a pox on clericalism. From Pope Francis to the back pew widow, from seminary rectors to lay ecclesial ministers, clericalism, it's agreed, is crippling the pastoral mission of the church while at the same time strengthening the secularists' claim that Catholic clergy are nothing more than papal agents bent on enforcing rigid moral controls which smother our human instinct for pleasure and freedom. So, let's end clericalism in the Church.

It is time to heed the growing consensus that clericalism must go. But something tells me "not so fast." This "cancer" crippling the Catholic world—from local communities to Vatican offices—is so deeply embedded in our past and present church fabric that a careful pre-surgery examination is called for. So, pull on your surgical gloves and join me in the pre-op room.

We know clericalism when we encounter it, whether on the parish level or in the media's often skewed portrayal of priests and bishops. But like pornography, although we know clericalism when we see it, it's not so easy to define. Here's how I see it: Clericalism is an attitude found in many but not all clergy who have made their status as priests and bishops more important than their status as baptized disciples of Jesus Christ. In doing so, a sense of privilege, preferment, and entitlement emerges in their individual and collective psyches. This, in turn, breeds a corps of ecclesiastical elites who think they're not "like other men."

Clergy caught up in this kind of purple-hewed seduction are incapable of seeing that it freezes their humanity—their ability to simply connect on a human level with the various sorts of God's holy people. Of all the sour fruits of clericalism, this inability to connect or to relate with others might be the most damaging. When the ordained come across as somehow superior to their parishioners and the various people they encounter, the playing field is tilted. The non-ordained sense the imbalance and metaphorically—and sometimes in real space—step back. This kind of disconnect can be fatal to a priest's efforts to build a sense of community in his parish. It's often difficult for parishioners to feel comfortable with a clerical priest. They simple don't find "Father" approachable. The same can be said of bishops who are all too comfortable thinking of themselves as princes by divine selection. They connect neither with their priests nor with the people they're meant to shepherd. And you won't find the smell of the sheep on them.

Often that's exactly what clergy caught up in clericalism want. They believe a certain distance from the non-ordained is fitting and right. Of course, priests need not be chummy with their parishioners and the pastor-parishioner relationship certainly requires maturity and prudence on the part of the ordained. Most pastors are all too aware of the smothering demands of some of their parishioners. Without question, they do need to safeguard their privacy and find regular time and space when they are, so to speak, "off the clock." But clericalism by its nature exaggerates this need. And without fail, it breeds artificiality and superficiality in pastor-parishioner relationships and encounters. Though often unrecognized, something "real" is missing.

Orthodox priest and theologian Alexander Schmemann observes, "Clericalism suffocates; it makes part of itself into a whole sacred character of the church; it makes its power a sacred power to control, to lead, to administer; a power to perform sacraments, and, in general, it makes any power a 'power given to me!'"[1] Clerical priests and bishops (and yes, clerical deacons) come to see their power to confer sacraments, to preach and teach and administer, as the bedrock of their identity. When this happens, they lose sight of the truth that the church's power is ultimately the power of the Holy Spirit. Without words, they seem to say "We are clergy . . . and you're not."

Years ago, when I worked at my diocese's headquarters as vicar for priests, I spoke with a highly placed lay diocesan official who related his fear that he was being co-opted by the system—that he was becoming "clerical." I told him not to worry. The very fact that he sensed the danger was his deliverance. We agreed that a number of his lay colleagues apparently didn't see the danger. These lay chancery workers thought of themselves as insiders. And in a real sense they were. And like many of their ordained colleagues, their first loyalty was now to the church as institution rather than to the gospel and to the faithful they served. So, the cancer of clericalism, in its broadest sense, is not restricted to deacons, priests, and bishops.

---

1. Schmemann, *Journals.*

~ ~ ~

It's clear to many church observers that clerical culture is the breeding ground for the disease of clericalism. The two, however, are distinct. We best understand this before any attempts to surgically excise the cancer of clericalism. Most professionals and most skilled workers and artisans develop over time a culture, a pattern of behavior and language and image that shape the identity of those who belong. Such cultures can foster a healthy *esprit de corp.* So, clerical culture itself isn't the culprit here. Priests regularly speak of the brotherhood of the ordained. They share a similar seminary training, they understand the joys and sorrows of parish ministry, the freedom and loneliness of celibacy, the daunting responsibility of preaching God's word. But a healthy clerical culture fosters a spirit of humility and gratitude in the hearts of deacons, priests, and bishops. It leads a priest to say to himself, "By the grace of God I'm a priest. But I'm first a baptized disciple in need of ministry myself, in need of mercy and the fellowship of lay men and women." However, a clerical culture that exaggerates the role and status of the ordained minister in the life of the Church becomes fertile soil for the cancer of clericalism.

So, what can we do to end clericalism? The following three surgical steps should excise the cancer or at least put clericalism into remission:

1. Bishops, priests, and deacons are called by the gospel—and by Pope Francis—to see discipleship and service as foundational to ordained ministry. Baptism confers all the dignity they need. Many clergy get this. Many still do not. So let our seminaries teach candidates for the priesthood that baptismal discipleship rooted in prayer is the foundation of priestly ministry.

    Cardinal Leon Joseph Suenens expanded on this issue in an address on the ministerial priesthood at a symposium of European bishops in 1969. He noted that Vatican II's focus on the church as the people of God and the ministries of all the baptized called for a genuine rethinking of the theology of ministerial priesthood. In his words, "The ministerial priesthood is distinct from the general priesthood though directed toward the latter . . . The ministerial priesthood, for the bishop as well as the priest, is secondary to the status and mission of these people as baptized."[2]

2. Some clergy insist on being addressed with their title, *Father* or *Monsignor* or *deacon*. And some prelates insist on their courtly honorifics,

---

2. De Broucker, *Suenens Dossier.*

Excellency or *Eminence*. Titles have their place, but we shouldn't insist on them. We might smile at a lay person who insists on being called *Mister, Mrs., Doctor, Professor* or *Judge*. Calling a physician *Doctor* is appropriate in the consulting room or hospital and addressing a pastor as *Father* is likewise appropriate in parish settings. But most people, I believe, wince when an individual insists on being addressed with his or her title.

3. Mandated celibacy needs to be revisited. It's true that we find clericalism in the married clergy of Eastern rite Catholic and Orthodox churches. But the inherent burdens of celibacy lead some clergy to a sense of entitlement and privilege, hallmarks of clericalism.

Isn't our critique of clericalism an attack on the priesthood? The logic behind this question goes something like this. It's difficult to exaggerate the dignity and spiritual power of the priesthood. Think of how many, if not most, of the laity perceive the priest primarily in terms of offering Mass and forgiving sins. So great a vocation, it's concluded, requires that a priest be someone "set apart." And with being set apart comes responsibility and privilege. In other words, this line of thinking assumes and accepts as natural a certain clericalism in Catholic priests because they belong to a kind of noble spiritual class. And while nobility has its obligations (*noblesse oblige*), nobility has its perks.

But Pope Francis has answered this way of thinking. For Francis, the priest is not so much a man set apart as a servant-pastor placed in the center of the community. The pope believes a priest and bishop should have a missionary heart, the antithesis of a clerical heart. He writes, "A missionary heart . . . makes itself 'weak with the weak . . . everything for everyone' (I Cor. 9:22). It never closes itself off, never retreats into its own security, never opts for rigidity and defensiveness. It realizes that it has to grow in its own understanding of the Gospel and in discerning the paths of the Spirit, and so it always does what good it can, even if in the process, its shoes get soiled by the mud of the street." (*Evangelii Gaudium*, 45)

So, yes, let's end clericalism and follow the example of our non-clerical pope. He keeps reminding his bishops, priests, and deacons that they are ministers of mercy, trail guides for a pilgrim people, ministers of mercy . . . with muddy shoes.

Conclusion

We have tried to assess the worthiness of the priesthood vis-à-vis the *Church in the Modern World* and *the Decree on the Apostolate of the Laity* and, indirectly, the pastoral vision of the Second Vatican Council itself.

Worthiness, you might agree, is a tricky Christian category. The scandal of the gospel is that while no one by herself or himself is worthy of communion with the divine, by the gift of abounding grace we are God's beloved, God's holy people. So, while reflecting on a priesthood worthy of *Gaudium et Spes* and *Apostolicam Actuositatem*, we have, in effect, been taking the measure of the priesthood's reception of these two documents.

The priesthood of the nineteenth and early twentieth centuries—I'm thinking here of Msgr. George Talbot and Pope Pius X—would have had considerable difficulty, to put it mildly, receiving these documents.

Their reception by today's priesthood is mixed and could be understood in part by the two models of the priesthood discussed earlier. Clericalism's hold on many priests will likewise affect their reception or non-reception of *The Church in the Modern World* and *The Decree on the Apostolate of the Laity*.

But here we stand, hopefully with mud on our shoes and the smell of the sheep on our clothes, grateful beyond words for the liberating, challenging, and pastoral vision of the Second Vatican Council.

Bibliography

De Broucker, Jose, ed. *The Suenens Dossier*. Dublin: Gill & Macmillan, 1970.

Francis. *Evangelii Gaudium*. November 24, 2014. w2.vatican.va/content/francesco/en/apost_exhortations/documents/papa-francesco_esortazione-ap_20131124_evangelii-gaudium.html.

Schmemann, Alexander. *The Journals of Father Alexander Schmemann, 1973–1983*. Translated by Juliana Schmemann. New York: St. Vladimir's Seminary, 2000.

Second Vatican Council. *Apostolicam Actuositatem*. November 18, 1965. www.vatican.va/archive/hist_councils/ii_vatican_council/documents/vat-ii_decree_19651118_apostolicam-actuositatem_en.html.

Second Vatican Council. *Gaudium et Spes*. December 7, 1965. www.vatican.va/archive/hist_councils/ii_vatican_council/documents/vat-ii_const_19651207_gaudium-et-spes_en.html.

———. *Presbyterorum Ordinis*. December 7, 1965. www.vatican.va/archive/hist_councils/ii_vatican_council/documents/vat-ii_decree_19651207_presbyterorum-ordinis_en.html.

18

Rebuilding a Vital Parish Culture[1]

—Michael White and Tom Corcoran

Michael White

As two guys working in a local church, the Church of the Nativity, in Timonium, Maryland, we have seen God accomplish some great things and bring a transformation in our church. There has been an increase in volunteerism as several hundreds have gotten involved in volunteer ministry. We have seen a great increase in financial support of the parish, and we have seen an improved spirit and momentum at the parish. I, pastor at the church, and Tom Corcoran, associate to the pastor, want to tell you a little about our story and the key strategies that have driven this transformation.

Did you ever have an experience where suddenly you ask "*Why am I here?*" or "*Why am I doing this?*" Sometimes it can happen at a party where we don't know many people and we feel out of place. Or we step into a situation and it's not what we thought it was going to be. It's a little uncomfortable. It happens in school a lot, as you're sitting in class saying, "I will never

1. Scripture quotations in this chapter are taken from the New Revised Standard Version Bible: Catholic Edition, copyright 1989, 1993, Division of Christian Education of the National Council of the Churches of Christ in the United States of America. Used by permission. All rights reserved.

need this information." It's not really a big deal, unless . . . until . . . we have that feeling about more significant things in our life.

In the busyness of life, the "*why*" question usually doesn't get asked soon enough, and often enough. We are usually running around and just trying to get through a day or complete our to-do lists. But answering the question "*why*" is vitally important. It provides purpose and meaning and adds value, and it will get us through the difficult times and make the good times far more enjoyable. Knowing why you do what you do matters.

So why does the Catholic Church exist? Why does the local church exists? Why do we do what we do?

When we first began working in the church we thought our job was to provide better service to church people. We came to a parish that did not have a lot of activities or programs running. We thought the problem with the parish was the low energy and lack of programs, and that if we invested energy into programs and services for parish members, we would be a successful parish. In other words, we fell into a consumer mentality, that the people in the pews should be thought of as consumers. The people in the pews are here to consume religion and it was our job to help them consume.

And so both Tom and I, who for a while were pretty much it when it came to staff, set about trying to do that with as much energy as we had. We expanded kids and student programs. Tom put together all kinds of activities to try to get students involved. We launched new musical programs and offered concerts and all kinds of fellowship programs, receptions, bus trips, lectures. We expanded member care as far as we could, hosting complimentary lunches following funerals and coffee service following daily Mass.

It was a waste of time.

In hindsight, the situation was reminiscent of the Red Queen's race in Lewis Carroll's *Through the Looking Glass*. The Queen says to Alice: "Now here you see, it takes all the running you can do, to keep in the same place, if you want to get anywhere, you'll have to run at least twice as fast as that." The more we provided, the faster we had to run just to stay in the same place. But, the more was provided, the more was demanded. Just like Alice, who didn't pause to reflect on why she was running an absurd race for the insatiable Queen, we hadn't considered why we were doing what we were doing or what we were accomplishing.

The net effect of our efforts was creating consumers in which nothing was different after than before. We spent our energy for nothing except creating demanding consumers. This all came crashing in on me during a program we ran for about five years, during Lent. There was Mass and Stations of the Cross and a featured speaker, but the draw was dinner, which was free; we also had childcare and a student program. And hundreds and hundreds and hundreds of people came. It was called "Family Friendly Friday" but it wasn't really that friendly, at least for our staff. We piled this program on top of everything else we were trying to do.

Well, it was the sixth and final evening, and by the time we got to that point it had seemed like we had been doing it forever and the staff was burnt out. Anyway, I was serving dinner and a woman approached me to complain about the food (that would be the *free* food). Not only did she complain but she was nasty about it. And she was quickly joined by a chorus of like-minded friends who all wanted to complain about the *free* food.

Something snapped, some artery exploded: I knew in an instant (if you didn't count the previous five years) that I could no longer do this. I was wasting my time . . . this was my life and I was wasting my time. It wasn't the ingratitude but the lack of purpose and lack of impact we were having.

Why am I doing this?

When we lose our why and lose our purpose, we are adrift on a dangerous sea of disillusion and disappointment that can lead to depression (as it did in my case) and even despair.

Tom Corcoran

So when it comes to a parish, what is our "*why?*" If you are working in parish ministry, how do you know if you are succeeding? As we have found it isn't necessarily getting more people to come to your programs. We had succeeded in getting more people to programs, but that only burnt us out.

When Jesus left this earth, He was very clear about what He wanted the church to accomplish and do. In Matthew 28, He said, "All authority on heaven and on earth has been given to me." Jesus through His work on the cross had won authority over heaven and earth. So now that He won it back He passed on that authority to the apostles and said, "All authority on heaven and earth has been given to me, go therefore and make disciples of all nations, baptizing them in the name of the Father and of the Son and the Holy Spirit, and know I am with you until the end of the age." Jesus tells us the purpose of all we do. We are to go and make disciples. And if we are wondering how many disciples Jesus wants us to make, He says, "Make disciples of all nations." That's our mission. That's why we exist as a church. We exist to make disciples. That's it. As a parish we don't have a responsibility for making disciples everywhere; our job is specifically to make disciples in our zip code. If you work in a parish, you exist to make disciples of Jesus Christ of the people in your zip code. As a parish, it means we don't exist just for the people in our church nor have responsibility for the people in the pews, but a parish means we have care for all people in our geographical boundaries, seeking to bring everyone in our parish boundaries into a relationship with Christ. The church exists to make disciples of Jesus Christ. This parish, the why of this parish is to make disciples of Jesus Christ. That is why we exist. That's it.

What are disciples? Students, just students. Not saints, not fully formed followers, not perfect people, just students of Jesus Christ. People who are trying to live more like Him and grow in Him a little more today than yesterday. When we define a disciple at our church we say that disciples Love God, Love Others as themselves, and Make Disciples.

In the Great Commandment, Jesus summed up the whole law when He said, "The Greatest commandment is to love God with all your heart, all your soul, all your mind and all your strength . . . And the second is like it, love your neighbor as you love yourself."

Disciples are students who love God with all their heart, soul, and strength. As a church we try and help people love God with all they have through a few disciplines.

This begins with weekend worship at Mass. Mass should be an experience where people draw closer to their heavenly Father through music, which helps them to lift up their hearts and soul to God. Each week we want them to be challenged and encouraged to grow through the weekend message.

Aside from weekend worship, disciples love God through private disciplines, specifically prayer, fasting, and giving. To help people grow as disciples means they are developing their own personal relationship with Him in prayer. They are reading the Bible and growing in His word. They are learning more to hear His voice. As Jesus says in John 10, the sheep hear His voice, they know the voice and the call of the shepherd. They fast at times so they can hear His voice more clearly and know more clearly His will.

Disciples love God with all they have by giving generously. Disciples see everything they have as a gift from God. They honor God with their money and resources by giving to His church and by giving money to build His kingdom and to the poor.

We are trying to make disciples who are loving God. Disciples are people who are learning more and more to love people as they love themselves. Loving people means valuing people as Jesus valued them. Loving people means serving them. So this means just being kind to the people around them. It means serving the people around them. Living in fellowship with them.

Disciples love people as they love themselves. This means disciples know how to practice self care. As Jesus modeled for us in the Scriptures,

He often took time to get away and be with His heavenly Father because He knew He needed to care for Himself. He knew He needed that time in order to minister to the crowds and crowds of people.

Disciples love God, love others as they love themselves and make disciples of Jesus Christ. When Jesus called the first disciples, He said follow me and I will make you fishers of men. And we see throughout the Scriptures that Jesus makes disciples of people so that they will go out and make other disciples. After Jesus heals the Gerasene demoniac, the demoniac wants to go with Jesus in the boat. He asks to go and follow Jesus. Jesus though doesn't let him. Instead He tells the man to go and share with the people in his town what God has done for him. And the next time Jesus returns all the townspeople go out to greet Him. After Jesus speaks to the woman at the well, she gets the whole townspeople to come out and greet Him.

So Disciples Love God, Love Others and make disciples of Jesus Christ. We are to be forming disciples of Jesus Christ. But if we are honest, many times our programs create more consumers than disciples. Rather than creating people who serve and mutually encourage one another, they create people who are less loving. So the change in our church began when we realized we weren't creating disciples and that whatever it was we were doing wasn't really succeeding as Jesus called us to succeed.

Our journey took off when we humbled ourselves to learn from others. Eventually we did the obvious thing: we looked to successful churches, intentionally growing churches. So we set out to learn from growing, healthy churches what we could do, even if that meant turning to Protestant churches.

We started at a place called Saddleback Church, in Orange County, California, which is Rick Warren's church, though nobody knew who he was at the time. We remember the first time we went out there, which was about ten years ago now. We felt scared to go. We worried about being "outed" as Catholics in an Evangelical setting. Being on their campus felt like being on a different planet—it was overwhelming. I remember parking the car and approaching what I assumed was the church building only to find out it was a nursery building. It was big and new and beautiful and totally dedicated to Sunday school for nursery students. On the other hand, when we finally made our way over to the church it was big, for sure, but entirely plain, a Wal-Mart with chairs. In my experience of churchworld, big churches meant expensive churches, churches with fancy finishes. Nothing fancy here. But it wasn't even primarily the buildings or the campus, it was the people. There was something different about the people of Saddleback than those of our church. They were so friendly and happy and happy to see us. We walked through the front door and were so warmly greeted, I went out a side door and circled back around to enter and be greeted again. Why were these people so happy? What did they have to be happy about? I grew up in church, and have been in church my whole life. I lived in Rome. I'd never seen people actually happy to be in church, much less happy to see me.

Along with Saddleback, we studied some other growing, healthy mega-churches including Willow Creek in Chicago, Fellowship Church in Dallas, and North Point in Atlanta. We learned several lessons from those churches, but three most vital were:

1. Change our focus from churched people to unchurched people.

2. Prioritize the weekend above all our other efforts.

3. Move church people into action.

Let me repeat those.

1. Change our focus from churched people to unchurched people. We started trying to think of the church experience from the perspective of the person *not* coming to church instead of the person already attending.

2. Prioritize the weekend above all efforts. We have an axiom we borrowed from another pastor. It's about the weekend, stupid. The weekend experience has become our top priority.

3. Move church people to maturity and action. Challenge them to take ownership of the parish. So let's look at these in a few deeper ways.

Focus on Unchurched People

Change in our church came when we took the focus off the church people and thought about creating an environment unchurched people would want to be a part of. If you think about it, in your community there is a much bigger market for unchurched than churched people. More people aren't going to church on a regular basis than are going to church. We began to focus on the unchurched person, and we began by describing him, what he looks like. Being in Timonium, we call him Timonium Tim. Tim is a good guy. He grew up Catholic, was probably confirmed Catholic, but once his parents stopped making him go to church he stopped going. What he knows from Catholicism is a muddled mess of what he thinks he remembers from Confirmation classes and what he learned from *The Da Vinci Code*.

Tim has a stressful life, especially during the week. He's got a long commute and he often finds himself driving his three kids in three different directions. He's racked up a bunch of debt because he is living beyond his means. So on Sunday mornings, Tim wants to relax or do what he wants to do, which means Tim usually finds himself at a Ravens game or playing golf, or running around for his kids' sports or just staying home, but it does not find him at church because for him church is boring and bad.

When we evaluated our church, we realized it wasn't very welcoming toward Tim. We didn't have a great experience. As a church we are competing with the NFL and golf courses and the mall for people's free time. As a church we are still under the impression that if we open the doors people will come. We are expecting people to come out of obligation or guilt or habit. But those days are dead and gone.

I realized the appeal of just staying in and missing church this past summer. I was visiting my in-laws in Connecticut. They have a pool, so on Sunday morning, my oldest three sons got up and went swimming. Pretty soon they were calling me to jump in. So I did. All of a sudden, I had an insight: so this is why people don't go to church. I could see how I could very easily make an argument for skipping Mass. I am spending good quality time with my kids. I was very relaxed sitting by the pool.

So if we want to be attractive to be people who are not going to church, we need to make sure we create a welcoming environment on the weekend for people to be a part of. We have to have provide excellence and put our very best energies into the time Tim comes to church, which is on the weekend. This was a key strategy we changed. We began making the weekend a priority.

Prioritize the Weekend

The weekend is the greatest opportunity to make an impact on people. Most people are on our campus on a weekend. Even when we run other programs, you never get as many people gathered as you do on the weekend. In those Family Friendly Fridays, we worked so hard to get 600 or so people to come out on a Friday night, which was only a third of our weekend attendance at the time. It's much smarter to invest more and more of our energy on weekend experiences than on events where we get far fewer people attending.

If people have a bad or mediocre experience on the weekend, then they assume the church has nothing to say to them otherwise. If you go to a restaurant that has bad service or poor food, you don't care how well they keep their books and do their accounting. You aren't going to go there again.

Your experience has ruined you. If people come to a church and it isn't a great experience, they assume we don't have anything to say to them. On the other hand, if we create an excellent experience, they believe we have something to offer them.

The Mass is the source and summit of our faith and it deserves our very best efforts, so that people come to see the importance of the Mass. It is important to note that the unchurched don't see the inherent value of the Eucharist. If the Eucharist were enough, every Catholic Church would be full. We help people to see the value the Eucharist by bringing our efforts to it. The three elements we bring to the Mass are music, message, and ministers. To maximize the weekend, we need music, message, and ministers working together.

Music

Focusing on the weekend from the perspective of lost people means . . . "It's the music!" The weekend experience should be a form of transportation, taking the participant on an emotional, intellectual, and ultimately spiritual journey to the higher things of God. The United States Conference of Catholic Bishops' *Sing to the Lord* says, "God has bestowed upon His people the gift of song. God dwells within each human person, in the place where music takes its source. Indeed, God, the giver of song, is present whenever His people sing His praises. A cry deep within our being, music is a way for God to lead us to the realm of higher things."

We like to say that music is the water on which the experience sails. "Music does what words alone cannot do. It is capable of expressing a dimension of meaning and feeling that words alone cannot convey." More than any other element in the church's weekend experience it is the music that can touch and change people's hearts for better or for worse.

Historically at Nativity, music was a huge problem. As is typical in many places, the program included some musical options: three weekend Masses were designated as "organ and cantor" one as choir, one "folk" and one blessedly as the "quiet mass." The folk Mass was far and away more popular than the other musical choices, perhaps because it was the easiest to listen to and the easiest to tune out. The group tried their best, but they struggled. Their presentation was flawed and the music they played was dated and uninteresting. At the other masses, the music was worse—far, far worse.

Many of the choir members were more convinced of their skills than they had reason to be and their accumulated sound was grievous. Most of the cantors were prima donnas in clear performance mode. The organist was a wonderful person who struggled mightily with a poorly designed organ. Traditional hymns, as well as more recent additions to the compendium of sacred music, were simply slaughtered Mass after Mass and week after week. And no one sang—we really mean no one! If people sang, you knew they were visitors and everyone stared at them until they shut up or went away. Not surprisingly, on some weekends the most popular weekend Mass was the early one, without music.

Early on we had a town hall meeting to listen to the range of concerns we inherited. While most people were generally apathetic toward the parish, the evening turned into a virtual riot of bitter complaint all about the music. And we had to agree with much of what was said. They were right. We had terrible music, and it made the weekend experience terrible. And that made people angry. Want to know what we did about the problem? Absolutely nothing. We didn't want to hurt anybody's feelings (if you don't count the parishioners as anybody) so we did nothing for two years.

Music has the greatest potential to reach people. And because it has the greatest ability to reach people, it is often the most difficult one to get right. And because it is such a struggle, often that's why we give up on it or just settle for mediocre music. You cannot do that. Keep investing your time and energy as a pastor until you get it right. Our music grew mostly from prayer and begging God to send good people to us. As we got the right people on our music team, other talented people became a part of it.

Message

The second component of the weekend experience is the message. Words are powerful. Proverbs 18:21 says that life and death is in the power of the tongue. For unchurched people who don't value the Eucharist, this is even more important because it is where they are being fed.

Ministers

Ministers create the energy of the church. They are the "there" there. They make our church a welcoming environment. When people describe why they are joining our church, they cite the welcoming environment as one of the most important reasons they chose to join. So we have a whole set of ministries that are put in place to help create a welcoming environment: parking team, greeters, and host ministers. Parking ministers help people find a parking spot. This sets the tone right from the beginning. Then there are greeters at the door to open the door and smile at people. Then there are host team members who help people to find a seat. Information ministers help with information. Café ministers serve coffee and doughnuts and other food after Mass. All this has to do with creating an irresistible environment people want to be a part of. The point is that they team together to serve others and serve one another.

Along with the ministries that support the guest experience have been our children's programs. One of the important things to note about our children's programs is that they are available at most Masses. We have our Kidzone, which is for kids three and under. All Stars for 4–6 year olds and a program we call Time Travelers, which is our children's liturgy of the Word program. We have Kidzone and All Stars and Time Travelers on Saturday nights and all three Sunday morning Masses. This has been very important in attracting families to our church. So often it is kids that bring their parents to church, and if you can create a great environment for kids, they will beg their parents to come to church. Also, if you give parents a break so that church becomes an opportunity where they are nourished and able to look forward to that time, they will keep coming back to church.

Motivate Church People to Move and Act

The book of the Bible that describes the life of the church's early exuberance, fruitfulness and momentum is called Acts of the Apostles. They got moving, they did something. The core church people need to be challenged beyond simply consuming to creating an environment unchurched people want to be a part of and to caring for one another. It's everyone's job. So often we challenge unchurched people and comfort insiders or churched people. We get it exactly backwards. We need to challenge church people in a few ways.

We challenge them to get into a ministry to create a welcoming environment. Michael White consistently preaches the need for people to volunteer in the parish in some way. In fact, we just had a pretty challenging message on that recently. We tell people that in order to grow spiritually, they need to be serving. We get people moving and active by getting people into ministry. How do you get people serving? Make it accessible. One reason we have so few volunteers at the church is because often the commitment starts out so high. People will give you a few hours a month; it is much harder for them to give you a few hours a week. So set the initial commitment to volunteering low.

Also set volunteers up for success by giving them tasks they know they can accomplish. We set them up for success by giving terms of service. One of the other problems with volunteering at church is that it can get to the feeling of being forever. People get into teaching and they can never get out. Give volunteer ministers a beginning, middle and an end. This is especially true for new volunteer ministers.

Another way we challenge them is by getting them into a small group where they can help care for one another. Small groups are our main delivery system for pastoral care. A few years ago, we had a very sad funeral as one of the members of the parish lost a child at birth. It was a heartbreaking situation as the family knew early on in the pregnancy that this child was not going to make it. At the funeral her small group came and provided support. They brought up the gifts. They did the readings. They surrounded the family with love in a way we could not even if our whole staff had invested in the funeral.

Personally I have benefitted in several ways from people in my small group. I have had help putting in a garbage disposal, taking down tree branches, and fixing my heating system. Small groups are where our great big church becomes small. It is how we practice loving one another, accepting one another, and serving one another. They are where there is mutual care for the body.

Application

1. We would encourage you to read our book, *Rebuilt: Awakening the Faithful, Reaching the Lost, and Making Church Matter* (Ave Maria, 2013). In the book, you will find many sections called "You can do this." Also go to the book website Rebuiltparish.com where you can find additional resources. See also our other books: *Tools for Rebuilding: 75 Really, Really Practical Ways to Make Your Parish Better* (Ave Maria, 2013); and *Rebuilding Your Message: Practical Tools to Strengthen Your Preaching and Teaching* (Ave Maria, 2015).

2. Get rid of extra programs and events, especially those that distract from the weekend. One of the biggest problems going on in so many churches is that we are doing too many things.

3. Take some time to think of the perspective of the unchurched person in your area.

4. Figure out the one way you need to focus your energies and key volunteer leaders on the weekend experience.

I believe God has a great vision for our parishes. People have left the Catholic Church in droves in the United States, giving up on connecting to God through the church. You and I are here because that bothers us. A growing number of Catholics see this and it bothers them and they want to do something about it, but they have no vision. They don't have a vision for how a modern-day parish can engage the culture. And so their parishes continue to languish.

The Book of Esther takes place during the heartbreaking exile of the Jews. At this point in the story they've lost their homeland and their freedom, but worse still is in store for them. An evil counselor to the ruler of the land, the king of Persia, plots the extermination of the entire Jewish people. Meanwhile, God raises up a simple Jewish girl and places her in the unlikely position of queen of Persia. And then He plants a vision in Esther, to save His people. It comes in the words of a friend who tells her she must go to the king and intercede (a dangerous thing for even the queen to do). Her friend tells her:

> If you remain silent at this time,
>
> relief and deliverance for the Jews will arise from another place,
>
> but you and your father's family will perish.
>
> And who knows but that you have come to royal position
>
> for such a time as this? (Esth 4:14)

Of course, she gets to work and saves the day. God placed her in a position of influence and gave her a vision for exactly the time and the circumstances she was in. Who knows if God hasn't placed you in your parish for such a time as this?

19

The Legacy and Challenge of the Council in a World Church

Lessons from Pope Francis on Preaching
and the Transition from "Lay Vocation"
to "Missionary Discipleship"[1]

—J. Matthew Ashley

I APPROACH MY THEME with a view to the demands and delights of preaching. I am taking a shot at this not as someone who preaches—I don't—but as one of those baptized sitting in the pews, who has had the great privilege of learning that something really, really important happened while he was a young lad memorizing Latin Mass prayers in the early sixties so that he could be an altar boy at St Patrick's Catholic Church. Vatican II happened, and if we reflect on and celebrate these documents that appeared fifty years ago it is because they set a course for a church that we are on the way to becoming, a church that the Holy Spirit has called us to be. But the journey has been a rocky, difficult one, and, being still on the way, we are all together in that anxious situation of being in between a church that many of us only

---

1. Scripture quotations in this chapter are taken from the New Revised Standard Version Bible, copyright 1989, Division of Christian Education of the National Council of the Churches of Christ in the United States of America. Used by permission.

dimly remember, and growing numbers of Christians don't remember at all, and a church that we can only see through a glass darkly.

So, let me propose to you, first, that among other things, good preaching gives people hope for this journey, and that is why it is worthwhile to take stock of where we are on that journey. Let me propose to you, second, that the extraordinary impact that Pope Francis has had derives in good part from the fact that he is giving the church as a whole hope for the journey. He is able to do this, I propose, third, both because he understands the event of the Second Vatican Council and because he understands the people: he "smells of the sheep," as he famously remarked when talking about bishops. So, good preachers should smell of the sheep. Now smelling of the sheep doesn't just mean hanging around with them and rubbing up against their wool; it means *understanding them*, and this takes thinking, and yes sometimes (not always, but sometimes) ivory tower academics can help us think about our situation. I think Pope Francis has done a good deal of thinking on the situation of the church on the difficult path toward the church envisioned fifty years ago in Rome, and so what I would like to do here is to see what we can learn from him about what we *all* share as baptized Christians called to live on the way.

Lots could be said about Francis' preaching and about how his actions have been calculated to give hope—just the fact that he radiates joy and peace, the fact that he has heeded his own advice that "an evangelizer should never look like someone who has just come back from a funeral."[2] In his presentation at our "What We Have Seen and Heard" conference at Notre Dame in June of 2015, Ed Hahnenberg gave us some useful basic principles on preaching that are also found in Francis: from below; from a prayerful immersion accompanying the people—or as Francis likes to name this in reliance on *Lumen Gentium* "the holy faithful people of God"; directed to the peripheries. For my part, I want to start from Hahnenberg's point about the shift in universities from focusing on *instructor teaching* to *student learning*, to take a somewhat different tack on the question. It is just as important to look at the qualities of a student community that is receptive to good teaching, and on how to build such a student community, as it is to focus on my own expertise and rhetorical habits as a teacher. Might not the same be true for the ministry of preaching, understood as a relational reality with the people of God? Isn't building a community of missionary disciples an important element of successful preaching? Francis is very concerned about this, and what I would like to do is talk about principles that Francis has articulated to guide the formation of a community of missionary disciples,

---

2. Francis, *Evangelii Gaudium*, 10.

which will be a community that will *hear* good preaching and maybe even draw it out of the preacher. Oscar Romero once famously said that "with this people it is not difficult to be a good pastor"; might we think about how to build up church communities so that it is not difficult . . . or at least, not *as* difficult, to be a good preacher? Isn't that part of what we *all* need to do, whether we preach or not? In the various tasks we fulfill in the church, be it as teachers, scholars, pastors, homilists, ministers, or administrators, we are called to cooperate in building a community of missionary disciples who will, as Francis has also said, recognize the voice of the shepherd. Francis worked very hard on this, and learned from his mistakes, as provincial and local superior of the Jesuits in Argentina, and then as auxiliary bishop and archbishop of Buenos Aires. He did it in difficult, difficult years in that country's history, which saw dictatorship, the Dirty War, rampant corruption (including in the church) and economic collapse—difficult times in the church, too. The first pope to have been ordained *after* Vatican II (during the council years he was finishing his first studies and teaching high school), Francis has experienced the struggle to carry the council forward. He rose to prominence in part because he was so instrumental in the Latin American church's attempt to appropriate Vatican II, *Gaudium et Spes* in particular, for itself, evident in his work for the most recent meeting of the Latin American Bishops' conference, in 2007 in Aparecida, Brazil. And now he is trying to do the same for the universal church.

Francis gave us a short summary of his fundamental principles for building community in *Evangelii Gaudium*, paragraphs 222–237. He provides these principles in a section on "the building of a people where differences are harmonized within a common pursuit" (227)—or, to put it another way, and recalling Archbishop Joseph Tobin's words, a people who embody a "culture of encounter," one in which we meet in our differences (even a difference as dramatic as between theist and atheist) in our common effort to do good. As Francis' biographer, Austin Ivereigh, points out, he formulated these four principles from an eclectic set of sources, including Ignatian spirituality, a variety of Latin American and European intellectuals, and, most of all, from his own experience. I will suggest that each of these principles encapsulates part of the way that Francis has adopted the legacy and challenges of the council, aiming toward a church of missionary disciples in which it might be *less* difficult to be a good preacher. They intersect with the principles that Hahnenberg has proposed on preaching. In addition to *Evangelii Gaudium*, I will use Francis' recent encyclical on the environment, *Laudato Si'*, as an illustration of how he puts these principles into practice to give the church hope for the journey.

One: The Whole Is Greater than the Sum of the Parts

For Francis our road forward must navigate a tension between globalization and localization. This was already evident at the Second Vatican Council, which was the first really global ecumenical council. One of its results was an awareness of the different needs and gifts of the great regional churches, like the one in Latin America—an awareness that, encouraged by Paul VI, led to the founding of the regional bishops conferences such as what is now called the USCCB, and the further development of the Latin American Episcopal Council, or CELAM. This led to difficult questions on the relationship of the teachings of these regional groups of bishops vis-à-vis Rome, which complicated the questions raised in council documents on the collegiality that should exist between the college of bishops and the pope. Now, the former question is one on which earlier pontiffs took a decisive option for Roman centralism. For example, with then-Cardinal Ratzinger's approval, John Paul II issued a motu proprio in 1998 (*Apostolos Suos*), denying that teachings of regional conferences shared in any way in the magisterium. Francis clearly thinks that this denies the contributions of the "parts" to the whole. In *Evangelii Gaudium* he states that "it is not advisable for the pope to take the place of local bishops in the discernment of every issue that arises in their territory,"[3] and you can see this in *Laudato Si'* by the many references he includes to documents of regional conferences: the USCCB and CELAM, but also the bishops of the Philippines, of southern Africa, of Bolivia and of Germany. He also quotes extensively from the "Green Patriarch"—Bartholomew, ecumenical patriarch of Constantinople. The whole is greater than the parts might also take us back to Maxwell Johnson's chapter on "the whole" that is made up by *all* the baptized.

This principle asserts that in working with our communities we have to pay attention to our global context in order avoid banality and narrowness while keeping our feet firmly on the ground in our local context. "The global need not stifle nor the particular prove barren," he writes. *Within* our communities we have to realize that they are wholes made up of parts that have their unique contributions to make. With his penchant for metaphor, Francis proposes that we image the church not as a sphere, with all points equally distant from a center against which everything is measured and oriented, but as a polyhedron, in which local churches are like the different planes of the polyhedron, each having its own value. Everyone has something to offer and our task is to draw that rich harvest in: first and foremost from the poor and those marginalized persons to whom we relatively privileged members

3. Ibid., 16.

of society habitually pay little or no attention. Who can deny that we can learn from, and should preach from out of, the experience of Emmanuel African Methodist Episcopal Church in downtown Charleston—even though it may be a learning that involves weeping? And, Francis goes on to write, "even people who can be considered dubious on account of their errors have something to offer which must not be overlooked." So the atheist, the couple in an irregular marriage, gays and lesbians. The premise—again remembering Archbishop Tobin's reflections—is that we are united, or striving to be united, in "a society which pursues the common good, which truly has a place for everyone" (236).

For Francis this principle has, ultimately, an evangelical basis. "The whole is greater than the sum of the parts" evokes for him "the totality or integrity of the Gospel which the Church passes down to us and sends us forth to proclaim" (237). This is a Gospel which blooms in places we might not expect to find it—in people's sometimes inarticulate prayer, in their struggles for justice, and in their celebrations. Indeed, it blooms in the "the joys and the hopes, the griefs and the anxieties of the men and women of this age, especially those who are poor or in any way afflicted." We might allow Francis to ask us—in the communities and institutions we serve and over which we have some charge—where do we look, and where do we not look, to harvest the riches of the Gospel for the whole community? What "part" have we overlooked? To which "part" do we need to call our local community to attend?

Two: Unity Prevails over Conflict

Francis has lived his adult faith life in a society and a church with many conflicts. This was even, and painfully, true of the Jesuits of Argentina, who, like many religious communities, were divided over how to respond to the call for renewal of religious life in that other document promulgated fifty years ago (*Perfectae Caritas*) as well as to the poverty and injustice evident in Latin America, and highlighted by the Latin American Bishops Conference at Medellín and beyond. Bergoglio got caught up in those tensions and spent two painful years in virtual exile in Argentina while a new province leadership took the province in a very different direction than the one he charted as provincial and local superior of one of the most important Jesuit communities in Argentina.[4] It was a purgation for him, a dark night, as

---

4. From June 1990 to May 1992, he was "in exile" in Córdoba, Argentina, hearing confessions and leading retreats.

Ivereigh notes. But he learned from it about the nature of conflict and what it means to deal with it.

There can be no doubt at all that there has been deep and painful conflict in the Catholic Church over how to interpret and implement the council. It is a source of deep pain, I think, that what should be a cause for celebration and hope—the work of the Spirit in an ecumenical council—has become instead a source of division and disillusionment for many. This too is a part of the legacy and challenge of the council fifty years later, and this principle is part of Francis' response to give people hope for the journey.

Francis writes that conflict cannot be ignored or concealed, but neither should we become trapped in it.

> When conflict arises, some people simply look at it and go their way as if nothing happened; they wash their hands of it and get on with their lives. Others embrace it in such a way that they become its prisoners; they lose their bearings, project onto institutions their own confusion and dissatisfaction and thus make unity impossible. But there is a third way, and it is the best way to deal with conflict. It is the willingness to face conflict head-on, to resolve it and make it a link in the chain of a new process. "Blessed are the peacemakers" (Matt 5:9).[5]

In this way, he goes on, we work toward a "reconciled diversity" (a term that Francis has taken from Cardinal Walter Kasper's definition of the goal of ecumenical dialogue): not a bland tolerance of "let a thousand flowers bloom," or a negotiated settlement between power blocs. Rather, it is "a way of making history in a life setting where conflicts, tensions and oppositions can achieve a diversified and life-giving unity" (228). What does this require? First that we find the locus of this reconciliation in our own hearts, "in our own lives, ever threatened as they are by fragmentation and breakdown." This comes only by encountering the merciful Christ—perhaps *the* most pervasive theme in Francis' writings, as Archbishop Tobin noted. On that basis we see everyone, especially those with whom we disagree, "in their deepest dignity." Our unity, as Maxwell Johnson noted, goes deeper than all conflict, because we are united in Christ, who "has made peace by the blood of his cross." In this light I can take up a question asked earlier: how do we preach to and within conflict? My answer: by hearing the continual exhortations of the Gospel: "Do not be afraid." "Peace be with you." This is no cheap advice that Francis offers, because he has taken it on and suffered from it, as I just noted. His recent practice at the Synod on the Family of surfacing conflict is evidence of that, as well as his willingness to write an

---

5. Francis, *Evangelii Gaudium* 227.

encyclical on the environment that likely no one will be fully happy with. Yet he keeps the lines of communication open while maintaining his own position. This is where the first principle complements this one: because the whole is made up of and is greater than the parts (even the parts represented by our opponents) we are also compelled in faith and hope to work on the premise that unity prevails over conflict.

Three: Realities Are More Important Than Ideas

This is a principle of incarnation and discipleship; it is "the principle of a word already made flesh and constantly striving to take flesh anew" in us and our vocations as the baptized, to be "missionary disciples." As Archbishop Tobin noted, Francis begins *Evangelii Gaudium* with a quote from the opening of Benedict XVI's encyclical *Deus Caritas Est*: "Being a Christian is not the result of an ethical choice or a lofty idea, but the encounter with an event, a person, which gives life a new horizon and decisive direction."[6] So when Francis talks about "reality," he does not mean atoms and molecules arranged this or way or that, nor historical events strung together in random sequences of cause-and-effect—he means that place where alone we find God—which is *not* in our heads. Karl Barth used to say that one of the best ways to avoid God was to spend your time thinking about God, and Jesuit philosopher Ignacio Ellacuría added that one of the best ways to avoid reality is to spend all your time thinking about it. Thinking is not unimportant, but it must follow upon engaging reality. Francis writes that "this means unmasking the various means of masking reality: angelic forms of purity, dictatorships of relativism, empty rhetoric, objectives that are more ideal than real, brands of ahistorical fundamentalism, ethical systems bereft of kindness, intellectual discourse bereft of wisdom" (231)—nice pointers both for the preacher and the academic theologian. You can see this principle in Francis' leadership. I think this is even true in his famous (or infamous) tendency for the off-the-cuff remark or gesture. While he now has two long, carefully thought-out documents (*Evangelii Gaudium* and *Laudato Si'*), his often controversial remarks and gestures come, I think, from his insight that carefully controlled official discourse coming out of Rome needs to be complemented by these casual (or maybe not so casual) remarks and gestures—mirroring the unruliness of reality and challenging us not to take the formal doctrinal statements as a replacement for the reality of the Gospel.

6. Francis, *Evangelii Gaudium* 7, from *Deus Caritas Est* 1.

Francis, then, has always been a realist, but in the precise meaning of the term "reality" that I just indicated. Maybe this sense for "reality" or "the secular" is best captured by "God's Grandeur," the well-known poem of Francis' fellow Jesuit, the poet Gerard Manley Hopkins:

> THE WORLD is charged with the grandeur of God.
> It will flame out, like shining from shook foil;
> It gathers to a greatness, like the ooze of oil
> Crushed. Why do men then now not reck his rod?
> Generations have trod, have trod, have trod;
> And all is seared with trade; bleared, smeared with toil;
> And wears man's smudge and shares man's smell: the soil
> Is bare now, nor can foot feel, being shod.
>
> And for all this, nature is never spent;
> There lives the dearest freshness deep down things;
> And though the last lights off the black West went
> Oh, morning, at the brown brink eastward, springs—
> Because the Holy Ghost over the bent
> World broods with warm breast and with ah! bright wings.[7]

We are to "find God in all things," as the Ignatian motto goes. This is not an insight or a way of seeing easily attained, and reality can afflict us—"seared, bleared, smeared," even confronting us with "crucified peoples" as liberation theologians Ignacio Ellacuría and Jon Sobrino assert. The necessity of this attention to reality was precisely the point of *Gaudium et Spes's* famous opening lines, and is behind Francis' call to "go out to the margins," or at least out to what appear to be margins based on the maps we have come up with in our heads, maps that delineate our own comfort zones, that precisely locate and cordon off the places we are accustomed to find God, and those places to which we need not go. It is also the principle that keeps the Gospel and the church's teachings alive and life-giving. This is evident in Francis' encyclical on the environment in which he not only recapitulates and interweaves prior social teachings of the church, but stretches it by going out to find God in a sphere of reality where until recently many had seldom thought to find God: in the natural world. Francis writes:

> At the end, we will find ourselves face to face with the infinite beauty of God (cf. 1 Cor 13:12), and be able to read with admiration and happiness the mystery of the universe, which with us will share in unending plenitude.[8]

7. Hopkins, "God's Grandeur."

8. Francis, *Laudato Si'*, 243.

Yes, Fido will go to heaven, as will we—but all as part of the whole universe. Reality is, indeed, more important than ideas. The whole is, indeed, greater than the sum of the parts. Deep unity will finally encompass and harmonize conflict.

Four: Time Is Greater Than Space

Perhaps the most puzzling of Francis' principles, "time is greater than space," is also one that begins showing up only after his time as provincial of the Jesuits of Argentina, perhaps mirroring what he had learned in that difficult work of trying to be faithful to the principle that unity prevails over conflict. He names this one as coming from the "constant tension between fullness and limitation" (222)—technically speaking, then, this introduces "eschatology" into his principles—attention to the "already" but always "not yet" of God's kingdom. "Broadly speaking," he says, "'time' has to do with fullness as an expression of the horizon which constantly opens before us, while each individual moment has to do with limitation as an expression of enclosure. People live poised between each individual moment and the greater brighter horizon of the utopian future as the final cause which draws us to itself" (222). Both are real: our efforts now are always limited; we lay only a few stones in the cathedral. But we contribute to a work of the Spirit that is greater than us, and which calls us to be patient. Francis continues:

> Giving priority to space means madly trying to keep everything together in the present, trying to possess the spaces of power and of self-assertion; it is to crystallize processes and presume to hold them back. Giving priority to time means being concerned about initiating processes rather than possessing spaces . . . What we need then is to give priority to actions which generate new processes in society and engage other persons and groups who can develop them to the point where they can bear significant fruit in significant historical events (223).

I think what Francis is talking about is captured by a common metaphor: "turf wars." How many of us have tried to initiate some new program, project or plan, only to be stymied by others who need to "protect their turf," hold onto their "space"? Or do *we* sometimes initiate a process and then decide that *we* need to control it completely, keep it from wandering out of the imaginary space we have defined for it? It's connected to the other principles: the whole is greater than the sum of the parts—in ways that I cannot ultimately understand in advance. Reality is greater than ideas—even my best ideas. For Francis this allows us to take the long view and to find hope without having to be obsessed with immediate results, to endure setbacks and the inevitable changes in plans. As Francis notes, Jesus warned the disciples that there were things they did not yet understand and that they would have to await the Holy Spirit to understand them. Referring to one of his favorites parables from Matthew 13, we plant seeds and "an enemy comes" and plants weeds. Our task is not to rip out the weeds but continue caring for the wheat, in the trust and hope that over the long haul, "the goodness of the wheat will prevail" (224). Maybe this principle is behind his remark, "Who am I to judge?"

This insight dovetails with a point that Ed Hahnenberg has made about the legacy and challenge of the council—not the building of a sky-scraper whose plan we already have laid out before us (space over time), but a patient toiling away at a cathedral that will take generations to complete. This reminds me of a prayer, often attributed to Oscar Romero, but really written (in Romero's honor) by Bishop Ken Untener of Saginaw:

> We cannot do everything, and there is a sense of liberation in realizing that.
>
> This enables us to do something, and to do it very well.
>
> It may be incomplete, but it is a beginning, a step along the way, an opportunity for the Lord's grace to enter and do the rest.
>
> We may never see the end results, but that is the difference be-tween the master builder and the worker.
>
> We are workers, not master builders; ministers, not messiahs.
>
> We are prophets of a future not our own.

This principle, too, is amply present in *Laudato Si'*. Francis is uncompromis-ingly critical of our current, unsustainable way of life, and calls for "radical change" in political policy, economic practice, and technological manipula-tion vis-à-vis the environment. Yet (inspired by Thérèse of Lisieux and her "little way of love") he *also* insists that little acts of asceticism, renunciation, sacrifice, and generosity when it comes to "our common home" are equally important. They may not have spectacular results all at once in the here and now; they do not take up a lot of space, as it were; but they are crucial, Francis insists, for any ecological conversion and spirituality. They make a difference—but only for someone for whom time is greater than space. And, speaking as someone who has taught on the environment, this priority gives people real hope. In the face of a catastrophe that seems unstoppable, there are things that are in our power to do, although they are difficult and require sacrifice. I think that the application to preaching is not too difficult to discern. Yes, be challenging, as Francis is in this encyclical, but, to recall his admonitions under the principle that realities are more important than ideas, don't preach "objectives that are more ideal than real," or "ethical systems bereft of kindness."

Conclusion

- The whole is greater than the sum of the parts
- Unity prevails over conflict
- Realities are more important than ideas
- Time is greater than space

These are the principles that Francis proposes for "the building of a people where differences are harmonized within a common pursuit," which is the way missionary disciples realize their mission to make of the church a leaven in the world. They don't provide a cookbook recipe either for pastoral administration, good teaching, or good preaching; rather they are basic principles of discernment that govern how Francis has understood and shouldered the legacy and challenges of the council fifty years later. I think that they intersect fruitfully with these principles that Ed Hahnenberg proposed in thinking about preaching, with my notes in parentheses:

- Preaching begins from below, respecting the reality that people live ("realities are more important than ideas").
- Preaching ministers from within the people, on the same journey they are on ("time is greater than space").

The preacher and his or her preaching become evangelical by turning to the peripheries in mission, even tense and conflictual peripheries ("the whole is greater than the sum of the parts"; and "unity prevails over conflict").

I suppose that what I might be leaving those of you who preach with is good news and bad news. Good news: take heart. All the good homiletical technique in the world will not reach a community that has not yet developed fully enough to "recognize the voice of the shepherd." You can appropriate for yourselves Francis' insight that "time is greater than space." Instead of waiting until you occupy an imaginary space of the "perfect preacher," armed with the best ideas, you can make a beginning, initiate processes, plant seeds. Bad news, or challenging news: I would think that your task as preachers, using these principles, is to stretch the community that you preach to, discerning and calling them in small ways to a reality that is greater than their thinking about it right now. Calling them out of their comfort zone. Realizing that they actually might be further along than you think! Not easy work! The task for all of us is to think about whether by the decisions we make, the things we write, the example we give, we might do a better job of encouraging the transition toward a community of missionary disciples. To the extent that you can do this as preachers, and those of us who struggle in other ministries to build a community of missionary disciples can do this as well, we give each other mutual encouragement and hope for the journey—and this, much more than any academic lecture I can give or chapter I can contribute, is the best way to take up the legacy and the challenge of the council in a global church.

Bibliography

Benedict XVI. *Deus Caritas Est*. December 25, 2005. w2.vatican.va/content/benedict-xvi/en/encyclicals/documents/hf_ben-xvi_enc_20051225_deus-caritas-est.html.

Francis. *Evangelii Gaudium*. November 24, 2014. w2.vatican.va/content/francesco/en/apost_exhortations/documents/papa-francesco_esortazione-ap_20131124_evangelii-gaudium.html.

——. *Laudato Si'*. May 24, 2015. w2.vatican.va/content/francesco/en/encyclicals/documents/papa-francesco_20150524_enciclica-laudato-si.html.

Hopkins, Gerard Manley. "God's Grandeur." Poetry Foundation. https://www.poetryfoundation.org/poems-and-poets/poems/detail/44395. London: Milford, 1918.

Ivereigh, Austen. *The Great Reformer: Francis and the Making of a Radical Pope*. New York: Henry Holt, 2014.